"As a teacher of graduate and undergraduate courses in public relations management, I have long sought this book, *Business for Communicators*, to give my students a business mindset for their public relations careers. This book is an essential guide to organizational livelihoods – e.g., finance, marketing, and data analytics within the broader perspective of the US economy. A very welcome book for our classrooms and industry."

Elizabeth L. Toth, *Professor, Department of Communication, University of Maryland, USA*

"This easy-to-read and oftentimes entertaining book provides a wide range of business knowledge that is essential for corporate communicators, for students who aspire to such careers, and for educators whose business literacy may be limited. In a sole volume that includes a brief history of capitalism, the book's uniquely qualified author teaches contemporary business practices, including micro- and macroeconomics, financial statements, operational management, legal considerations, and a range of related topics that are insufficiently covered in existing communication textbooks."

Dean Kruckeberg, *Professor, University of North Carolina at Charlotte, USA*

"A must read for communications professionals seeking to advance and enrich their leadership. Dr. Duhé's insightful and highly readable book will help you gain a vital second language – *business*, the vocabulary of big decision-making. The book provides a rich breadth and depth of business knowledge highlighted by case studies and real examples. Read it and become business smart."

Bruce K. Berger, *Professor Emeritus, Advertising & Public Relations, University of Alabama, USA*

"Since the days of Eddy Bernays, when public relations went mainstream and corporate communicators claimed the mantle of a profession, a serious credibility gap has existed. Far too many communication specialists have no business acumen. They don't understand how the organizations that employ them make money. They have no real understanding of how business and economics function to produce prosperity, wealth, and opportunity.

Sandra Duhé's brilliant new book, *Business for Communicators*, is a serious first step in closing that gap. Short of getting your own MBA, this is the resource you'll need to fully understand the levers of commerce and inner-workings of the enterprise you've chosen. Her work is carefully researched, thoughtfully organized, and exceptionally well expressed. Keep this one on the shelf and read it periodically. You'll never again be regarded as an amateur."

James Scofield O'Rourke, IV, *Professor of Management, University of Notre Dame, France*

"*Business for Communicators: The Essential Guide to Success in Corporate and Public Affairs* by Sandra Duhé fills an important gap. She understands firsthand how to build trust and credibility, the essential currencies that enable communicators to influence decision making and company success. I wish I had had a book like this to help develop my business mindset when I embarked on my journey to the C-suite!"

Carolyn Covey Morris, *Corporate Communications and Agency Leader*

"Sandy's work dissects the daily grind of C-suite corporate communicators, extracts the most salient lessons, and provides a simple to follow guide for students looking to find a differentiator that can last a lifetime. There's a reason why her students are among our best strategic communicators, and she graciously uncovers those secrets here."

Chris Murphy, *AT&T, CEO Communications*

"Oh, how I wish this book had been available when I started my communications career! Skillful communications informed by data and business acumen are a powerful combination. Sandra Duhé has written the quintessential MBA for communicators. This book is required reading for those who want to advance their careers, their profession, and their organizations."

Kathleen Beathard, *Vice President, Strategic Communications, Medical City Healthcare*

"It is difficult to effectively communicate from what we do not understand. Since communicators work with and within businesses, it's important that we internalize the business mindset to craft strategies and tactics that move the business forward. This reinforces the communicator's role as that of a trusted advisor to senior management, while also emphasizing the importance of keeping the discipline in the front lines to support business decisions. From an individual's perspective, an effective business mindset enhances lifetime career potential and broadens the scope of prospective trajectories. *Business for Communicators* is the foundation for new communicators (or those new to business) to understand basic business, while also acting as a refresh or reference for experienced communicators."

Linda Beheler, *Head of Communication, North America, Diodes Incorporated; Immediate Past President, Corporate Communication & Public Affairs (CCPA) Advisory Board, Southern Methodist University, USA*

"We have enjoyed working with prominent educators like Sandy Duhé to advance the level of business acumen within the communications profession and contribute more to strategic decision-making. Sandy's new book, *Business for Communicators*, is an important addition to this vital conversation."

Matt Ragas and Ron Culp, *College of Communication, DePaul University, USA*

Business for Communicators

Business for Communicators provides future and current professional communicators with a hands-on, working knowledge of how businesses profit, grow, and adapt in their competitive environments.

Corporate communicators aspire to sit at the decision-making table but too often fall short because of an inability to speak the language of business or effectively apply a business mindset to communication strategy. *Business for Communicators* provides the in-depth business literacy these professionals need, beyond just building the case for business intelligence or explaining business basics. The text delves into the details of corporate finance, accounting, marketing, strategy, operations, and economics to provide a theoretical grounding and a working knowledge that business communicators can apply to every decision they make. Real world applications illustrate concepts covered, focus on the communication implications of business outcomes, and provide opportunities for extended learning and discussion.

This book is an essential resource for advanced undergraduate and graduate students, as well as professional corporate communicators ready to enhance their influence and advance their careers with business acumen.

An accompanying website, blog, email, and social media platforms provide additional resources, interaction, commentary, and responses to questions from educators and practitioners, as well as teaching materials for educators, at www.thecommunicatorsmba.com.

Sandra Duhé is Associate Professor and Chair of Corporate Communication and Public Affairs at Southern Methodist University, USA.

Business for Communicators

The Essential Guide to Success in Corporate and Public Affairs

Sandra Duhé

NEW YORK AND LONDON

First published 2022
by Routledge
605 Third Avenue, New York, NY 10158

and by Routledge
2 Park Square, Milton Park, Abingdon, Oxon OX14 4RN

Routledge is an imprint of the Taylor & Francis Group, an informa business

© 2022 Taylor & Francis

The right of Sandra Duhé to be identified as author of this work has been asserted by her in accordance with sections 77 and 78 of the Copyright, Designs and Patents Act 1988.

All rights reserved. No part of this book may be reprinted or reproduced or utilised in any form or by any electronic, mechanical, or other means, now known or hereafter invented, including photocopying and recording, or in any information storage or retrieval system, without permission in writing from the publishers.

Trademark notice: Product or corporate names may be trademarks or registered trademarks, and are used only for identification and explanation without intent to infringe.

Library of Congress Cataloging-in-Publication Data
Names: Duhé, Sandra C., 1968– author.
Title: Business for communicators: the essential guide to success in corporate and public affairs / Sandra Duhé.
Description: New York, NY: Routledge, 2022. |
Includes bibliographical references and index.
Identifiers: LCCN 2021011052 (print) | LCCN 2021011053 (ebook) |
ISBN 9780367430078 (hardback) | ISBN 9780367430085 (paperback) |
ISBN 9781003000600 (ebook)
Subjects: LCSH: Success in business. | Business–Vocational guidance. | Communication in management.
Classification: LCC HF5386 .D84 2022 (print) |
LCC HF5386 (ebook) | DDC 650.1–dc23
LC record available at https://lccn.loc.gov/2021011052
LC ebook record available at https://lccn.loc.gov/2021011053

ISBN: 978-0-367-43007-8 (hbk)
ISBN: 978-0-367-43008-5 (pbk)
ISBN: 978-1-003-00060-0 (ebk)

DOI: 10.4324/9781003000600

Typeset in Sabon
by Newgen Publishing UK

Access the Support Material: www.thecommunicatorsmba.com

To my father, Byron Core, who taught me business,
To my professor, Kathleen Kelly, who taught me public relations, and
To my husband, Brad Duhé, who made it possible for me to succeed in both.

Contents

List of Figures xiii
List of Tables xiv
List of Sidebars and Boxes xv

Introduction to *Business for Communicators* 1
   My Path from Corporate Finance to Public Affairs 1
   My Transition from Corporate Life to the Classroom 3
   The Call from Communicators for Business Literacy 3
   What's Inside and Available Online 4
   Acknowledgements 6

1 Why You Need to Speak the Language of Business 7
   A Business Mindset 7
   An Informed Seat at the Table 8
   Don't Go It Alone 9
   Business Acumen is More than Numbers 10
   What Women Leaders Are Missing 11

2 Capitalism: Its Benefits and Discontents 13
   Origins of Political Economy 13
   Political Economy and Public Affairs 14
   A Political Economy Approach to Understanding Capitalism 15
   Classical View of a Self-Regulating Market 16
   Neoclassical View of the Market 17
   The Firm's Purpose: Shareholder and Stakeholder Perspectives 19
   Capitalism in the U.S. 21
   A Brief Note on Capitalism Abroad 23
   CSR and ESG 24
   Corporate Governance 25
   Communicating Capitalism 34

3 A Micro and Macro View of the Economy 39
   Ten Principles of Microeconomics 39
      #1: Economic Agents Seek to Maximize Their Utility with Limited Resources 40

#2: Supply and Demand Drive Price and Quantity 40
#3: Elasticity of Demand Determines Consumer Sensitivity to Price Changes 42
#4: Consumer Reactions to Price Changes Indicate Which Goods Are Substitutes and Which Goods Are Complements 42
#5: Diminishing Returns, Marginal Analysis, and Opportunity Costs Apply to Individuals and Firms 43
#6: Sunk Costs Are Not Recoverable, No Matter What 45
#7: Bigger is Better for Economies of Scale 46
#8: Perfect Competition is a Theory, Not Reality 47
#9: Firms, Markets, and Industries Are Organized in a Variety of Ways 47
#10: Information and Expectations Drive Markets 48

Ten Principles of Macroeconomics 48
#1: Aggregate Demand and Aggregate Supply Represent the Sum Total of Goods and Services Produced in an Economy 49
#2: GDP is a Key Indicator of a Country's Economic Health 50
#3: Fiscal Policy Dictates How the Government Taxes and Spends 51
#4: Monetary Policy Governs an Economy's Money Supply 52
#5: Interest Rates Are a Key Component of Monetary Policy 53
#6: Inflation is a Good Thing, Until There's Too Much of It 54
#7: Declining Macroeconomic Indicators Can Signal a Recession 55
#8: Employment Reflects How Well an Economy is Reaching Its Potential 56
#9: Currency Exchange Rates Can Be Flexible or Fixed 57
#10: International Transactions Drive the Global Economy 58

Economics, Communication, and You 59

4   **The Art and Science of Financial Statements** 65
Financial Reporting Standards: FASB and GAAP 66
The Big Three: Three Statements, Three Formulas, Many Different Names 69
  The Income Statement 69
  The Balance Sheet 73
  The Cash Flow Statement 77
Those All-Important Footnotes: Read Them 79
Caveats and Communication Roles for Accounting and Finance 79
When Creative Accounting Leads to Crisis 81
A Closer Look at the WorldCom Debacle 82

5   **How and Why Finance Rules the Business World** 89
The Focus on Creating Value 89
Three Functions of Corporate Finance 91
  Capital Investments and Budgeting 91
  Capital Access and Financing 96
  Shareholder Returns 100
Public vs. Private Companies 102
The Stock Market 103
  Stock Exchanges 104

Stock Indices 104
Shareholder Activism 106
   Shareholder Resolution 106
   Proxy Fight 109
   Hostile Takeover 110
Regulatory and Reporting Requirements 111
Ratio and Margin Analysis 114
Quick Case Study: Wendy's and ROE 114
The Journey from Startup to IPO 117
Focusing on Growth 119
   Top-Line vs. Bottom-Line Growth 119
   Organic vs. Inorganic Growth 120
Mergers and Acquisitions 121
Company Valuation 123
   Public Company Valuation 124
   Private Company Valuation 125
Increasing Your Value to an Organization 126

6 Marketing Envy and Other Observations   133
Marketing Beyond the Customer 133
The Business of Branding 135
Seven Ps of Marketing 136
Types of Marketing 137
Key Marketing Concepts 137
   B2B vs. B2C 139
   Types of Goods 140
   Perceptions of Value 140
   The Sales Funnel 141
   Life Cycle: Products, Businesses, and Markets 141
   Cash Cows and Other Product Categories 142
   Competing on Something Other Than Price 144
ROI and Other Nifty Marketing Metrics 144
Learn from Marketing 147

7 Getting Comfortable with the Quants   150
The Need for Unicorns 150
Data Science and Data Scientists 151
Artificial Intelligence, Machine Learning, and Deep Learning 152
Data Big and Small: Use and Privacy 153
Cybersecurity Risk Management 154
Competitive Advantages of Data 156
Data-Driven Communication Strategy 156

8 Why You Cannot Ignore Operations Management   159
A Focus on Efficiency 159

The Supply Chain 160
Lean Manufacturing 162
Demand Forecasting 163
Horizontal vs. Vertical Integration 163
Understand Operations, Improve Communications 164

9 The Care and Feeding of Human Capital 167
The Future of Work and the Employee Experience 167
Attracting, Retaining, and Incentivizing Employees 169
The Psychology of High-Performing Teams 172
Diversity and Inclusion 174
HR Risk Management 176
The Dual-Brand Challenge 177

10 What is Strategy? 179
The Business Model 179
What Business Are We In? 180
The What, Who, Why, and How of Strategy 181
Porter's Forces: Strategy and Competition 181
Competitive Advantage and Strategic Choices 183
Three Levels of Strategy 185
Innovation: The S Curve and Blue Ocean Strategy 187
Strategic Communication 189

11 And Here Comes Legal 192
A Global View of Enterprise Risk 192
Key Aspects of U.S. Employment Law 194
Intellectual Property 195
Product Liability 197
Fiduciary Duty 198
Foreign Corrupt Practices Act 200
Legal Communication 200

12 Last but Not Least: Business Ethics 204
Values, Morals, Law, and Ethics 204
The Psychology of White-Collar Criminals 205
Keeping Self-Interest in Check 206
Whistleblower Protections 207
Communication and Ethics 208

Concluding Thoughts 211

Index 213

List of Figures

3.1a	Change in Quantity Demanded	41
3.1b	Change in Demand	41
3.2	Diminishing Marginal Returns	44
4.1	Income Statement Example	73
4.2	Balance Sheet Example	76
4.3	Cash Flow Statement Example	78
5.1	Sample Proxy Card	107
5.2	Sample Shareholder Resolution	109
5.3a	Form 10-K	112
5.3b	Annual Report	113
6.1	The Sales Funnel	141
6.2	The Product Life Cycle	142
6.3	The BCG Growth-Share Matrix	143
7.1	Data Science Illustrated	152
7.2	Three Essential Sources of Knowledge	157
7.3	Data-Driven Communication Strategy	157
8.1	Conventional Supply Chain	161
8.2	E-Commerce Supply Chain	161
9.1	Target Corporation Diversity and Inclusion Goals and Results	175
9.2	Diversity and Inclusion Best Practices	176
9.3	Human Capital Risk Treatment Options	177
10.1	Porter's Competitive Forces	182
10.2	Achieving Competitive Advantage	184
10.3	Three Levels of Strategy	186
10.4	The S Curve	187
10.5	Red vs. Blue Ocean Strategy	188

List of Tables

5.1	Capital Investment Choices	94
5.2	Capital Investment Choices With NPV for Each	95
5.3	Key Financial Ratios	115
5.4	Startup Series Funding	119
6.1	A Seriously Long List of Types of Marketing	138
6.2	General Marketing Metrics	145
6.3	Website and Blogging Metrics	146
6.4	SEO Metrics	146
6.5	Social Media Marketing Metrics	146
6.6	Email Marketing Metrics	147
6.7	Pay-Per-Click (PPC) Metrics	147
11.1	Major Laws Governed by U.S. Department of Labor (DOL)	193
12.1	Whistleblower Protections	208

List of Sidebars and Boxes

Sidebars

0.1	What's in a Name? Public Relations, Public Affairs, and Other Variations	2
3.1	Long Run vs. Short Run	49
3.2	Nominal vs. Real Terms	50
4.1	Debits and Credits	68
4.2	Recognizing Revenues	68
4.3	Internal vs. External Audits	69
4.4	R&D, Brands, and Goodwill	71
4.5	Book Value	74
4.6	Operating Expenses vs. Capital Expenditures	84
5.1	Financial Lingo to Know	91
5.2	Understanding Securities	97
5.3	Bankruptcy 101	98
5.4	Types and Classes of Shareholders	100
5.5	Stock Splits and Dilution	102
5.6	Reading the Market	103
5.7	Bulls, Bears, and Investor Psychology	105
5.8	Market Cap and Volatility Defined	105
5.9	M&A Deal at a Glance	121
6.1	Market Share and Market Growth Strategies	134
7.1	Blockchain 101	155
9.1	Sweetgreen's Company Culture	168
9.2	Employee Engagement	170
9.3	Three Types of Workplace Intelligence	173

Boxes

2.1	Darden Corporate Governance Guidelines	26
3.1	Supply and Demand Illustrated	40
5.1	10-K vs. Annual Report	112

Introduction to *Business for Communicators*

My father started his career like most college grads: Working for someone else. Then, one day not long after the birth of his first child, my oldest brother, he went to the movies instead of going to work, quit his job, and informed my unsuspecting mother that he was starting his own business. Over the next several decades, he and my mother experienced the exhilarating highs and fretful lows well known by entrepreneurs.

Daddy grew, nurtured, and built a reputation for his firm that still thrives today. Along the way, he insisted that I, his youngest child and only daughter, understand business. My lessons began when he opened a checking account for me when I was in third grade. And yes, I grew up in a small town where retailers actually took my checks. I'm proud to say I never bounced one of them.

His plan for me, which I readily accepted long before the checkbook arrived, was to attend business school and then law school to serve the companies he started. I went humming along through my undergrad business studies and in my senior year decided I was moving away for the oil and gas business instead of going to law school and returning home. That announcement didn't go over entirely well, but he came around and remained exceedingly proud of me.

My Path from Corporate Finance to Public Affairs

I began my career with Conoco (now ConocoPhillips) as a financial analyst, not knowing a darn thing about how petroleum deposits could be extracted from the depths of the earth and transformed into hundreds of products I found essential to my quality of life. In a short time, I learned a lot about my company and industry from the network of engineers, operators, plant managers, executives, senior analysts, and, yes, administrative assistants (take note: they know *everything*), who surrounded me, allowed me to shadow them, and answered my numerous questions.

Admittedly, the numbers part of my job didn't thrill me. Running calculations and analyzing figures were more fun in college, and it was difficult to see the outcomes or benefits of my work. My soft skills – an anomaly among my fellow number crunchers – landed me for a brief stint in corporate training, where I got the teaching bug I'd pursue years later.

After surviving my first of many waves of downsizing (or *rightsizing* as our high-priced consultants called it), I should have been thrilled when a senior manager approached me

DOI: 10.4324/9781003000600-1

with a transfer offer to a new city and a transition into community relations. Instead, I was horrified. Anything with "relations" in its title sounded like sheer fluff to me. I was a "business" person. Community relations couldn't possibly be a real job. I went home crying to my new husband, who reminded me to put my soft skills to work so we could pay our new mortgage. At least that got me thinking about numbers again.

I interviewed elsewhere. Nothing. I sent out dozens of resumes. Rejection. Tears. Angst. Time was running short, and with no viable alternatives, the company movers arrived, and off I went. My new external-facing position was completely foreign to me (see Sidebar 0.1: What's in a Name?). Public speaking was the closest I ever got to a communication class in business school. I ran to the nearby University of Louisiana at Lafayette where I met Kathleen Kelly, Ph.D., who introduced me to the science behind public relations. I hung on to her every word, pinching myself over the accidental and highly resisted discovery that I could have more influence on a business as a communicator than I ever could as an analyst.[1]

Sidebar 0.1 What's in a Name? Public Relations, Public Affairs, and Other Variations

Organizational communication is an umbrella term describing how firms interact with internal and external audiences, also known as **publics** or **stakeholders**. **Internal communication** focuses on employees. **Public relations** refers to communicating with publics external to the firm, including customers, communities, and the media. **Public affairs** is the term most often used in business. As a function, public affairs can focus on policy, lobbying, and government affairs, or it can be as broad as including corporate, employee, and external affairs. The bottom line? Names are used interchangeably and depend on the organization. If your job involves communicating with one or several business audiences, this book is for you.

I earned my Master's in Public Relations while enjoying success in community relations. Soon after, I made a major move to public affairs manager for Mobil's largest U.S. refining and petrochemical complex. My career progressed with increasing responsibility and visibility, including upstream (i.e., exploration and production) and more downstream (i.e., refining) operations. Then came a rarified opportunity to work on the public affairs team for the $80 billion ExxonMobil merger, the largest in corporate history at the time. While at ExxonMobil's global headquarters in Irving, Texas, I completed a Master's in Applied Economics and a Ph.D. in Political Economy, having learned firsthand how significantly (and quickly) political, social, and economic forces can impact stakeholder relationships and, consequently, a company's ability to achieve its goals.

My 14-year career in the energy sector provided me with extensive experience in financial, risk, and crisis communication; international media relations; community and government relations; and corporate brand management. I've done my share of live television to promote good causes and respond to bad incidents. I've been in the trenches with trusted colleagues, on the floor of the New York Stock Exchange, in the C-suite working with executives, and in the field learning from activists. All the while, my business acumen distinguished me as a communicator and provided me opportunities I wouldn't trade today.

My Transition from Corporate Life to the Classroom

I serendipitously entered the classroom in 2004 via Kathleen Kelly's former office at the University of Louisiana at Lafayette. I transitioned from industry to academia with the requisite scholarly achievements, but I never left my business mindset behind. I've been fortunate to find academic homes with colleagues who share my passion for preparing students to serve as business-minded communication leaders in industry, government, and civil society.

Currently, I serve as chair of the Division of Corporate Communication and Public Affairs (CCPA) in the Meadows School of the Arts at Southern Methodist University (SMU) in Dallas, Texas. I earned my MBA with honors at the SMU Cox School of Business in 2016. In CCPA, we offer undergraduates the opportunity to focus their studies in organizational, political, and nonprofit communication, in addition to public relations and strategic communication. Regardless of which area(s) students choose, our faculty ensure and insist each one graduates with a firm grasp of data analytics and applied business acumen. Their early-career accomplishments and advancements indicate we're on the right track.

CCPA is an exciting place to develop what I've heard referred to as "unicorns," that is, highly effective communicators who are data- and business-savvy. A good portion of our success is attributed to Ph.D. and adjunct faculty who not only have significant field experience, but also maintain an active presence in each of the sectors we teach. Those are the unicorn professors every school longs to have, and they are in short supply.

Practitioners often reach out to me when considering a move to the classroom, whether part- or full-time. It's been my experience that a corporate background gives one the knowledge, work ethic, and tolerance to navigate academia while enjoying the flexibility to consult and offset the (no kidding) salary cut. I maintain an active consulting practice with energy, higher education, and pharmaceutical clients facing high-risk situations that fits my schedule and enriches my teaching. That said, there's no getting around the research and publication expectations that accompany most tenure-track positions. Industry experience alone doesn't provide the graduate-level scholarly and theoretical credentials required for conventional tenure lines, but programs are increasingly designing positions to meet their particular needs.

The Call from Communicators for Business Literacy

I'm a firm believer in the need for corporate communicators and educators to work together in preparing students for the workplace. Since 2013, I've served in various capacities on the Board of Directors for the Commission on Public Relations Education (CPRE) and, at the time of this writing, serve as an at-large director. Comprising both practitioners and educators, CPRE is the leading global authority offering public relations curriculum recommendations for undergraduate and graduate programs.[2]

CPRE's latest report, "Fast Forward: Foundations and Future State. Educators and Practitioners," is the outcome of a three-year study of the knowledge and skills public relations practitioners and educators believe are essential for college graduates entering the field. I chaired the data analysis and writing for Chapter 4 "Undergraduate Curriculum: Courses and Content to Prepare the Next Generation of Public Relations

Practitioners," which includes business literacy along with content creation, analytics, digital technology, and measurement and evaluation as key topics undergraduates need exposure to before joining the workforce.

Business for Communicators responds to this call for business literacy, which, like the other key topics identified, can be difficult to provide within conventional communication programs limited by credit hour restrictions, accreditation requirements, and faculty expertise. Communication professors typically don't attend business school, and business schools most often limit course enrollments to business majors. With support from SMU and Routledge, I am committed to helping educators bring business literacy to their communication classrooms.

Additional inspiration for *Business for Communicators* came from countless communicators now well advanced in corporate and agency ranks. They've shared with me their stories of entering the workforce and soon realizing the need for business acumen to move beyond entry-level and middle management assignments. With a mostly liberal arts education under their belts, their business literacy was wanting, but required. They scrambled to get the knowledge they needed. I wrote *Business for Communicators* to help aspiring communicators avoid that struggle.

Hiring managers have told me they seek graduates in economics, anthropology, sociology, psychology, and information technology to diversify thinking around communication strategy. Having entered corporate communication as an "outsider" myself with no former study of the field, I didn't have the framework to help anyone with communication strategy, no matter the quality of my business skills. Once I sought the education I needed, however, I could readily connect business to communication. Although I'm an avid proponent of interdisciplinary study,[3] I also maintain communication deserves its due attention as a social science. To think someone could be successful in corporate communication without any communication expertise, is, in my opinion and experience, foolhardy. *Business for Communicators* is foremost a business book for those who already understand the intricacies, challenges, and opportunities communication offers.

What's Inside and Available Online

This text provides the business literacy needed to facilitate your success in corporate communication and public affairs. It's your one-stop, go-to source to gain a business mindset and apply it to every decision you make as a communicator. I've filled these pages with insights on corporate finance, accounting, operations, economics, and more gained from two business degrees completed with honors, world-class industry experience, and years of interdisciplinary study to become the business-minded educator and consultant I am today. Unlike other "business for non-business types" books, this one is written by a communicator who understands business specifically for communicators who need to understand business. Both the practitioner and the professor in me will guide you through chapters that cover the essentials of business literacy, as follows:

Chapter 1: Why You Need to Speak the Language of Business explains the importance of developing a business mindset, why business literacy is essential for corporate communicators, and how to build an internal network that enhances business acumen.

Chapter 2: Capitalism: Its Benefits and Discontents provides the political and economic origins of today's thinking about market-oriented capitalism, including its outcomes and criticisms that permeate the firm's operating environment.

Chapter 3: A Micro and Macro View of the Economy guides you through the principles of microeconomics and macroeconomics, global impacts of economic activities, and the overlapping systems that move markets.

Chapter 4: The Art and Science of Financial Statements dissects the three accounting statements that together reveal a company's financial health, what you can learn from each, and the regulatory and reputational importance of accurate reporting.

Chapter 5: How and Why Finance Rules the Business World covers the practices, terminology, and regulations that govern how the firm attracts, secures, and uses capital; reports and tracks its value-creating activities; and positions itself for growth.

Chapter 6: Marketing Envy and Other Observations explains how marketers readily quantify their contribution to the bottom line, build brand value, and adapt their practices throughout a product's lifecycle.

Chapter 7: Getting Comfortable with the Quants explores the gathering and uses of data big and small, how analytics (can and should) drive communication strategy, tools of the trade, data breaches, and the competitive advantages of data.

Chapter 8: Why You Can't Ignore Operations Management reviews how firms manage seasonality, demand projections, supply chains, vertical integration, and other operational issues rarely discussed in a communication context.

Chapter 9: The Care and Feeding of Human Capital looks at how corporate culture, talent management, retention, and engagement initiatives affect and motivate employees as front-line communicators and the firm's most valuable asset.

Chapter 10: What is Strategy? draws on the preceding content to review the variety of objectives and business models a firm can pursue while discerning its competitive advantage and navigating the inescapable forces of a market economy.

Chapter 11: And Here Comes Legal focuses on key aspects of enterprise risk, employment law, intellectual property, product liability, fiduciary responsibilities, global operations, and other issues relevant to the C-suite.

Chapter 12: Last but not Least: Business Ethics reviews the psychology of white collar criminals, moral hazard, and control mechanisms used to keep self-interest in check and firms in business.

Concluding Thoughts captures my parting advice and how to access me and other resources for additional help as you build and apply your business literacy on the job.

Each chapter draws content from MBA coursework and provides what you need to know in a communication context. Case studies, examples, and sidebars help you "connect the dots" between concepts that at first may seem removed from the work you do but upon closer examination illustrate an untapped opportunity for communication counsel, or, at the very least, enable you to be a more informed source of counsel.

Read the entire book in chapter order, focus on the chapters most important for you, or use the table of contents and index to get the exact bit of info you need when you need it. Visit The Communicator's MBA website (thecommunicatorsmba.com) to find resources for practitioners, educators, and students; post questions; and explore how the everyday conduct of business affects, and is affected by, how we communicate on behalf of firms.

Acknowledgements

My deepest appreciation goes to Kevin Moloney and Jacqueline Curthoys for first reviewing this book proposal for Routledge and graciously sharing it with business and management editor Meredith Norwich. Meredith enthusiastically onboarded *Business for Communicators* before handing it off to Sophia Levine and Emmie Shand who stewarded the project through publication. I look forward to continuing our collaboration for forthcoming editions and whatever other opportunities may come our way. Hard work is always more enjoyable when done alongside great people.

The devil is in the details, and everyone needs an editor. I am grateful to have worked with the highly focused reviewers, editors, and production team members who shared their time, wisdom, and belief in the book's mission to create what you're now reading. With a nod to the legendary band Queen, I thank them for being fastidious and precise. I'd go to press with nothing less for a project I started contemplating in 2013.

I cannot mention a rock band without thanking my favorite digital guru and bona fide rock-and-roll photographer Steve Lee who is the mastermind behind the website and digital platforms that support *Business for Communicators* and The Communicator's MBA. I've learned much from my accomplished, caring colleague and friend who delivers a lot of wisdom over sushi lunches.

My family of relatives, colleagues, and students deserve my gratitude for cheering me on through this project while I did my best to keep up with the many other responsibilities I have to each of them. They know all too well that now this is done, I'll be looking for what's next to fill its place on my already full plate. I'm thankful they accept and love me anyway. My current station in life is a great and blessed one.

And finally, dear reader, my thanks go to you. I'm excited to work with you, whether you are a student, new professional, or about to embark on the C-suite. Perhaps you've been in the field a while and will use this book as a reference for yourself or your team. In any case, reach out at thecommunicatorsmba.com, and let me know how I can help you. Business is better when communicators are at the decision-making table, so let's get to work!

Notes

1. A similar account of my journey from corporate finance to public affairs appears in *Teaching Business as a Second Language* published by the Institute for Public Relations at https://instituteforpr.org/teaching-business-second-language/. See also *Observations of a First-Semester MBA Student* at https://instituteforpr.org/observations-first-semester-mba-student/ for related commentary.
2. Learn more about the Commission on Public Relations Education and its publications at http://www.commissionpred.org.
3. See my related remarks in *The Three Pillars of PR Education in the Future* at https://instituteforpr.org/view-future-public-relations-education/.

Chapter 1

Why You Need to Speak the Language of Business

A seat at the table: *A position as a member of a group that makes decisions.*[1] The quest for a place among decision-makers is neither new nor limited to communicators. The term "a seat at the table" is commonplace. It's not a term, however, I recall hearing much in business school.[2] Perhaps we assumed business majors would always have a say in company matters.

Conversely, I heard extensively about this longing for a seat at the table with senior executives as a grad student in communication. "Why wouldn't we be at the table?," I wondered. And as my years in industry and grad school progressed, it occurred to me that it was my initial grounding in business that provided me decision-maker access as a communicator. My business mindset was second nature to me, so I didn't take notice of it. It was just always there. My business sense informed the questions I asked, the proposals I made, and the way I interacted with stakeholders without my realizing it. It motivated me to write this book so you, too, can have a business mindset as a communicator.

A Business Mindset

What exactly is a business mindset, you ask? Duncan (2014) explains that having a business mindset means understanding the purpose of a business is to make money, knowing the results you want before investing in any business activity, and grasping how what you do contributes to profitability. She argues:

> Every business decision you make today affects your business today, tomorrow, and in the future – so **become a good strategist**. A good strategist looks at all facets of their business today in context of where they are trying to go. A good strategist reacts to problems positively instead of negatively. A good strategist also welcomes change and turns it into an opportunity. A good strategist can react quickly with the unexpected. **A good strategist has a business mindset.**
>
> (para. 11, emphasis in original)

We're going to cover how businesses create value, earn profits, devise strategy, and much more, but first it's important to understand the *mental models* you'll encounter as a corporate communicator. The decision-makers you seek to influence either went to business school or got fully immersed in a business mindset while advancing in their own careers.

DOI: 10.4324/9781003000600-2

Sure, there are exceptions, like the college drop-out who eschews conventional thinking and launches a multi-billion-dollar enterprise. But here, we're focusing on the mindset of most business executives you'll encounter. And if you happen to find yourself in the employ of an unconventional mastermind, or even with an activist group working against corporate interests, you'll still need to understand business fundamentals to influence how business is run.

Mental models are belief systems held by managers (Rust, Moorman, & van Beuningen, 2016). They exist at both the individual ("I believe…") and collective ("We believe…") level. In business, mental models guide thinking about revenues, costs, quality, customers, firm performance, and so on. Interestingly, individual mental models converge to become collective mental models, and vice versa.

You won't find your company's mental models neatly captured in a manual (sorry), but the communicator in you will pick up on clues provided in meetings, speeches, company publications, priorities, goals, etc. Specifically, which ways of thinking about problem solving, innovating, learning, and investing are prevalent in your company? What mantras, approaches, and frameworks are repeated, emphasized, and, particularly, rewarded when acted upon? Corporate communicators create messages based on mental models. Don't skim over them. Understand them. Your business literacy will feed your business mindset and help you internalize your company's predominant mental models.

A business mindset is unlike a liberal arts mindset. There's a stark difference in each field's educational approach and one that I experienced firsthand. Business thinking is linear, mostly black and white, predictive, and highly quantitative, with defined outcomes and relatively low tolerance for uncertainty, risk, and excessive narrative. In a nutshell: Get to the point, and get to the point using numbers. A liberal arts mindset, however, is highly narrative, exploratory, open to ambiguity and change, qualitative, and descriptive with a much higher tolerance for the gray that falls between the black and white. Although complex business issues benefit from a liberal arts mindset, many Fortune 500 CEOs have degrees in business, engineering, or computer science, and about half are MBAs (Williams, 2018). Business thinking drives their mental models.

There was a 30-year span between the time I started business school as an undergrad and later crossed the stage as an MBA graduate. Although the business landscape changed significantly over those three decades, the pedagogical approach used in business school was remarkably similar: Case studies, spreadsheets, graphs, and analyses. Course titles. Study groups. Lectures, exams.

My graduate liberal arts education in between two business schools greatly expanded my business way of thinking. I thoroughly enjoyed pondering issues from an interdisciplinary perspective and examining how politics, economics, and social/cultural variables affect both business and communication. My newfound liberal arts orientation enriched my thinking, but my business mindset still did the talking in the C-suite, and it still does. Why? Because it's the language executives and I together understand. In the chapters that follow, I'm going to help you speak the language of business so you can more effectively present, defend, and implement your communication strategies.

An Informed Seat at the Table

Having a seat at the table isn't sufficient for you to be an effective strategist. You need to be an informed presence at that table, that is, deeply conversant about whatever business you are in. Bad things happen when communicators aren't at the table. The heads of finance, legal, and operations don't have communication impacts at the forefront of their thinking, nor frankly should they. It's your job to understand how communication supports, detracts from, and otherwise affects the business. But here's the rub: You need to understand their mindset before you can ever be persuasive about yours. Corporate communication is a staff function that supports line, or profit-making, functions (see, for example, Broom & Sha, 2013). That's a fact, not something to bemoan.

You're in a unique position to make business better financially, socially, and operationally, but you must first understand business to support it effectively. Bad things happen when *uninformed* communicators are at the table. For example, if you blindly charge ahead in promotions that increase demand for your midsize company's products without any knowledge of your company's financial or operational capacity to meet that demand, you could actually do more harm than good. And where does that leave the communication function? Far away from the table and back to creating employee newsletters. That's not where we do our best work.

My favorite Harvard Business School case to teach the importance of being an informed seat at the table is *Ceres Gardening Company: Funding Growth in Organic Products* (McArthur & Yong, 2009). In it, the VP of marketing has a practically exclusive role in advising the CEO on an aggressive growth strategy. The Chief Financial Officer is glaringly absent. And trouble ensues. While the VP of marketing pushes more sales to retailers, operating cash flow tanks and long-term debt terms are violated. The favorable terms that undoubtedly drove more retailer sales also posed a significant threat to the company's financial health and ability to attract more capital. Chapters 4 and 5 cover this terminology in more detail, but suffice it to say anyone not fully informed about the potential, broader implications of business decisions shouldn't devise promotional strategies in a vacuum.

Don't Go It Alone

There's a table of advisors to the CEO because it takes a team with various skillsets to make and keep a business profitable. No one at the table, including the CEO, is an expert in finance, law, human resources, operations, and marketing, which is why the CEO needs the best thinkers in these functions at the table. Whether or not communication has a seat at that table, in my experience, comes down to the CEO's choice, based on his or her reliance on and past experience with communicators. You won't have multiple opportunities to make a good impression, but if your counsel proves to be wise, you're much more likely to have your counsel sought again. Your relationship to the CEO and others in the C-suite greatly (and I'd dare say solely) depends on the trust and confidence they have in your abilities to support the business.

To make every C-suite impression count in your favor, build your contacts in the key line and staff functions early and proactively. How do you know which functions? Look at an organizational chart to see which functions report directly to the CEO, or, depending on the structure, one level below. Some variation of finance, law, human resources, operations, and marketing are most common, though titles and functions will vary. Start building relationships with counterparts at your level in these functions, whatever your level may be. Jump at good opportunities to work, socialize, and collaborate cross-functionally.

You'll be surprised how quickly you pick up functional ways of thinking and speaking. In fact, the more time you spend with other functions, the more ingrained these parts of the business will become in your thinking about communication strategy. Along the way, you'll gain an extraordinary store of business knowledge that will inform your own work and conversations.

In his classic text, Steven Covey (1989) includes *Seek First to Understand, Then to Be Understood* as the fifth of his *7 Habits of Highly Effective People*, which is decidedly relevant as you cultivate cross-functional relationships. As you seek to first understand your colleagues' focus areas, you'll then have an opportunity to share more about yours. Developing these relationships proactively is key. You don't want to be in a crisis, need information from Human Resources, and then try to establish a relationship in the midst of chaos. I once had a VP ask me how I got the head of trademark law to return my call so quickly. Now you know my secret.

No one is going to direct you to do this relationship building, so get going. This is the same principle we follow in cultivating stakeholder relationships externally. Your internal connections are even more critical to your success. In public affairs, we work on the periphery of organizations, and our boundary-spanning role requires we navigate information flows both from within and outside of the company (see, for example, White & Dozier, 1992). Your internal connections are vital sources of information and learning. Without internal support, you cannot do anything for your external stakeholders.

Don't delay, and don't go it alone. Public affairs is a collaborative effort that necessarily draws on knowledge across your organization. You need those internal alliances to enhance your business literacy, strengthen your work, and make your way to the C-suite. In return, serve as a source of communication counsel for your cross-functional contacts. Those mutually beneficial relationships will provide you a trusted sounding board when you need to test your thinking, vet a presentation, or confirm you have your company facts in order. Be quick to return the favor, and you'll discover these relationships are among your most valuable professional assets.

Business Acumen is More than Numbers

Business for Communicators focuses on helping you to understand, apply, and leverage business knowledge in every aspect of your corporate communication career. Hastings (2008) differentiates business literacy – understanding financial statements and how a business makes and loses money – from business acumen. Business acumen, she argues, is not only having, but also acting on, business literacy. This means every strategy, proposal, and budget request reflects a deep understanding and ability to advance business objectives. Business knowledge without application benefits no one. When you have business acumen, however, your business mindset shines through everything you do.

Business acumen will get you noticed and increase your chances of being tagged as *high potential,* or, in other words, as an employee worthy of additional investment, mentoring, and grooming for fast-track advancement.[3] It's a good place to be. You don't "sign up" or apply to be considered high potential. In most organizations, it's an organic process that emerges from seeing you in action. Don't be afraid to ask how high-potential identification works in your company.

Hastings (2008) draws on additional sources to explain how being able to lead, knowing how to things get done, and knowing where to go for help (Note: that internal network you're building) are key to business acumen and, consequently, advancement in a competitive setting. Business acumen, she writes, is not dependent on an MBA but rather an ability to effectively grasp business fundamentals and demonstrate well-informed efforts to impact business results.

But you ask, isn't it difficult to show how communication drives business results? It's true that communicators have searched decades for the holy grail of measurement, return on investment, and business impact metrics for our field. Line functions, like marketing, operations, and sales, are in the enviable position of readily demonstrating their contribution to the bottom line. Support functions, including corporate communication, public affairs, legal, and human resources, given the nature of our work, are less able to do so. If you take us away, however, there's going to be a negative impact on the bottom line. That's not, however, a formidable business case working in our favor.

The Institute for Public Relations (n.d.) Measurement Commission continues to advance the discussion on business results from communication. Follow the progress they're making, and implement measurements for your own programs. Most importantly, make every communication decision with your company's relevant business strategies in mind, not in a vacuum of uninformed optimism that your plan will work. Draw on your internal network to sharpen your business acumen and heighten your confidence discussing how what you do supports the business. Quantify wherever possible. Get to the point. Apply the predominant mental models. This is business thinking. Effective, well-informed stakeholder communication is essential to driving business results.

What Women Leaders Are Missing

In her TED Talk, *The Career Advice You Probably Didn't Get*, leadership expert and author Susan Colantuono (TED Summaries, 2014) discusses what keeps women from rising out of middle management and into executive positions, or the C-suite, as we've discussed here. I'm easily lured by intriguing titles, and this one actually delivered. From the summary:

> Women now occupy 50% of middle management positions, but less than a third of that portion in upper management. Leadership skills are required at all levels of management – defined by using your own skills and engaging with others to help the organisation achieve its goals. However in the highest positions, the most important skill is 'Business, strategic, and financial acumen' – or the ability to understand the business, and people's roles. This is the skill that is missing in the advice given to women – not because they are incapable of achieving it but because it isn't recognised as a skill they are advised to acquire.
>
> (para. 2)

Business acumen. It's the missing factor that prevents many women from ascending to more senior positions. It's the essential combination of business knowledge and the ability to apply that knowledge that most often keeps women out of the C-suite. It's equally true that a lack of business acumen will exclude men from the C-suite.

But there's more to Colantuono's (TED Summaries, 2014) observations. Few women in her study were ever told to increase their understanding of the business. Instead, they were told to focus on the soft skills of negotiating, personal branding, networking, and self-confidence. Furthermore, one male executive told Colantuono that when he mentored a man and a woman, he helped the man learn the business and helped the woman learn self-confidence without realizing he was treating them differently.

This isn't about laying blame, pointing fingers, or feeling slighted. This is about looking in the mirror and knowing – whether you're male or female – that you can and should take ownership of your corporate communication career and develop your business acumen. This book and its accompanying resources online (thecommunicatorsmba.com) are a start. If your university or company offers courses in business fundamentals, take them. Note in your annual (or other cycle) performance evaluations that you want development in business acumen. Even if don't think you want to be Chief Communication Officer, take advantage of every opportunity to develop your business acumen and advance your standing while you're with the company. Doing so will only enhance your resume and give you highly transferable skills that will provide you with more career choices down the road.

Notes

1. From the Macmillan Dictionary at www.macmillandictionary.com/us/dictionary/american/a-seat-at-the-table.
2. See the full account of my journey from business school to communication professor in Introduction to *Business for Communicators*.
3. See Chapter 9 The Care and Feeding of Human Capital for additional discussion of employee development.

References

Broom, G.M., & Sha, B-L. (2013). *Cutlip and Center's effective public relations*. Boston, MA: Pearson.

Covey, S. (1989). *The 7 habits of highly effective people: Powerful lessons in personal change*. New York, NY: Fireside.

Duncan, S. (2014, March 14). *Do you have a business mindset?* Retrieved from www.businessknowhow.com/manage/mindset.htm.

Hastings, R.R. (2008, February 1). *Business acumen involves more than numbers*. Retrieved from www.shrm.org/resourcesandtools/hr-topics/behavioral-competencies/leadership-and-navigation/pages/numbers.aspx.

Institute for Public Relations. (n.d.) *IPR Measurement Commission*. Retrieved from https://instituteforpr.org/ipr-measurement-commission.

McArthur, J.H., & Yong, S. (2009, May 15.) *Ceres Gardening Company: Funding growth in organic products*. HBS No. 4017. Boston, MA: Harvard Business School Publishing.

Rust, T.R., Moorman, C., & van Beuningen, J. (2016, March). Quality mental model convergence and business performance. *International Journal of Research in Marketing*, 33(1), 155–171.

TED summaries: TED talks worth sharing. (2014). *Susan Colantuono: The career advice you probably didn't get*. Retrieved from https://tedsummaries.com/2014/10/11/susan-colantuono-the-career-advice-you-probably-didnt-get/.

White, J., & Dozier, D. (1992). Public relations and management decision-making. In J. Grunig (Ed.), *Excellence in public relations and communication management* (pp. 91–108). Hillsdale, NJ: Lawrence Erlbaum.

Williams, T. (2018, October 11). *America's top CEOs and their college degrees*. Retrieved from www.investopedia.com/articles/professionals/102015/americas-top-ceos-and-their-college-degrees.asp.

Chapter 2

Capitalism: Its Benefits and Discontents

To understand capitalism, you need to first understand its origins. As a corporate communicator, you also need to understand how the principles and outcomes of capitalism attract both vehement supporters and antagonistic opponents. The larger your firm, the more likely you will encounter both ends of this spectrum in your corporate career, as each group places significant change pressures on companies. We're going to trace the roots, priorities, and varieties of capitalism through the lens of political economy in this chapter.

Origins of Political Economy

The term "political economy" dates back to the 18th century and Adam Smith's (1776) publication of *An Inquiry into the Nature and Causes of the Wealth of Nations*, more commonly referred to as *Wealth of Nations*. This point in history is significant for a number of reasons, including a fundamental shift in want satisfaction (Gilpin, 2001; see also Duhé & Sriramesh, 2009). Specifically, the means to satisfy one's wants (e.g., food, clothing, shelter, livelihood) was becoming an increasingly political process. Think of the early colonists in what would become the United States of America. They left England for a new life in a new settlement, with increasing dependence on others outside of their families to get by. Similar shifts were taking place globally. Major political and economic changes were underway as nations defined their sovereignty and expanded commerce beyond their borders. This time in history was ripe for Smith's observations and insights.

The "political" in political economy refers to the public role of the state, or government. The role of the state was debated in these early settlements, asking how much or how little government should be involved in the lives of citizens. The "economy" in political economy refers to the web of interdependent relationships, including individuals, institutions, and organizations, also known as the market, that facilitates an individual's pursuit of self-interest. Economic matters are private matters (Duhé & Sriramesh, 2009).

Political economy, then, recognizes the inescapable interplay of economic, political, and sociological interests and outcomes. The public and the private aspects of a society – how people are governed and how they earn a living – are connected and overlapping. As such, conflicts and special interests are sure to arise. Political economists draw on three disciplines – economics, political science, and sociology – rather than just one, to analyze societal issues and improve overall social welfare (Duhé & Sriramesh, 2009).

DOI: 10.4324/9781003000600-3

Consider healthcare, education, and the environment as examples. If each issue were addressed from only an economic (the cost), political (the will of the majority), or sociological (the cultural considerations) perspective, there would be very different outcomes, none of which would be optimal solutions. A political economy perspective presumes an interdisciplinary approach to resolving issues will render better policy and societal outcomes.

As a field of study, political economy began as an integrated discipline grounded in Adam Smith's (1759) moral philosophy. Its focus, however, gradually shifted almost exclusively toward the price and efficiency concerns of economics regarded as being more "scientific." Levin-Waldman (2012; see also Ławniczak, 2009; Milgate & Stimson, 2009) describes political economy's transition away from its initial political and social grounding as a narrowing of the field's vision of creating a better society. Over the years, the integrated perspective of political economy has fallen in and out of scholarly favor and applied practice in policy analysis. Recent coverage of a "new political economy" (e.g., Besley, 2007) in related literature suggests a re-marrying of political and social perspectives with economic ones. Regardless, the multi-faceted view of political economy aligns well with the multiple stakeholder concerns of corporate and public affairs. Let's explore a bit more.

Political Economy and Public Affairs

How does a political economy perspective apply to corporate and public affairs? When you consider why we do what we do, it becomes evident that the crux of corporate practice is cultivating, sustaining, and negotiating *relationships* that enable the firm to reach its goals. Upon further reflection, you likewise realize the goals of the firm are economic, social, and political in nature and, in fact, parallel a political economy perspective.

Management scholar R. Edward Freeman (2010) explains the objective of the firm is to effectively balance a number of stakeholder interests through these relationships. Firms in decline, he argues, are failing at this crucial balancing act (see also Corporateethics, 2009). Stakeholders include employees, shareholders, suppliers, customers, activists, governments, and "any other group or individual who can affect, or is affected by, the achievement of a corporation's purpose" (Freeman, 2010, p. vi). In the public relations field, the term *public* is often used interchangeably with stakeholder and conveys the same idea of groups imparting influence and change pressures on the firm's activities (Hallahan, 2000).

Think of which groups or individuals can help or hurt your organization. In Freeman's (2010) view, this line of thinking is the foundation of strategic management. By their very nature, stakeholder interests are going to be varied, broad, and even conflicting at times. The larger your organization, the more visible your ability to navigate and negotiate these relationships will be. And even small firms can be shaken or bolstered by stakeholder actions. No organization exists in a vacuum, regardless of size, industry, or type. Stakeholder interaction and information exchange are essential to the continuing life of the firm and central to your work in public affairs. Freeman insists that effective management is considering, addressing, and, yes, aligning these interests so *value* is created for all stakeholders.[1] This is no short order at an organizational level.

Imagine, for instance, if you considered only the interests of shareholders (economic interests), elected officials (political interests), or activist groups (sociological interests) if you were considering sites for a large, new retail store. Your shareholders would expect your company to maximize profits, the elected officials would expect you to hire from the surrounding community, and the activist groups may not want you there at all. If you focused exclusively on only one of these interests, you wouldn't have a successful enterprise.

Now think of operating internationally. If you're a U.S.-based organization wanting to set up shop in Sierra Leone, you'd best well understand market viability (economic interests), government structure (political interests), and local customs pertaining to retailers and consumers (sociological interests) if you hope to sustain your presence there.

In public affairs, you must balance the interests of a variety of stakeholders, not operate in the interests of one at the exclusion of others. That balancing act represents a view of your business from a political economy perspective.[2] It's a perspective I encourage you to always keep in mind by asking: How can my firm be affected economically, politically, and socially by this particular issue or stakeholder group? Thinking through a political economy lens will give you a more comprehensive base from which to build your communication strategy.

A Political Economy Approach to Understanding Capitalism

We return to Adam Smith (1776) to understand the roots of modern-day capitalism (see also Duhé & Sriramesh, 2009). A key takeaway from his voluminous *Wealth of Nations* is the assertion that society is best served by each individual pursuing their self-interest with minimal interference from the state. Much is implied in this synopsis, so let's examine each underlying component of this political economy perspective on the market:

- **Each individual pursuing their self-interest.** Individual freedoms are essential in providing citizens the opportunity to pursue their dreams of how best to contribute to society. Smith (1776) writes how the butcher, the brewer, and the baker provide their goods not out of benevolence or charity, but rather out of their self-interest in earning a living. In Smith's view, no government bureaucrat should dictate a citizen's role in the economy. Rather, that role is motivated, supported, and, if necessary, altered according to an individual's self-interest. Interested in shoes? Be a shoemaker. No one wants to buy your shoes? Try dressmaking instead. The individual is free to adapt and adjust to changing market conditions.
- **Profit is a critical signal.** Pursuit of self-interest must be profitable to be sustainable. Smith ("Adam Smith," 2019) argues that profit benefits not only the individual, but also society because profit-producing activities provide goods and services that have value for others. Furthermore, when individuals seek to maximize the value generated by their goods and services, they benefit not just themselves but all of society, thus increasing the wealth, or prosperity, of a nation. Consider how a profitable business serves more than just its owner. A ripple of economic benefits flows to employees, customers, suppliers, communities, and so on, tracing back to the founder's self-interest. This cascading effect occurs without the founder ever realizing the full reach of their self-interest. The profit signal is key and essential: Profits encourage continued investment in a business and thus expansion of these benefits to society. Unprofitable ventures cannot sustain this overflow of benefits. These businesses will close permanently or reorganize in order to earn a profit.[3]

- **Minimal market interference from the state.** Smith (1776) and his contemporaries had little faith in the ability and experience of government bureaucrats to regulate markets for the exchange of goods and services. He instead proposes that an *invisible hand* would better guide economic transactions toward maximum benefits for society. Specifically, Smith relies on the forces of supply, demand, competition, and profits – his notion of an invisible hand – to provide cues to business owners, guide efficient markets, and optimize the distribution of limited resources, namely land, labor, and capital (i.e., money or other assets).[4] Let's go back to the shoemaker pursuing her self-interest. If she makes too many shoes (a supply issue), she'll have extra inventory on hand that needs to be discounted, donated, or discarded. If a particular style isn't selling (a demand issue), she'll produce fewer of that style, mark down the price, or discontinue a style altogether. If a competing shoemaker opens a shop nearby (a competition issue), she's certain to think about how she can differentiate her styles, service, and customer experience to keep her profits flowing and stay in business. Smith's point is this: Why would a business owner need government bureaucrats to tell them what to make, how much, and how to price it when market signals provided by this invisible hand guide the business owner much more efficiently and effectively?
- **Minimal role for government.** Smith (1776) assigns economic, or profit, pursuits to the private sector and leaves the state, or government, also known as the public sector, to address only three key areas of national interest: defense, justice, and public works. Government must provide a national defense to protect its interests; a system of law to regulate behavior and transactions among citizens; and public works, such as roads and bridges, to provide and preserve necessary infrastructure for its people. In Smith's view, these three areas are essential to the wellbeing of a nation and thus fall under the purview of government. If left to the private sector, defense, justice, and public works would only be provided if they were profitable. Their importance is too great to be subjected to the uncertainties of profits and hence are left to the government's responsibility. In areas of profitability, however, Smith is adamant that these belong to the private sector and are guided more competently by market cues (supply, demand, competition, profits) than any government entity.

Classical View of a Self-Regulating Market

Smith's (1776) fundamental principles of how the market, the state, and citizens should interact in public (political) and private (economic) matters to maximize social welfare inform what's known as the *classical view* of a self-regulating market. From a classical perspective, each person brings their property (labor, goods) to the marketplace, seeking a voluntary exchange for something of value (wages, price). The classical view holds that self-interest and the allocation of resources (land, labor, and capital) are optimized through mutual exchanges.

Self-interest, voluntary exchange, and mutual benefit are key concepts here, so let's more closely examine each. Self-interest is the person doing what they want to do, what they feel drawn to do, or called to do, to sustain a living. Voluntary exchange means that exchanges in the marketplace – for example, I'll pay this amount for that item, or I'll do this amount of work for that fee – are voluntary for all parties involved. That is, no one is coerced or ordered by a government entity or other authority to buy, sell, manufacture, or set a particular price on goods (including labor) offered in a marketplace free of such restrictions. In this way, self-interest is sustained by the individual who finds a way to offer their desired goods or services to the market in a way that brings mutual benefit to others who find value in those goods or services. Essentially, everybody wins by enhancing their *utility*, which is the economic term used to describe one's pleasure or happiness with a particular product or service (Moffatt, 2019).

The crux of the classical view of the market is that market cues – supply, demand, competition, and profits – and not the state – regulate these transactions and keep everyone in check. If someone's labor is not providing the wages they need, the classical view says that person is free to improve their offering or provide something different in the marketplace that can garner a higher level of pay. Ultimately, self-interest, voluntary exchange, and mutual benefit support the functioning of Smith's (1776) invisible hand forces of supply, demand, competition, and profits.

Very simply, the task of the individual is to find what people value, and provide it. When that no longer works, they need to try something else. Hardships occur and require adjustment on the part of *economic agents*, that is, individuals seeking profits in the marketplace. This unrestricted freedom to pursue self-interest and decide what, how much, and at what price to bring one's goods or services to the marketplace – without government intervention – is essential in the classical view. This is the notion of *laissez-faire*, which translates into "let do" or "leave it alone" when referring to the economy (Chappelow, 2019b). The self-regulating interplay of market forces, profits, and self-interest are trusted to optimize the allocation of scarce, or limited, resources, namely, land, labor, and capital. In other words, land, labor, and capital are put to their highest and best use in a self-regulating market. Each resource is limited in supply, but a free market in the classical view ensures land, labor, money, and other assets flow to those opportunities that optimize self-interest, mutual benefit, and, ultimately, social welfare. In the classical view, markets cannot fail.

Neoclassical View of the Market

The *neoclassical view* of the market was introduced at the end of the 19th century and is the predominant model of capitalism in the U.S. today (Gilpin, 2001; see also Duhé & Sriramesh, 2009). Capitalism is an overarching term describing the organization of economic activity in which the means of production (facilities, materials, machinery, etc.) are owned by private individuals or businesses (Chappelow, 2019a).[5] The purest form of capitalism is the classical view of the free market, or laissez-faire, which is unrestrained by government intervention.

For our purposes, there are two key turning points as we transition from the classical view to the neoclassical view of the market that require our attention. The first is the neoclassical recognition that markets can fail, which is in direct opposition to the classical view of market infallibility. And when markets fail, the neoclassical view acknowledges there is a somewhat broader – but still limited – role for government to play beyond Adam Smith's (1776) classical view focusing only on defense, justice, and public goods. The second difference in the neoclassical view compared to its classical predecessor is the introduction of cost-benefit, or marginal, analysis in economic decision-making. We'll cover three types of market failures and the concept of cost-benefit analysis to understand how the neoclassical view emerged to better address the needs of a modern economy. As economies develop and advance, so, too, does economic thinking.

Monopolies as market failure. As self-interest began organizing beyond just individual interests and morphed into large corporate entities in the 18th and 19th centuries, new challenges arose to the notion that markets could fully regulate themselves (Kenton, 2020a; "What is the History," 2019). Some early corporate founders were labeled "robber barons" because of their monopolistic tendencies to maximize profits while restricting competition, a key component of a self-regulating market. Consider this: If a business has monopoly status, that is, if it's the only provider of a widely used good or service, like a cellular network, owners can provide inferior service and charge whatever they wish. Customers, then, are forced to pay set rates until they figure out another means of mobile communication. We're not talking about monopolies that occur organically, like a start-up with a brand-new business idea that no one has yet developed.[6] Rather, monopolies are market failures when economic power is so massive and concentrated that customers lack alternative, viable choices for a particular good. Without competition, monopolies have no incentive to cut prices or improve service. Hence, the market fails to regulate itself without competition as a key signaling device that gives customers a choice of providers and keeps businesses motivated to keep customers happy.

Market failures like monopolies require government intervention (i.e., correction) in the neoclassical view. This is a major shift from the classical view, which greatly restricts government involvement in the marketplace. An example of neoclassical government intervention is the Sherman Antitrust Act of 1890 (Kenton, 2020b).[7] The Sherman Act is landmark U.S. legislation that prevents high concentrations of economic power and preserves competition. Consumers benefit when they have a choice of where to purchase their goods and services, and businesses are forced to compete on price (among other factors) when they are not the sole provider of some product. As such, monopolies are considered market failures in the neoclassical view and require government intervention to ensure the benefits of competition are preserved.[8] Even so-called *natural monopolies*, such as water, gas, nuclear energy, and electricity providers, in which high infrastructural costs limit the number of providers to consumers, are regulated by state and federal agencies to ensure fair pricing and reasonable returns on investments ("Natural Monopolies," 2019).[9]

Negative externalities as market failure. The neoclassical view still holds that profit seeking provides benefits to society. But a market failure is recognized when the pursuit of profits has a negative impact on others who don't benefit from the profits created. Industrial pollution is a classic example of a negative externality ("Negative Externality," n.d.). If a manufacturing plant is polluting the air while maximizing profits, the plant's owners benefit from the profits while neighbors living near the plant bear the "cost" of the pollution (e.g., noise, odor, health concerns) without receiving any direct benefits from the profits. Government intervention in this case of market failure could take the form of more restrictive environmental policies, taxes, or fines to curtail the plant's negative externality, or impact, on the community. The neoclassical view of the market sees government intervention used to lessen the impact of negative externalities as justified and necessary.

Missing markets for public goods as market failure. In economic terms, public goods are non-excludable and non-rival, meaning all consumers have access (non-excludable) and one person's use of a public good doesn't diminish the amount another person can use of that same good (non-rival) ("Missing Markets," 2019; "Public Goods," n.d.). Public goods include clean air, public parks, lighthouses, and street lights. When public goods are not provided, their absence is classified as a market failure. Why? Because the private market, focused on profit-making, wouldn't produce public goods *because* they are non-excludable and non-rival. As such, public goods are also known as missing markets. Instead of the private market, the public sector (or government) decides which public goods are essential to society and funds them with tax dollars. And herein lies the *free rider* problem: A person can use public goods without ever paying for them (not everyone pays taxes) or having their access restricted. Neither of these conditions is appealing to a profit-seeking capitalist who wants to charge customers based on consumption of their products and services. The neoclassical view recognizes public goods that are regarded as necessary but missing as market failures and thus justifies a role for government to provide them.

Introduction of cost-benefit analysis. A concept so fundamental to business decision-making that it almost escapes notice is that of weighing the costs alongside the benefits of numerous options for achieving an objective, and then choosing the option that maximizes the benefits and minimizes the costs. Cost-benefit analysis is embedded in the neoclassical framework and found in both private market and public sector decision-making (Argyrous, 2017).[10] What's important for our purposes in understanding capitalism is the assumption that every cost and every benefit can, or at least should, be reduced to a numerical figure for comparative purposes.

The Firm's Purpose: Shareholder and Stakeholder Perspectives

The neoclassical perspective provides a limited-government model for the conduct of business that acknowledges markets can fail and, when they do, require government intervention in the form of regulation, penalties, or taxes to alleviate burdens associated with those failures. The economy, or market, has grown considerably more complex since Adam Smith's (1776) 18th-century reflections on the enlightened self-interest of the butcher, the brewer, and the baker. Capitalism as a means of organizing economic activity still centers on the idea that pursuit of self-interest leads to prosperity for the whole of society. But the self-interest of a singular baker is undeniably simpler to grasp than the self-interest of a multibillion-dollar corporation. How did capitalism get so complicated? Let's begin by briefly tracing the history of the firm in a U.S. context.[11]

The late 18th century brought the Industrial Revolution to the United States and transformed a largely agricultural society into an automated, industrialized, and urbanized one ("Industrial Revolution," 2019; "What is the History," 2019). Goods once made by hand were mass produced by machines in factories. Global markets expanded through trade and commerce. As efficiencies and profits grew, so did attention to issues of workplace health, safety, child labor, and pollution. Corporations then, and today, played both an important and controversial role in U.S. political economy.

The late 19th century became known as the Gilded Age – a time of tremendous business growth both domestically and internationally ("What is the History," 2019). It was legally easy and, in most states, cost-free to form corporations, unlike today. And like today, corporations went in and out of public favor. The 1929 stock market crash and the Great Depression that followed raised public doubt about big business practices and raised questions about a perceived lack of shareholder control over management decision-making.

By 1945, however, American business was thriving unlike other industrial powers hit hard by WWII. In the latter part of the 20th century, U.S. corporations faced challenges from Japanese and German competitors, outcries for corporate social responsibility, and rises and falls in the stock market. The first two decades of the 21st century have brought major corporate scandals; a financial crisis with a global ripple effect of distrust in large, capitalist institutions; heightened regulation of business activities; and increased shareholder activism. The economic ups and downs of American business are evident, and so is the overflow of economic activities into politics, culture, and society.

A political economy perspective of the firm helps corporate communicators appreciate the breadth of stakeholders impacted by the firm's decisions and activities. In turn, economic, political, and social forces pressure firms to fulfil a variety of responsibilities, including shareholder returns, employee hiring practices, environmental policies, financial soundness, management quality, and, increasingly, a wide array of societal expectations of what a "good" company should and should not do. How does a firm navigate so many demands from so many stakeholders? Let's begin by looking at the purpose of the firm. That is, why does the firm exist?

The firm exists to create value (Bolton, 2015). And value takes on many meanings. For example, the firm's products and services need to be valued enough by customers that they are willing to exchange something of value (money, time) to receive these goods and services. Shareholders invest in the firm, providing money to support the firm's operations with the expectation that their returns on those investments will far exceed their initial investment – that is, they expect their investment value to increase by multiples over time. Value has meaning beyond financials, too. Firms need employees who not only bring value (skills, knowledge) to the firm, but also feel valued and appreciated by the firm, or they'll take their talents elsewhere. Communities value firms that provide jobs, tax dollars, volunteer hours, and donations to the arts, education, and other areas deemed worthy of support. In a communication context, journalists, customers, and business partners value firms that provide trustworthy information in a timely manner.

Value, value, value. It's a term used broadly in business with the underlying notion that the work of the firm should create value for others beyond the firm. Adam Smith (1776) describes the self-interest behind creating the firm as ultimately contributing to the wealth of nations, or the prosperity of all. A profitable firm hires more employees who buy homes, cars, and clothing. Those selling the homes, cars, and clothing benefit, albeit indirectly, from the profitable firm that hired the employees. Each of the people involved in these rippling transactions can then afford vacations, college tuition, and restaurant dining, and the cycle continues. The inherent economic and political freedoms associated with capitalism leverage self-interest to create value for people far beyond the one with the initial idea, or self-interest, to start a business. Value creation and sustainability of the firm go hand in hand (Bolton, 2015). The challenge for the business owner is to figure out which business elements best create value for profits and growth and maintain this cycle of benefits from capitalism (Hillstrom, 2019).

The idea of creating value wasn't always as broad-reaching as it is today. Back when corporations were just beginning to form in the United States, many, if not most, had monopoly status before competing firms and government regulations surfaced. It made sense that shareholder interests were a primary focus of the firm. These shareholders took a risk and invested their dollars toward making these early firms successful with an understanding that at some point in time they, too, would benefit from the firm's profits.[12] Think of the early railroads, connecting parts of the country for the first time via transportation and commerce. Being first, they weren't concerned about competitors luring away customers or employees, or government regulators encroaching on their operations. It made sense that the primary concern of railroad management was to maximize shareholder value. Shareholders were the one public, or stakeholder, that commanded their full attention and were (literally) banking on their success. As management found ways to increase profits, they were able to share more of those profits with the shareholders who provided the capital to get the railroad up and running. Increasing shareholder value was a win for shareholders and management: Each benefitted financially from a successful railroad.

Shareholder primacy is a management approach to business that places shareholder interests above that of other stakeholders ("What is Shareholder Primacy," 2019). Shareholders actually own "shares" of the corporation and have the ability to influence and even control a company's operations. Thus, maximizing shareholder wealth becomes a company's top priority. Today, shareholder value is tracked through the rising and falling of stock prices and dividend payouts, among other measures. Investor relations staff focus their communications with shareholders on how firms are contributing to and increasing shareholder wealth.

Not surprisingly, the shareholder primacy approach to business has its critics. Concerns include management making short-term decisions to improve financial performance rather than taking a more thoughtful, long-term approach that serves more than just financial interests ("What is Shareholder Primacy," 2019). Companies focused solely on increasing shareholder wealth may avoid risk-taking and investing in new areas of growth for fear that potential setbacks could negatively affect shareholder value. Or, firms mainly concerned with returns to shareholders could put cash into dividends paid to shareholders instead of, say, research and development that could ultimately bring comparatively more long-term value to the company.

Counter to shareholder primacy is Freeman's (2010) previously discussed stakeholder model that insists the firm consider the interests of multiple stakeholders, not just shareholders (see also, Pfarrer, 2010). Today, businesses have multiple responsibilities to suppliers, partners, employees, regulators, customers, and, yes, investors and other financiers. A stakeholder approach demands that the firm identifies, prioritizes, and addresses a variety of stakeholder interests to maximize its value. It follows, too, that when firms enhance value across multiple stakeholders, shareholders and other investors benefit in the long term, too. From a public affairs perspective, focusing solely on shareholders may seem less complicated, but the realities of modern business dictate that value creation applies to a breadth of stakeholders that drive a firm's success, not just one.

Capitalism in the U.S.

The U.S. form of capitalism is *market-oriented capitalism* in which the primary purpose of the market is to benefit consumers and maximize value creation (Gilpin, 2001; see also Duhé & Sriramesh, 2009). Capitalism in the U.S. is profit-centered, taking its cues from classical political economic thinking that profitable firms benefit the whole of society. Both economic and political freedoms are essential to the U.S. model. These freedoms contribute to the notion of "the American dream" whereby any person, regardless of background, origin, or means can go from rags to riches by bringing their self-interest to a market that discriminates only on one's ability to navigate the forces of supply, demand, and competition.

Famed classical economist Milton Friedman (1982) credits U.S. market-oriented capitalism as the greatest wealth generator in human history with its ability to lift people out of poverty, improve living conditions, and advance societies (see also Safvio, 2007). Whole Foods CEO John Mackey (Mackey & Sisodia, 2014) praises U.S. capitalism as heroic in its power to transform societies and the wellbeing of masses of people, not just a chosen few. The track record of U.S. capitalism is compelling, drawing generations to the country's shores in search of the American dream and placing the U.S. among the world's greatest economic powers.

The U.S. model of capitalism is not without its critics, however (Duhé & Sriramesh, 2009). The inherent freedoms associated with the profit-seeking focus of U.S. capitalism also give rise to activist voices that vehemently oppose a widening gap between "winners" who succeed in the marketplace and outcomes imposed on "losers" who aren't as successful. Arguments for and against globalization – the expansion of business practices beyond a firm's home country and into international markets – fall along these lines as well. Corporate misconduct, exorbitant executive pay packages, and the plight of those either left behind or unable to participate in the wealth-building benefits of capitalism only exacerbate public distrust and frustration with large companies. And where the public goes, public policy in the form of harsher regulations and "safety net" programs tend to follow. As such, capitalism in the U.S. isn't a pure laissez faire system but rather a mixed model including government support for welfare payments, unemployment benefits, health care, and wealth transfer programs including a progressive tax structure[13] that essentially shifts money from those who earn more to those who earn less (see also, Chappelow, 2019a).

The cost-benefit analysis introduced in the neoclassical view of the economy likewise attracts criticism of corporate interests and is highly relevant to corporate communication practice (Duhé & Sriramesh, 2009). As profit-seeking entities, firms will invest in any worthwhile initiative to the point where cost equals benefit, but usually not beyond where cost exceeds benefit. Firms don't stay in business if they're incurring extensive losses without some promise of recovery. Although it's true that some investments have short-term losses before realizing long-term gains, generally speaking, the benefits of an investment must exceed its cost. This formula gives rise to activist pressures against corporations, too. Publics and firms can disagree on what is a "reasonable" cost and a "worthwhile" benefit.

An example is helpful here. Think of cases where companies are following the letter of U.S. law on product ingredients, design, or safety. Baby products are a good example. Around 2009, consumer and environmental watch groups began protesting the presence of formaldehyde, a chemical used in embalming, in baby shampoos and other care products (Boyles, 2009; Thomas, 2014). Apparently, chemical byproducts considered offensive by activists and parents alike were banned from baby products in other countries but still permitted in the U.S. "But we're adhering to current regulations," companies may say, and object to incurring additional costs associated with going above and beyond what the law requires.

In this particular scenario, there is a cost associated with removing certain chemicals in a manufacturing process that already meets the standards of the law. But what of public opinion and consumer behavior? In this case, major consumer product provider Johnson & Johnson (J&J) reconfigured its manufacturing process to remove the unwanted chemicals, thus demonstrating that the benefits of *not* being targeted by pressure groups outweighed whatever cost was necessary to remove the chemicals from baby care products. The company went as far as working with lawmakers to strengthen Federal Drug Administration oversight of chemical safety even though J&J's global toxicologist stated there is more formaldehyde in one apple than in 14 bottles of baby shampoo (Browning, 2012).

What's the lesson here? When faced with opposition, companies can choose to stick to their guns and defend their actions or materially respond to customer concerns. There's also room to maneuver between those two extremes. Ultimately, companies must assess the costs and benefits associated with any decision – these are still *business* decisions. More often than not, however the calculation is derived, companies will land on a solution perceived as delivering more benefits than cost. Communicators with business acumen are needed in that decision-making process to fully account for stakeholder costs and benefits that may not otherwise be considered by management. The J&J case illustrates, too, how one issue can have overlapping effects in a firm's economic, political, and social operating environment.

A Brief Note on Capitalism Abroad

Capitalism is not a one-size-fits-all model of organizing economic activity. Nor should the U.S. model be considered the standard bearer against which all other capitalist models are judged better or worse.[14] Variations of capitalism could fill an entire book, but, for our purposes, we'll cover just a few highlights illustrating differences in political economies across borders. Each country has its unique political economic structure. As a corporate communicator, learn more about those structures before you work with or in those countries. Political economies dictate the publics, issues, and priorities you'll encounter and the freedoms (or lack of freedoms) you have to work as a communicator (Duhé & Sriramesh, 2009). Never assume! Knowledge always trumps uninformed judgment.

For example, compared to the U.S. model of market-oriented capitalism focused on consumers, wealth creation, and individual self-interest, Japan instead practices *collective capitalism* in which societal interests are more important than individual interests, and there is a strong commitment to national image and social harmony (Duhé & Sriramesh, 2009; see also Gilpin, 2001). Germany, on the other hand, balances social harmony and market efficiency with social concerns and supports a highly collusive relationship between labor, government, and business we would consider unusual in the U.S. Again, different isn't better or worse, just different – and worth understanding why and how capitalism varies around the globe.

Some initial questions to jump-start your understanding of political economies abroad include: What's the primary purpose of the nation's economy activity – power, wealth, or harmony? What is the role of the state in the economy – interventionist and active, or minimal and relatively passive? How about the structure of the corporate sector and civil society[15] – what's their primary focus? Role in social welfare? Level of activism? (Gilpin,

2001; see also Duhé & Sriramesh, 2009). Answers vary widely across countries and directly inform communication strategies and tactics.

CSR and ESG

The idea that corporations should address responsibilities beyond that of shareholders, or generating profits, dates back to before 1970. *Corporate social responsibility*, or CSR, was famously addressed by Milton Friedman (1970) in his *New York Times Magazine* essay, *The Social Responsibility of Business is to Increase its Profits*. Friedman's prose is frequently cited as solely promoting shareholder primacy to the exclusion of other stakeholders. Although a closer read underscores Friedman's uncompromising belief in market, as opposed to political, mechanisms guiding an economy (which aligns with his classical view of economics), he also recognizes a need for firms to dedicate resources to support their communities. Whether business contributions are used to advance schools, governments, charities, or other causes, Friedman argues that these are justifiable business-driven investments that make it easier to attract and retain employees or reduce costs. He is opposed to hypocritically labeling these contributions as acts of "social responsibility" when they clearly align with and serve to promote business interests. In his words:

> In each of these – and many similar – cases, there is a strong temptation to rationalize these actions as an exercise of "social responsibility." In the present climate of opinion, with its widespread aversion to "capitalism," "profits," the "soulless corporation" and so on, this is one way for a corporation to generate goodwill as a by-product of expenditures that are entirely justified on its own self-interest.
>
> (Friedman, 1970, p. 5)

Semantics aside, there is ample evidence in today's business climate that firms are taking stances on social issues, actively supporting causes, and addressing social ills as part of their business models. In many cases, shareholders and customers seek to do business with firms that are more active in the social realm. Firms can lose some customers in the process of taking social positions (or supporting certain causes) while gaining others.[16] But the cost-benefit calculation remains even in these circumstances. When you see a company partaking in these activities, you can bet that the benefits of speaking out, investing resources, and expanding the company's reach into areas perceived as more "social" than "business" are viewed by the firm as ultimately exceeding any related costs.

Not far removed from CSR is ESG, or *Environmental, Social, and Governance* criteria used by socially conscious investors to screen companies for potential investments (Chen, 2019). In particular, firms are evaluated on the quality of their environmental stewardship; business relationships across stakeholder groups; and corporate governance of executive pay, internal controls, and shareholder rights. Proponents of tracking ESG activities claim firms performing well in these areas are less likely to encounter crises that can plummet stock prices and significantly diminish shareholder (and other stakeholder) value. On the company side, ESG management involves assessing, adjusting, and communicating policies, systems, and processes regarding issues such as climate change, labor practices, employee welfare, and consumer safety (Papadopoulos & Araujo, 2020; Price, 2018).

A number of rating systems exist that rank companies, and their financial performance, based on ESG initiatives.[17]

Corporate Governance

In this chapter, we've covered the benefits and discontents associated with capitalism. Corporate governance is a key factor in placing appropriate checks and balances on corporate activity so that self-interest, profit-seeking, and other business activities are allowed to thrive yet still remain within the bounds of the law and ethical corporate practices.[18] Note how the definition of corporate governance takes a stakeholder – not just a shareholder – perspective:

> Corporate governance is the combination of rules, processes or laws by which businesses are operated, regulated or controlled. The term encompasses the internal and external factors that affect the interests of a company's stakeholders, including shareholders, customers, suppliers, government regulators and management. The board of directors is responsible for creating the framework for corporate governance that best aligns business conduct with objectives.
>
> (Rouse, 2019, para. 1)

Corporate governance's reach is far and wide, encompassing business plans, human resource policies, decision-making models, compensation and incentive programs, dividend payouts, conflict resolution procedures, accounting methods, contracts, and so on. Principles of good corporate governance include treating shareholders fairly and equally (including informing them of their rights as owners in the firm), upholding obligations to stakeholders other than shareholders, operating with a commitment to accountability and transparency, and following an agreed upon code of conduct in the firm's business transactions.

A company's board of directors is its highest governing authority and, as such, responsible for the protection of shareholder assets and governance (Kennon, 2020). Directors are elected by shareholders to represent a variety of stakeholders on behalf of the company. Boards comprise both inside members, who are company executives, and outside, or independent, members who bring significant expertise that benefits the company. Outside members offer an objective perspective that helps to balance stakeholder interests with inside interests. Board committees are designed to oversee particular areas of business practice, including compensation, audits, appointments to the board, and evaluation of management performance ("Corporate Governance," 2019). Every publicly held company is required to have a board of directors.

The Sarbanes-Oxley Act of 2002, or SOX (pronounced "socks"), is a far-reaching regulatory response to a glut of corporate scandals, including WorldCom and Enron.[19] Chapter 5 covers elements of SOX designed to protect investors. Here, our focus is SOX implications for board governance, which include requirement of an independent audit committee able to bypass management in the hearing of complaints regarding internal controls or accounting matters from within the company (Johnson & Sides, 2004). Further, the majority of the board must be independent, non-management directors able to meet outside of the presence of company management. The New York Stock Exchange (NYSE) requires listed companies to adopt and disclose corporate governance guidelines that address director qualifications, responsibilities, and access to management, among other policies.

We conclude our governance discussion by taking a look at Darden's Corporate Governance Guidelines (2018), provided in Box 2.1. Darden Concepts, Inc. is a restaurant conglomerate of brands including Olive Garden, Cheddar's Scratch Kitchen, Seasons 52, The Capital Grille, and Eddie V's (Darden, 2020). Note how the company's governance guidelines fall under the purview of the Board's Nominating and Governance Committee and are reviewed by the Board annually. The Board is elected by shareholders and, in turn, selects the CEO. Working with the CEO, the Board selects, advises, and monitors the performance of the senior management team. The Chairman (of the Board) and CEO are separate positions at Darden, but other companies combine the two roles into one position. Their responsibilities, along with that of directors, are outlined, as are the qualifications to serve as a director. Independent directors must meet the *bright-line standards* set by the NYSE that define and determine qualifications for independence. The Board committee structure is formalized in this document, as are requirements to evaluate the effectiveness of both Board members and the CEO. Remaining sections include codes of business conduct, director communications and access to pertinent parties, director compensation, and confidentiality.

Box 2.1 Darden Corporate Governance Guidelines

(Reprinted with the permission of Darden Restaurants, Inc.)

The following corporate governance guidelines have been approved by the Board of Directors (the "Board") and, along with the charters of the Board committees, provide the framework for the governance of Darden Restaurants, Inc. ("Darden" or the "Company"). The Nominating and Governance Committee will review the corporate governance guidelines and other aspects of Darden's governance as necessary, but no less than annually, and will report its findings and recommendations to the full Board. If necessary, the corporate governance guidelines shall be revised and updated by the Board based on the recommendations of the Nominating and Governance Committee.

ROLE OF THE BOARD AND MANAGEMENT

Darden's business is conducted by its employees, managers and officers, under the direction of the chief executive officer (the "CEO") and the oversight of the Board, to enhance the long-term value of the Company for its shareholders. The Board is elected annually by the shareholders to oversee management and to assure that the long-term interests of the shareholders are being served. The Board selects the CEO and, in consultation with the CEO, selects the senior management team, acts as an advisor and counselor to senior management and ultimately monitors its performance. Both the Board and management recognize that the long-term interests of shareholders are advanced by responsibly addressing the concerns of other stakeholders and interested parties including employees, recruits, customers, suppliers, Darden communities, government officials and the public at large.

CHAIRMAN AND CEO

It is the policy of the Company that the positions of the Chairman of the Board and CEO be held by separate persons and that the position of Chairman be held by an independent director.

DIRECTOR RESPONSIBILITIES

The Board shall have at least four regularly scheduled meetings a year at which it reviews and discusses reports by management on the performance of the Company, its plans and prospects, as well as immediate issues facing the Company. In addition, special meetings may be called from time to time as determined by the needs of the business. Directors are expected to attend all scheduled Board and committee meetings, and the annual meeting of shareholders. In addition to its general oversight of management, the Board, acting itself or through one or more of its committees, performs a number of specific functions, including:

A. Selecting, evaluating and determining the compensation of the CEO and overseeing CEO succession planning;
B. Providing counsel and oversight on the selection, evaluation, development and compensation of senior management;
C. Reviewing, approving and monitoring fundamental financial and business strategies and major corporate actions;
D. Assessing major risks facing the Company, and reviewing options for their mitigation; and
E. Ensuring processes are in place for maintaining the integrity of the Company, including the integrity of the financial statements, the integrity of compliance with law and ethics, the integrity of relationships with customers, suppliers, Darden communities, government officials and the public at large, and the integrity of relationships with other stakeholders.

DIRECTOR QUALIFICATION STANDARDS

Darden's mission is to be financially successful through great people consistently delivering outstanding food, drinks and service in an inviting atmosphere making every guest loyal. This mission is supported by the Company's core values of integrity and fairness, respect and caring, diversity, always learning – always teaching, being "of service," teamwork and excellence. Directors should reflect these core values, possess the highest personal and professional ethics, and be committed to representing the long-term interests of the shareholders. They should also have an inquisitive and objective perspective, practical wisdom and mature judgment. Darden endeavors to have a Board representing diverse experience at policy-making levels in business, government, education and technology, and in areas that are relevant to the Company's restaurant activities. Recruiting, hiring and nurturing the careers of women and minorities and increasing the diversity of the Company's suppliers are top priorities at Darden, and the Board intends to maintain its diversity as well. Further information concerning director qualification standards will be provided in the Director Nomination Protocol that is attached to and made a part of the charter of the Nominating and Governance Committee.

Directors must be willing to devote sufficient time to carrying out their duties and responsibilities effectively, and should be committed to serve on the Board for an extended period of time. Directors are expected to offer their resignation in the event of any significant change in their personal circumstances, including a change in or termination of their principal job responsibilities. The resignation will be considered by the Nominating and Governance Committee, and it will recommend to the Board the action, if any, to be taken with respect to the resignation. Directors should also offer their resignation in writing upon leaving the Board for any reason.

Directors should not serve on more than four other boards of public companies in addition to the Company's board. No member of the Audit Committee of the Board should simultaneously serve on the audit committee of more than three public companies, including the Company's. Directors should notify the Nominating and Governance Committee in advance of becoming a director or a member of the audit committee of another public company.

The Board self-evaluation process described below will be an important determinant for board tenure. Directors will not be nominated for election to the Board after their 73rd birthday, except when the full Board determines that special circumstances exist. Directors will be subject to stock ownership guidelines recommended by the Nominating and Governance Committee and approved by the full Board.

INDEPENDENCE OF DIRECTORS

It is the policy of the Company that at least two-thirds of the directors must be independent directors as defined under the rules of the New York Stock Exchange ("NYSE").

Historically, transactions of any kind between the Company and its directors have been infrequent and immaterial, and the Company intends to encourage its outside directors to continue to limit their contacts with the Company. Nevertheless, the Company will in any event comply with the applicable independence standards of the NYSE. In accordance with the listing standards of the NYSE, a director is "independent" if the Board affirmatively determines that a director has no material relationship with the Company (either directly or as a partner, shareholder or officer of an organization that has a relationship with the Company), and the director meets the bright-line independence standards promulgated by the NYSE in its listing standards. Independence determinations will be made on an annual basis by the Board, on the recommendation of the Nominating and Governance Committee, at the time that the Board approves director nominees for inclusion in the proxy statement or at any time a director joins the Board between annual meetings. The Board will broadly consider all relevant facts and circumstances in determining director independence.

Members of the Audit Committee must satisfy the requirements of Rule 10A-3 under the Securities Exchange Act of 1934 (the "Exchange Act"), as amended from time to time.

Members of the Compensation Committee must satisfy the requirements of Rule 10C-1 under the Exchange Act, as amended from time to time.

The Company will not make any personal loans or extensions of credit to directors or executive officers. All directors are required to deal at arm's length with the Company and its subsidiaries and to disclose any material circumstances that might be perceived as a conflict of interest.

SIZE OF BOARD AND SELECTION PROCESS

The directors are elected each year by the shareholders at the annual meeting of shareholders. The Board proposes a slate of nominees to the shareholders for election to the Board. The Nominating and Governance Committee considers and makes recommendations to the Board concerning the appropriate size and needs of the Board. The Committee considers candidates to fill new positions created by expansion and vacancies that occur by resignation or any other reason. Shareholders may propose nominees for consideration by the Nominating and Governance Committee by submitting the names and supporting information to the Secretary of the Company in accordance with the deadlines and procedures indicated in the proxy statement for the annual meeting of shareholders and the Company's Bylaws. Between annual shareholder meetings, the Board may elect directors to serve until the next annual meeting. Subject to the Company's Articles of Incorporation and Bylaws, the Board also determines the number of directors on the Board. The Board believes that, given the size and breadth of Darden and the need for diversity of board views, the size of the Board should be in the range of eight to ten directors. The Board annually reviews the appropriate size of the Board.

BOARD COMMITTEES

The Board currently has established the following standing committees to assist the Board in discharging its responsibilities: (i) Audit Committee; (ii) Compensation Committee; (iii) Nominating and Governance Committee; and (iv) Finance Committee. The Board determines the responsibilities of each of the committees from time to time. The duties for each of these committees shall be outlined in the committee charters, which are published on the Company's website. The committee chairs report the highlights of their meetings to the full Board following each meeting of the respective committees. The Audit Committee, Compensation Committee, Nominating and Governance Committee and Finance Committee are made up entirely of independent directors. From time to time, the Board may provide for such other standing committees or special committees as may be necessary to carry out its responsibilities.

MEETINGS OF INDEPENDENT DIRECTORS

The Board will meet in executive session of independent directors without management present at least four times a year on the same day as the regularly scheduled Board meetings. Such sessions will be led by the independent Chairman of the Board. The Chairman will approve Board meeting agendas, including approving meeting schedules to assure that there is sufficient time for discussion of all agenda items, and other information sent to the Board, advise the committee chairs with respect to agendas and information needs relating to committee meetings, have the authority to call meetings of independent directors as he or she deems appropriate and perform other duties as the Board may from time to time delegate to assist the Board in fulfilling its responsibilities. The identity of the Chairman will be stated in the proxy statement for the Company's annual meeting of shareholders. The independent directors may meet without management present at any other times as determined by the Chairman.

ANNUAL PERFORMANCE EVALUATION OF THE BOARD

The Board and each of the committees will perform an annual self-evaluation. The directors will be requested to provide their assessments of the effectiveness of the Board and the committees on which they serve. The individual assessments will be organized and summarized for discussion with the Board and the committees. The Nominating and Governance Committee shall oversee the self-evaluation processes, summarize the results of the evaluations and present the results to the Board. In addition to the annual self-evaluations, no less often than every two years, the board will undergo an in-depth evaluation of its overall effectiveness, conducted by an independent facilitator.

EVALUATION OF THE CEO

The independent directors, led by the Chairman of the Compensation Committee, shall perform an annual evaluation in executive session of the CEO. The evaluation shall be based on a broad range of criteria and include objective criteria, including performance of the business, accomplishment of long-term strategic objectives and development of management succession.

SETTING THE BOARD AND COMMITTEE AGENDA

The Chairman of the Board sets the agenda for Board meetings with the understanding that certain items pertinent to the advisory and monitoring functions of the Board be brought to it periodically for review and decision. The Chairman or committee chair, as appropriate, will determine the nature and extent of information to be provided regularly to the directors before each regularly scheduled Board or committee meeting. Board and committee materials relating to agenda items are provided to directors sufficiently in advance of meetings to allow the directors to prepare for discussion of the items at the meeting. Directors are responsible for reviewing these materials prior to each Board or committee meeting. Any member of the Board may make suggestions to the Chairman or appropriate committee chair at any time that an item be included on the agenda, or that information be included in pre-meeting materials.

CODES OF BUSINESS CONDUCT AND ETHICS

All Darden employees, including the CEO, chief financial officer and principal accounting officer, are required to abide by Darden's Code of Conduct to ensure that the Company's business is conducted in a consistently legal and ethical manner. The Company has also adopted an additional Code of Ethics for CEO and Senior Financial Officers and a Code of Business Conduct and Ethics for Members of the Board of Directors. These Codes cover conflicts of interest; corporate opportunities; confidentiality; compliance with laws, rules and regulations; fair dealing; and encourage the reporting of any illegal or unethical behavior. The Codes are posted on the Company's website. The Board expects Darden directors, as well as officers and employees, to act ethically at all times and to adhere to these Codes. The Sarbanes-Oxley Act of 2002 also requires companies to have procedures to receive, retain and treat complaints regarding accounting, internal accounting controls or auditing matters and to allow for the confidential and anonymous submission by employees of concerns regarding questionable accounting or auditing matters. We currently have procedures in place, and a description of the procedures is posted on the Company's website. The Audit Committee oversees treatment of employee concerns in this area.

RELATED PARTY TRANSACTIONS

It is the policy of the Board that Interested Transactions with a Related Party, as those terms are defined below, are prohibited without prior approval of the Board. The Board shall review the material facts of each proposed Interested Transaction and either approve or disapprove of the entry into the Interested Transaction. In determining whether to approve an Interested Transaction, the Board will consider whether the Interested Transaction is in, or not inconsistent with, the best interests of the Company and its shareholders. The Board will take into account, among other facts and circumstances it deems appropriate, whether the Interested Transaction is on terms no less favorable than terms generally available to an unaffiliated third party under the same or similar circumstances, and the extent of the Related Party's interest in the transaction.

No director shall participate in any discussion or approval of an Interested Transaction for which he or she is a Related Party, except to provide all material information as requested. If an Interested Transaction will be ongoing, the Board may establish guidelines for the Company's management to follow in its dealings with the Related Party.

An "Interested Transaction" is any transaction, arrangement or relationship (or series of similar transactions, arrangements or relationships) in which (1) the amount involved exceeds $120,000 in any calendar year, (2) the Company is a participant, and (3) any Related Party has or will have a direct or indirect interest (other than solely as a result of being a director or a less than 10 percent beneficial owner of another entity), but does not include any salary or compensation paid by the Company to a director or for the employment of an executive officer that is required to be reported in the Company's proxy statement.

A "Related Party" is any (1) person who is or was since the beginning of the last fiscal year an executive officer, director or nominee for election as a director of the Company, (2) beneficial owner of more than five percent of the Company's common stock, or (3) immediate family member of any of the foregoing.

An "immediate family member" is any child, stepchild, parent, stepparent, spouse, sibling, mother-in-law, father-in-law, son-in-law, daughter-in-law, brother-in-law, or sister-in-law of the person in question and any person (other than a tenant or employee) sharing the household of the person in question.

COMMUNICATING WITH DIRECTORS AND SHAREHOLDERS

Shareholders may communicate directly with the Board, the Chairman or non-employee directors as a group by following the Shareholder Communication Procedures that are approved by the Company's independent directors and posted on the Company's website. It is the policy of the Company that management speaks for the Company. This policy does not preclude non-employee directors from meeting with shareholders, but any meetings between directors and shareholders generally are held with management present. In addition, the Chairman is available for consultation with major shareholders, if requested. Anyone who has a concern about the Company's conduct, or about the Company's accounting, internal accounting controls or auditing matters, may communicate that concern using the Shareholder Communication Procedures or by following the confidential process established for submission of employee complaints about accounting or auditing matters described in the Code of Business Conduct and Ethics section above. Concerns relating to accounting, internal controls, auditing or officer conduct will be sent immediately to the chair of the Audit Committee and will be simultaneously reviewed and addressed by the Company's internal auditor in the same way that other concerns are addressed by the Company. The Company's Code of Business Conduct and Ethics prohibits any employee from retaliating or taking any adverse action against anyone who in good faith raises or helps to resolve an integrity concern.

DIRECTOR COMPENSATION

Directors who are also Darden employees do not receive additional compensation for serving on the Board. The Nominating and Governance Committee has the responsibility for recommending to the Board compensation and benefits for non-employee directors. In discharging this duty, the Committee will be guided by three goals: compensation should fairly pay directors for work required in a company of Darden's size and scope; compensation should align directors' interests with the long-term interests of shareholders; and the structure of the compensation should be adequate to enable the Company to attract and retain well-qualified directors. The Nominating and Governance Committee reviews the compensation of directors annually.

MANAGEMENT SUCCESSION PLAN

The Board approves and maintains a succession plan for the CEO and senior executives. To assist the Board, the CEO annually provides an assessment of senior managers and of their potential to succeed him or her. He or she also provides the Board with an assessment of persons considered potential successors to certain senior management positions.

ANNUAL COMPENSATION REVIEW OF SENIOR MANAGEMENT

The Compensation Committee will annually approve the goals and objectives for compensating the CEO. The Committee will evaluate the CEO's performance in light of these goals and objectives before making recommendations to the other independent directors who will, together with the Committee, determine the CEO's salary, bonus and other incentive and equity compensation. The Committee will also annually approve the compensation structure for the Company's executive officers, and will discuss with the CEO the performance of the Company's executive officers before approving their salary, bonus and other incentive and equity compensation.

DIRECTOR ACCESS TO SENIOR MANAGEMENT

Board members shall have complete access to management. Board members shall use sound business judgment to ensure that such contact is not distracting. At the invitation of the Board, members of senior management recommended by the CEO or the Chairman may attend Board meetings or portions of meetings to participate in discussions.

DIRECTOR ACCESS TO INDEPENDENT ADVISORS

The Board and its committees have the right at any time to retain independent outside financial, legal, accounting or other advisors.

DIRECTOR ORIENTATION AND CONTINUING EDUCATION

The general counsel and the chief financial officer will be responsible for providing an orientation for new directors and for periodically providing materials or briefing sessions for all directors on subjects that would assist them in discharging their duties. Each new director will, within six months of election to the board, receive a personal briefing by senior management at the Company's restaurant support center on the Company's strategic plans, financial statements, and key policies and practices. The Company will pay reasonable expenses and fees incurred for attendance at director continuing education institutes and programs, and will host continuing education for directors from time to time as appropriate.

RISK OVERSIGHT

The Board shall oversee the establishment and maintenance of the Company's risk management processes. The Board may delegate primary responsibility for oversight of specific risks to any one or more of its committees.

CONFIDENTIALITY

Pursuant to the Code of Business Conduct and Ethics for Members of the Board of Directors, directors should maintain the confidentiality of information entrusted to them by the Company and any other confidential information about the Company that comes to them, from whatever source, in their capacity as a director, except when disclosure is authorized or legally mandated.

Adopted by Board of Directors July 21, 2003
Amended March 25, 2004
Amended March 22, 2005
Amended September 12, 2008
Amended December 16, 2009
Revised October 12, 2010
Amended June 20, 2012
Amended June 18, 2013
Amended July 28, 2014
Amended November 11, 2014
Amended June 17, 2015
Amended June 22, 2017
Amended June 20, 2018

Communicating Capitalism

The 21st century has brought a tumultuous wave of change to U.S. business operations. Accounting frauds, restrictive regulations, a worldwide financial crisis, a global pandemic, and intense political divides have brought further attention to the perceived "winners" and "losers" in a capitalist economy. The overlapping of economic, political, and social concerns in contemporary debates is palpable. The fabric of U.S. capitalism – its founding principles, operating mechanisms, and minimal role for government – is under scrutiny by those who seek to dismantle its current functioning and viewed as under vicious attack by others who passionately defend its framework. There's a lot of room to maneuver between these opposing points of view. You may be steadfast or struggling in your own opinions of capitalism.

Meanwhile, in the midst of disagreements over capitalism in our modern economy, your company is working to stay in business. The role you serve as a corporate communicator, connector, and counselor is unique and vital in navigating public sentiment on economic, political, and social issues. Know your business well enough to understand how public sentiment, on certain issues, can impact your profitability. Listen to your stakeholders, even when you disagree with them. Challenge your colleagues, even when you agree with them. Maintain a comprehensive, current view of how your company benefits, frustrates, and interacts with its stakeholders – not through your usual digital platforms but more importantly by putting aside your laptop and reaching out to personally hear how stakeholders are affected by your business. Commit yourself to ongoing, actual conversations with employees, customers, suppliers, regulators, and even activists. Bring the positives and negatives you hear to your colleagues and executives. Then, draw on your business acumen and your communication expertise to figure out what comes next. Take an active role in helping your company not just survive, but thrive.

Notes

1 See www.stakeholdertheory.org for resources from R. Edward Freeman and other scholars who study stakeholder theory.
2 See Ławniczak (2009) for his specific call to a more holistic view of public relations through a political economy perspective.
3 See Chapter 4 The Art and Science of Financial Statements for an explanation of profit accounting and Chapter 5 How and Why Finance Rules the Business World to learn more about business bankruptcy and reorganization options.
4 See Chapter 5 How and Why Finance Rules the Business World for a more in-depth explanation of capital.
5 In comparison, and very simply, the state owns the means of production in socialism, and the community owns the means of production in communism. A brief comparison of political economic systems is found at www.webpages.uidaho.edu/engl_258/lecture%20notes/capitalism%20etc%20defined.htm.
6 See Chapter 10 What is Strategy? for a related discussion of "blue ocean" ventures.
7 U.S. monopolies date back to the time of the American Revolution when companies were granted exclusive contracts, or "trusts," to carry out certain public works, including the production of steel, oil, and tobacco. With little government oversight, these early firms were able to set national prices for these goods without competitive pressures to adjust those prices. The Sherman "antitrust" legislation gave the U.S. government power to dismantle these high concentrations of economic power and bring competition back into the market (Beattie, 2019; "What are the Most Famous Monopolies," 2020).
8 For a contemporary case example, see Kang, C. (2018, June 12). *Why the AT&T-Time Warner case was so closely watched*. Retrieved from www.nytimes.com/2018/06/12/business/dealbook/att-time-warner-trial-antitrust-ruling.html.

9 From a communication perspective, terms such as "fair" and "reasonable" are going to be differently defined and heavily debated by consumer advocates and utility producers.
10 Cost-benefit analysis relates to marginal analysis, which is covered in Chapter 3 A Micro and Macro View of the Economy.
11 The Smithsonian's National Museum of American History offers a helpful review of the corporate era in U.S. history at https://americanhistory.si.edu/american-enterprise-exhibition/corporate-era.
12 See Chapter 5 How and Why Finance Rules the Business World for an explanation of shareholder benefits and expectations.
13 A progressive tax structure is one in which the more one earns, the more tax one can expect to pay.
14 Highly recommended is Amy Chua's analysis of how the best of intentions to export the U.S. model of free markets and democracy can have detrimental effects abroad in Chua, A. (2003). *World on fire: How exporting free market democracy breeds ethnic hatred and global instability*. New York, NY: Doubleday.
15 Civil society is the third realm of society outside of business and government, including volunteer organizations, nonprofits, and NGOs.
16 Procter & Gamble's stances on toxic masculinity (see www.marketwatch.com/story/pgs-gillette-ad-asks-men-to-shave-their-toxic-masculinity-and-a-big-backlash-ensues-2019-01-15) and race (see www.cnbc.com/2019/06/27/pgs-latest-ad-takes-on-racial-bias-of-black-men-in-america.html) are good examples.
17 See, for example, "Best ESG Companies: Top 50 Stocks for Environmental, Social and Governance Values." (2020, October 26). Retrieved from www.investors.com/news/esg-companies-list-best-esg-stocks-environmental-social-governance-values/.
18 We focus on governance structure here. See Chapter 11 And Here Comes Legal and Chapter 12 Last but not Least: Business Ethics for additional topics related to acceptable corporate practices.
19 See Chapter 4 The Art and Science of Financial Statements for a discussion of WorldCom and other corporate accounting scandals.

References

Adam Smith 1723-1790. (2019). Retrieved from www.econlib.org/library/Enc/bios/Smith.html.
Argyrous, G. (2017). Cost-benefit analysis as operationalized neoclassical economics: From evidence to folklore. *Journal of Australian Political Economy, 80*, 201–211.
Beattie, A. (2019, August 2). *A history of U.S. monopolies*. Retrieved from www.investopedia.com/insights/history-of-us-monopolies/.
Besley, T. (2007). The new political economy. *Economic Journal, 117*(524), F570–F587.
Bolton, B. (2015). *Sustainable financial investments*. New York, NY: Palgrave Macmillan.
Boyles, S. (2009, March 12). *Report: Toxins common in baby products*. Retrieved from www.webmd.com/parenting/baby/news/20090312/report-toxins-common-in-baby-products#1.
Browning, D. (2012, August 22). *The real lesson of formaldehyde in baby shampoo*. Retrieved from http://ideas.time.com/2012/08/22/the-real-lesson-of-formaldehyde-in-baby-shampoo/.
Chappelow, J. (2019a, June 25). *Capitalism*. Retrieved from www.investopedia.com/terms/c/capitalism.asp.
Chappelow, J. (2019b, July 25). *Laissez-faire*. Retrieved from www.investopedia.com/terms/l/laissez-faire.asp.
Chen, J. (2019, May 10). *Environmental, social, and governance (ESG) criteria*. Retrieved from www.investopedia.com/terms/e/environmental-social-and-governance-esg-criteria.asp.
Corporateethics. (2009, October 1). *R. Edward Freeman on stakeholder theory* [video file]. Retrieved from www.youtube.com/watch?v=bIRUaLcvPe8.
Corporate governance structure and policies. (2019). Retrieved from www.complianceonline.com/dictionary/Corporate_Governance_Structure_and_Policies.html.
Darden. (2020). *Our brands*. Retrieved from www.darden.com.

Darden corporate governance guidelines. (2018). Retrieved from https://s2.q4cdn.com/922937207/files/doc_downloads/governance/2018/3-Corporate-Governance-Guidelines-as-amended-through-6-20-18-(v2).pdf.

Duhé, S. C., & Sriramesh, K. (2009). Political economy and global public relations research and practice. In K. Sriramesh & D. Vercic (Eds.), *The global public relations handbook: Theory, research, and practice* (2nd ed., pp. 22–46). New York, NY: Routledge.

Freeman, R. E. (2010). *Strategic management: A stakeholder approach*. New York, NY: Cambridge University Press.

Friedman, M. (1970). *The social responsibility of business is to increase its profits*. Retrieved from http://umich.edu/~thecore/doc/Friedman.pdf.

Friedman, M. (1982). *Capitalism and freedom*. Chicago, IL: The University of Chicago Press.

Gilpin, R. (2001). *Global political economy: Understanding the international economic order*. Princeton, NJ: Princeton University Press.

Hallahan, K. (2000, Winter). Inactive publics: The forgotten publics in public relations. *Public Relations Review, 26*(4), 499–515.

Hillstrom, L. C. (2019). *Value creation*. Retrieved from www.referenceforbusiness.com/management/Tr-Z/Value-Creation.html.

Industrial revolution. (2019, July 1). Retrieved from www.history.com/topics/industrial-revolution/industrial-revolution.

Johnson, L.P.Q., & Sides, M.A. (2004). *The Sarbanes-Oxley Act and fiduciary duties*. Retrieved from https://open.mitchellhamline.edu/cgi/viewcontent.cgi?article=1218&context=wmlr.

Kennon, J. (2020, June 18). *The role and duties of a corporate board of directors*. Retrieved from www.thebalance.com/corporate-board-of-directors-3960038.

Kenton, W. (2020a, March 13). *Robber barons*. Retrieved from www.investopedia.com/terms/r/robberbarons.asp.

Kenton, W. (2020b, October 20). *Sherman Antitrust Act*. Retrieved from www.investopedia.com/terms/s/sherman-antiturst-act.asp.

Ławniczak, R. (2009). Re-examining the economic roots of public relations. *Public Relations Review, 35*, 346–352.

Levin-Waldman, O.M. (2012, October). After Adam Smith: A century of transformation in politics and political economy [book review]. *Review of Political Economy, 24*(4), 669–673.

Mackey, J., & Sisodia, R. (2014). *Conscious capitalism: Liberating the heroic spirit of business*. Boston, MA: Harvard Business Review Press.

Milgate, M., & Stimson, S. C. (2009). *After Adam Smith: A century of transformation in politics and political economy*. Princeton, N.J.: Princeton University Press.

Missing markets. (2019). Retrieved from www.economicsonline.co.uk/Market_failures/Missing_markets.html.

Moffatt, M. (2019, February 1). *Economic utility: The pleasure of products*. Retrieved from www.thoughtco.com/definition-of-utility-1148048.

Natural monopolies. (2019). Retrieved from www.economicsonline.co.uk/Business_economics/Natural_monopolies.html.

Negative externality (n.d.). Retrieved from http://economics.fundamentalfinance.com/negative-externality.php.

Papadopoulos, K., & Araujo, R. (2020, September 23). *The seven sins of ESG management*. Retrieved from https://corpgov.law.harvard.edu/2020/09/23/the-seven-sins-of-esg-management/.

Pfarrer, M.D. (2010). What is the purpose of the firm? Shareholder and stakeholder theories. In J. O'Toole & D. Mayer (Eds.), *Good business: Exercising effective and ethical leadership* (pp. 86–93). New York, NY: Routledge.

Price, N.J. (2018, December 14). *Creating an ESG plan*. Retrieved from https://insights.diligent.com/esg/creating-an-esg-plan/.

Public goods. (n.d.). Retrieved from https://courses.lumenlearning.com/boundless-economics/chapter/public-goods/.

Rouse, M. (2019). *Corporate governance*. Retrieved from https://searchfinancialsecurity.techtarget.com/definition/corporate-governance.

Safvio. (2007, July 14). *Milton Friedman – Your greed or their greed?* [video file] Retrieved from www.youtube.com/watch?v=RWsx1X8PV_A.

Smith, A. (1759). *The theory of moral sentiments* [2009 reprint]. New York, NY: Penguin Books.

Smith, A. (1776). *An inquiry into the nature and causes of the wealth of nations (Vol. I & II)* [1981 reprint]. Indianapolis, IN: Liberty Fund.

Thomas, K. (2014, January 17). *The "No More Tears" shampoo, now with no formaldehyde.* Retrieved from www.nytimes.com/2014/01/18/business/johnson-johnson-takes-first-step-in-removal-of-questionable-chemicals-from-products.html.

What are the most famous monopolies? (2020, October 19). Retrieved from www.investopedia.com/ask/answers/032315/what-are-most-famous-monopolies.asp.

What is the history of corporations in America? (2019, August 3). Retrieved from www.investopedia.com/ask/answers/041515/what-history-corporations-america.asp.

What is shareholder primacy? (2019). Retrieved from https://corporatefinanceinstitute.com/resources/knowledge/other/what-is-shareholder-primacy/.

Chapter 3

A Micro and Macro View of the Economy

In Chapter 2, we covered the origins, benefits, and sources of opposition to capitalism. Capitalism is the organizing framework for economic activity in the U.S., and the economy is the marketplace where the pursuit of self-interest and profit takes place. Although the mathematics of economics can get complex, economics as a field isn't just about numbers. In my opinion, the most interesting parts of this social science focus on the intriguing relationships between limited resources, expectations, information, and the choices people make in their daily lives. Economics is, ultimately, a study of human behavior. Understanding how the economy works and what it means for your firm requires that we examine the economy from two different, but highly related, perspectives: the micro, or firm, level and the macro, or broader economy, level. Let's get started.

Ten Principles of Microeconomics

Microeconomics focuses specifically on how the actions of individuals and firms affect resource allocations related to the production, exchange, and consumption of goods and services in an economy (Chappelow, 2019c). *Factors of production*, including land, labor, money, and other assets, are obviously limited in quantity. There's not an endless supply of cash, time, production capacity, or labor force upon which a firm can draw. As such, choices must be made, and those choices fall on the shoulders of line management[1] who are primarily responsible for monitoring and growing the bottom line.[2] Staff functions, including public affairs, finance, human resources, and law, provide necessary support to line management who are tasked with meeting the company's goals and objectives. Doesn't it make sense, then, that as a support function to line management, we in public affairs understand the business so we can best assist with attainment of those goals and objectives? Ideally, that's how line and staff functions should work together, and this book will help you do just that.

Let's begin your economics briefing by outlining some key assumptions in microeconomics, or the economics of the firm. Microeconomics is the "ground-level" view of daily business operations and decisions made by individual stakeholders associated with the firm, whether they are employees, customers, operators, or managers. These decisions center on making optimum use of limited resources. In other words, if you cannot have an unlimited supply of money, workers, and supplies to run your business, how can you make the best use of what you've got? Microeconomic principles provide some guidance to answer these questions.

DOI: 10.4324/9781003000600-4

Microeconomics Principle #1: Economic Agents Seek to Maximize Their Utility with Limited Resources

Economic agents are individuals and organizations that impact the economy, including firms and governments (Boyd, 2019). Take consumers, for example. This first key concept of microeconomics relays the assumption that consumers will seek to maximize their *utility*, or happiness, with a particular mix of goods and services purchased within the constraints of their income. Firms are also economic agents, and they're competing for that consumer spend. In fact, customer preferences drive a number of business decisions.

As a famed MBA professor of mine once stated, the objective of marketing is to figure out how to increase your company's share of someone's wallet.[3] The wallet, as we all well know, has its limits. The same is true for a company's finances. Management strives to find a product mix that minimizes cost and maximizes profits (Chappelow, 2019c). Economic agents, whether individuals or firms, seek to optimize their satisfaction with whatever resources they have at their disposal.

Microeconomics Principle #2: Supply and Demand Drive Price and Quantity

We discussed Adam Smith's (1776) invisible hand in Chapter 2. Essentially, Smith believes the market forces of supply, demand, competition, and profits are sufficient cues to let merchants know if they are succeeding in the marketplace. He argues that profit-seekers don't need government bureaucrats telling them what to make, how much, and what to charge when they can observe the laws of supply and demand at work and figure out these things for themselves.

The interworking forces of supply, demand, and price are fundamental to understanding economics. Fortunately, they also make intuitive sense. The *law of supply* tells us that as price of a particular good gets higher, sellers will supply more of that good. However, the *law of demand* tells us that as price of a particular good gets higher, buyers will demand less of that good (Chappelow, 2019d). See the rub? All else being equal,[4] as price goes up, sellers are eager to supply goods for sale, but consumers become increasingly less willing to buy as those goods become more expensive (see Box 3.1: Supply and Demand Illustrated).

Box 3.1 Supply and Demand Illustrated

The downward sloping **demand curve** shows how the quantity demanded for a product increases as its price drops. The upward sloping **supply curve** shows the quantity supplied of a product increases as customers are willing to pay more for that product. In Figure 3.1a, **Point A** illustrates how at a price of $20 per unit, suppliers will provide 2,000 units to the market. **Point B** illustrates how, at $20 per unit, customers will purchase 4,000 units at that price. **Point C** is the **equilibrium price** where the market "clears." That is, as suppliers put more product on the market, and customers are willing to pay a higher price, quantity supplied equals quantity demanded (i.e., 3,000 units) at a price of $30.

A Micro and Macro View of the Economy 41

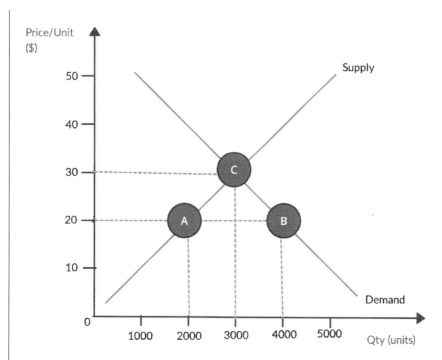

Figure 3.1a Change in Quantity Demanded

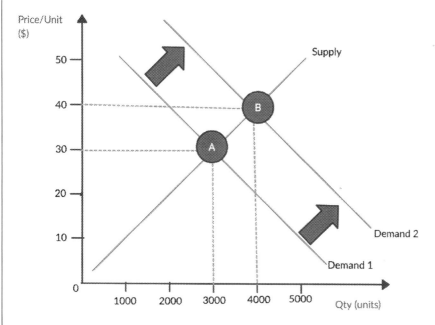

Figure 3.1b Change in Demand

> In Figure 3.1b, we have a **positive shift, or increase, in demand** that could result from an overall increase in consumer income or a favorable shift in consumer preference for a particular product. When the demand curve shifts upward (from Demand 1 to Demand 2), both customers and suppliers win. Customers get more of the product available for purchase (i.e., an increase from 3,000 units at Point A to 4,000 units at Point B), and suppliers increase revenue by $10 per unit (i.e., from $30 at Point A to $40 at Point B) when the **market clears** at **Point B**.

Essentially, consumers like lower prices, and sellers like higher prices. Consumers get more out of their limited income when things they enjoy cost less. Sellers earn more revenue, and presumably more profit, when prices are higher. What becomes obvious is that both sellers and consumers are watching price to guide their behavior. Economic theory tells us that supply and demand interact until the market *clears* and finds an *equilibrium price* that balances quantity demanded with quantity supplied for a certain product (Hall, 2018). In other words, by watching and responding to pricing cues, suppliers figure out how much product to put on the market based on what customers are willing to pay for that product.

Microeconomics Principle #3: Elasticity of Demand Determines Consumer Sensitivity to Price Changes

Think of a product you need and frequently rely on to sustain your quality of life – things like electric power, gasoline, and perhaps even coffee. If a supplier increases the price of something you consider vital, economic theory tells us that you'll find a way to pay that higher price, at least until you figure out how to do without that product (or make do with less of it). *Price elasticity of demand* indicates the percentage change in quantity demanded of a good given a percentage change in its price (Kenton, 2018). The easier a consumer can find a substitute for a product when its price increases, the more *elastic* their demand is said to be. Think of it as someone's ability to "stretch" (yes, like an elastic band) their preferences. If coffee gets too expensive, and consumers are willing to switch to tea, the price of coffee will go down. If the demand for coffee is *inelastic*, that is, the quantity demanded of coffee changes very little when the price goes up, this indicates that coffee isn't readily substitutable (and consumers need their java fix), regardless of a price hike. Time plays an important role in elasticity, however. Inelastic demand – the absolute need for a particular product regardless of price – becomes more elastic over time as consumers find acceptable, cheaper substitutes (Dolan, 2011).

Microeconomics Principle #4: Consumer Reactions to Price Changes Indicate Which Goods Are Substitutes and Which Goods Are Complements

The concepts of *substitutes* and *complements* are related to our discussion of demand elasticity and consumer sensitivities to price changes. Substitute goods are just that: substitutes. Let's revisit the price of coffee going up. If enough consumers switch to tea, the price of coffee will drop and the demand for tea will increase. Substitute goods have a *positive cross-price elasticity*, that is, as the price of one good goes up, the demand for the substitute good goes up ("Complementary and Substitute Goods," n.d.; Cross-Price Elasticity," n.d.). In the case of substitutes, the price of one good and demand for the other good both increase. Other examples of substitutes include blueberries versus strawberries, cola versus root beer, and liquid soap versus bar soap. Substitute products are highly similar. One can readily take the place of the other. If the price goes up on one product, consumers will switch to the lower-priced substitute product and increase demand for it. Liquid soap getting too expensive? Consumers will buy the bar soap. It still gets them clean.[5]

Complementary goods, however, go together. Think of hot dogs and hot dog buns, wine and cheese, and peanut butter and jelly. These are complementary goods that are typically purchased and enjoyed together. Complementary goods have a *negative cross-price elasticity*, that is, as the price of one good goes up, the demand for its complement, as you may have guessed, goes down ("Complementary and Substitute Goods," n.d.; Cross-Price Elasticity," n.d.). Complementary goods are related to each other. They're purchased together. If the price of one product (peanut butter) goes up, consumers will buy less of its complement (jelly) and decrease demand for it. A peanut butter and jelly sandwich just isn't the same without both fillings. If the peanut butter is too expensive, the jelly will be left behind at the store, too.

Microeconomics Principle #5: Diminishing Returns, Marginal Analysis, and Opportunity Costs Apply to Individuals and Firms

We've discussed a lot about utility, otherwise known as the happiness, satisfaction, or enjoyment an individual receives from consuming some product. Take ice cream, for example, or any product you enjoy a great deal. The first few bites will bring you the greatest enjoyment. Although you may continue to enjoy your favorite food for several more bites, excessive indulgence of that food will bring you *decreasing* enjoyment with each additional bite. Enjoying a scoop of ice cream is one thing. Eating an entire gallon of it is a wholly different matter. There comes a point in consumption when one additional bite, or one additional pair of shoes, or one additional hour of preparing for a big presentation no longer "pays off" in satisfaction (or productivity). Instead, the "return" you get from one additional unit of a *thing* begins to diminish. Economists refer to this occurrence as *diminishing marginal utility* (Kenton, 2019b).

Diminishing marginal utility applies in a business context, too. A firm may benefit from having a public affairs department of five people. Hiring a sixth person, however, would bring diminished utility because the benefit of another person doesn't outweigh the cost of another person.

Marginal analysis from a business perspective focuses on comparing the costs versus the benefits of making small changes and seeing how those small changes ripple – for better or worse – throughout the business (Hayes, 2019a). Suppose your firm manufactures winter coats. You don't want to produce so many coats in one season that you create an oversupply of coats that later needs to be discounted or otherwise discarded. You also don't want to produce so few coats that you cannot keep up with demand for the sought-after designs, colors, and features your firm offers.[6] If you under-produce, your customers are going to a competitor to find a suitable substitute.

44 A Micro and Macro View of the Economy

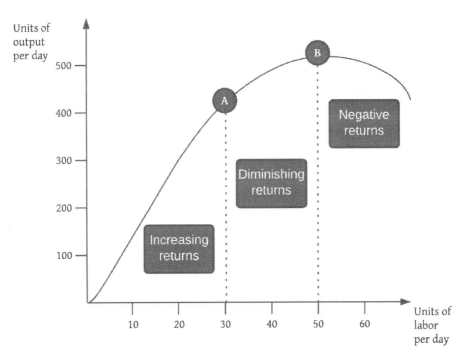

Figure 3.2 Diminishing Marginal Returns

Making business decisions "on the margins" means examining the cost versus the benefit of each additional unit of output. The area under the curve to **Point A** provides **increasing returns** to the firm in that each additional unit of labor is increasingly productive. **Diminishing returns** occur **between Points A and B**. Here, each additional investment in labor still provides more output, but not as much as under increasing returns. **Point B** indicates the optimal output and labor levels, beyond which are **negative returns** where cost of an additional unit of labor exceeds the benefits of that labor when production levels begin to drop.

A common phrase in business is "decisions are made at the margin" (e.g., "Decisions," 2019). This thinking directly relates to the cost-benefit analysis introduced in Chapter 2. A key point driving a firm's production decisions is the cost versus the benefit of one more "unit," whatever that unit may be – another winter coat, employee, or even an airplane. The unit doesn't matter, but the rationale does. In essence, a firm will produce (or purchase) one more unit of something, however big or small, if the marginal benefit of *one more unit* exceeds the marginal cost of that additional unit.[7] This analysis "on the margin" is used to determine the number of units a firm produces and the price per unit it charges (Hall, 2019a; see Figure 3.2: Diminishing Marginal Returns).

The business will maximize its profits at the point where marginal revenue earned from one additional unit equals the marginal cost of producing that unit. Any point beyond that "cost equals benefit" level of production is losing money. The adage, "We lose money on every sale, but make it up on volume" is a long-standing business joke (Popik, 2011). Why? Because if you're producing at a point where the cost of a unit exceeds the revenue you can get from that unit, you're losing money on each sale.[8] That's nothing to laugh about.

Even if producing another unit yields a net marginal benefit, the firm must ask: Could the business yield an even higher marginal benefit by investing those funds elsewhere (Hayes, 2019a; Henderson, 2019)? For example, the benefits of hiring an additional factory worker may be positive, but hiring an additional salesperson could provide an even greater benefit to the business. The *opportunity cost* of hiring the additional factory worker is the lost benefit the business could have realized from hiring another salesperson instead.

Opportunity cost applies to individuals, too. The classic example is that of a college education (Henderson, 2019). From an economist's perspective, the cost of a college education includes both the tuition and the income students forego, or could have earned, instead of going to college. Opportunity costs apply to every decision you make. The "cost" of however you decide to use your time, money, and talents is the next-best alternative you had to use your time, money, and talents. For instance, you could have spent a Saturday afternoon completing a work presentation, but you instead decided to watch a movie to clear your head. In this case, you as a rational economic actor concluded that the benefit of taking a break outweighed the cost of postponing your work.

Microeconomics Principle #6: Sunk Costs Are Not Recoverable, No Matter What

Ever heard the expression, "throwing good money after bad"? It means that just because you spent money on something you never used (a gym membership), underutilized (an expensive suit worn one time), or changed your mind about using (a bright orange coffee table) doesn't mean you should keep throwing dollars at it to "get your money's worth" out of those purchases.

This is the *sunk cost* fallacy, a psychological phenomenon identified by behavioral economists ("Sunk Cost Fallacy," 2019). A sunk cost is sunk. It's spent. It's not coming back. Continuing to throw money at a sunk cost is a bad idea when those limited funds could be put to more productive use. Both individuals and firms fall prey to the sunk cost fallacy.

From an accounting standpoint, sunk costs are not considered when deciding whether to continue an investment ("Sunk Cost," 2018). Sunk costs, also known as *stranded costs*, are not relevant because they are not recoverable. Pouring more cash into an unprofitable venture is not going to improve its economic outlook. The investment is gone. Written off. It's time to move on and cut the losses.

For example, suppose a company spends $2 million on new software product development, and the software fails to meet market demand. The company could continue to invest in the software in hopes of making it marketable, or abandon the project completely and begin investing in a more revolutionary product design. For accounting purposes, the $2 million spent on the failed software system is a sunk cost and is not considered relevant when calculating the cost of developing a more innovative product to better address market demand. The $2 million is sunk, gone, and done.

Investments in marketing studies, research and development, employee training, and even hiring bonuses can become sunk costs when the product, software, and employee don't meet expectations ("Sunk Cost," 2018; see also "What is a Sunk Cost?," 2019). If the product is a dud, the software is outdated, or the employee doesn't perform, there's no use in continuing to invest in a dead end. Those sunk costs are irrelevant when it's time to invest in new studies, products, and people.

Think about it, and you'll realize you've seen this happen in the workplace. "But we've already invested so much time, energy, and resources in this project!" cries the team leader, despite compelling data that demonstrate the project isn't worth continued funding. Or, "I've spent so much time researching and planning this event! What do you mean it's canceled?! If we just spend more money promoting it, more people will register."

Don't be fooled by the sunk cost fallacy. What's done is done, and sunk is sunk. Consider only relevant costs when making investments.

Microeconomics Principle #7: Bigger is Better for Economies of Scale

Economies of scale is the term used to describe the competitive advantage realized from being able to produce more products, at a lower cost, relative to your competition (Amadeo, 2019b; Nikolas, 2019). We'll begin by differentiating fixed and variable costs. For example, let's say your firm has a fixed cost of $25,000 per month to lease a production facility. Whether your firm produces 100 units or 10,000 units, the leasing cost is still $25,000 per month. A *fixed cost* is one that doesn't vary, and it's spread across your units of production. If you're spending $25,000 per month on a lease, it makes sense that you want to produce (and sell) as many units as feasible because you need to pay that fixed cost each month. That way, you "spread" the $25,000 across the number of units you produce. The more you produce, the lower the fixed cost per unit. However, the fixed total of $25,000 per month remains, regardless of production volume. That's why it's "fixed." It's unavoidable. The more fixed costs your firm has, the more revenue it needs to generate to cover those costs each week, month, quarter, or year.

A *variable cost*, on the other hand, is directly tied to the number of goods or services your firm produces (Amadeo, 2019b; Nikolas, 2019). If the materials and labor required to produce a bike lock, for instance, are $3, and you produce 1,000 bike locks, your variable cost is $3,000. If you produce 10,000 bike locks, your variable cost is $30,000. If you produce no bike locks, your variable cost is $0. The more you produce, the higher your total variable costs, but the cost *per unit* stays the same. Compare that to the fixed cost per unit that *decreases* as you produce more volume. Variable costs vary based on production volume, but their per-unit cost is the same (e.g., $3 per bike lock). Fixed costs are, well, fixed, whether you produce thousands of units or none at all, but the per-unit cost lowers as you produce more volume (e.g., spreading a $25,000 monthly lease across 100,000 units vs. just 1,000 units).

Getting back to economies of scale, the bigger the firm, the more it can produce, and the lower its costs per unit (Amadeo, 2019b). Those lower costs give both producers and consumers an efficiency advantage. Producers can meet growing demand at a lower cost, and thus customers benefit from lower prices, too. Alden (2012) likens economies of scale to moats – those deep, wide, water-filled defensive structures surrounding castles – that protect a company's profitability for years to come. Why? The companies with major economies of scale (think Wal-Mart, Procter and Gamble, and ExxonMobil) have infrastructure, cost management, and widespread operating practices in place that are practically impossible to replicate at the same scale.

Microeconomics Principle #8: Perfect Competition is a Theory, Not Reality

The study of economics includes a great number of assumptions, one of which is the notion of perfectly competitive markets. In *pure*, or *perfect*, *competition*, all firms sell the same, indistinguishable product; all firms are price takers; all buyers have complete, or perfect, information about the products they're purchasing; and firms can enter or exit markets without any hardships (Hayes, 2019b). Only commodity markets, like wheat or corn, come close to having these characteristics.

In reality, competition in a free market is quite imperfect (Liberto, 2019). Companies compete with differentiated products, set their own prices, and are either protected or frustrated by *barriers to entry*.[9] Barriers to entry include technological, regulatory, legal, infrastructure, and licensing requirements that make it difficult for a newcomer to enter a market ("What are Barriers," 2019). *Structural barriers to entry* include economies of scale already leveraged by current competitors (e.g., small-town retailers trying to compete with Wal-Mart), high start-up costs (e.g., starting a new airline), and ownership of scarce resources (e.g., a competitor already owns or has access to the raw materials needed). *Strategic barriers to entry* include brand loyalty, patents, and pricing. Each of these elements can be used to deter new competitors from entering a market. Monopolies (single firms with no close substitutes) and *oligopolies* (small number of large firms producing similar products, such as auto dealers) enjoy significant barriers to entry and are further examples of imperfect competition (Hall, 2019b).

Microeconomics Principle #9: Firms, Markets, and Industries Are Organized in a Variety of Ways

Firms can be organized as *sole proprietorships* (one individual doing business), *partnerships* (two or more individuals), or *corporations* (the most predominant form – a legal entity distinct from the individuals in it). Each way of organizing has its own legal and tax implications (Garrison, 2018). Further, firms can be *privately held* by founders, managers, or a group of investors, or *publicly held* by shareholders who have an ownership interest in the company's assets and profits (Majaski, 2019).[10]

Market structure and *industrial organization* are terms used to describe how certain segments of the economy are organized (Chappelow, 2019c). For example, the market for off-brand personal electronics is highly competitive, meaning products are plentiful and fairly interchangeable, and producers/sellers are *price takers* ("Perfect Competition," 2019). In microeconomic terms, price takers operate among many competing firms offering a similar product in the market. These firms, however, aren't large enough or differentiated enough to set their own price. Instead, they have to "take" whatever price is set by the market. If they attempt to set their price even slightly higher than the market will bear, they will have a difficult time making any sales. On the flip side, a *monopoly* firm can set whatever price it wishes. Until customers can figure out how to do without the monopoly's product or service, they have no other choice of where to get it.[11] In between the extremes of price takers and monopolies are competitive firms that differentiate themselves on attributes other than price, giving them leeway to adjust their prices based on what customers are willing to pay for their goods and services.[12]

Industries are classified in a number of ways. *Cyclical industries* tend to follow economic trends. That is, as the economy expands, so does demand for products provided by cyclical industries, such as raw materials and heavy equipment (Chamberlin, 2019). As the economy contracts, however, demand drops for these products while firms wait for economic conditions to improve before making major investments. *Counter-cyclical industries*, conversely, tend to increase their revenues in times of economic downturns. Pharmaceutical, educational, and discount retail firms in many cases attract more customers when uncertainties about employment and financial security run high.

Fragmented industries are those in which a number of firms compete, but no one firm dominates the market (Merlo, 2016). As such, barriers to entry are generally low. Fragmented industries offer attractive opportunities for *disruptors* – firms that forge a new way of organizing an industry and serving customers that is unmatched by current competitors (Rogers, 2016). Airbnb, Casper, Peloton, and DoorDash are examples of disruptor firms that entered fragmented industries and radically redefined how customer needs are met ("Meet the 2019," 2019). As fragmented industries mature, they become more *consolidated* (Deans, Kroeger, & Zeisel, 2002). That is, larger, more successful firms begin to acquire former competitors, and industry giants emerge.

Microeconomics Principle #10: Information and Expectations Drive Markets

This tenth microeconomic principle underscores the role of communication in the economy. As noted, economics is a behavioral science. Economic actors behave based on what they know, what they think they know, and what they expect to happen. The role of expectations is central to the study of economics (Robinson, 2017). Expectations can be rational, irrational, accurate, or ill-informed. Expectations drive choices made by individuals, firms, and governments.

And where do these expectations come from? Information. Information provided by spokespersons, journalists, elected officials, regulators, opinion leaders, friends, relatives, and next door neighbors feed expectations of how well (or not) the economy is doing and what will happen next. When consumers, investors, and business owners feel good about the economy, they tend to spend more. When they're feeling uncertain or concerned about their economic futures, they tend to spend less.

When you speak, post, and report on behalf of your firm, you're creating expectations. The larger your firm, the greater the potential that your words will not only inform, but also move markets. Even if you're the largest employer in a small rural town, what you say about the business climate and your outlook for the future can affect the choices customers, other businesses, and local government will make. Corporate public affairs is in the business of providing information to a broad range of internal and external stakeholders. Never underestimate the responsibility of communicating accurately and thoroughly. Stakeholders are making decisions based on the information you provide.

Ten Principles of Macroeconomics

Now that we've covered key concepts in microeconomics, we turn our attention to key concepts in macroeconomics. Whereas microeconomics focuses on the choices made by individuals and firms, macroeconomics takes a more aggregated view of the economy *as a whole* ("Definition," 2019). As you review the following concepts, you'll see how the purview of macroeconomics is much broader than its microeconomic counterpart, yet highly related. Macroeconomics focuses on how government policies, economic indicators, and employment affect overall economic health for nations, industries, and firms.

Macroeconomics Principle #1: Aggregate Demand and Aggregate Supply Represent the Sum Total of Goods and Services Produced in an Economy

The microeconomic illustration of supply and demand represents the interaction of these forces, along with price, for a particular good or service. In macroeconomic terms, *aggregate demand* and *aggregate supply* illustrate how these forces, along with price, interact for all finished goods and services in an economy.

Aggregate demand (AD) is the sum of consumer spending on goods and services (C), private/corporate investments and capital expenditures (I), government spending on public goods and social services (G), and net exports (exports, or products going out of the country for sale, minus imports, or products coming into the country for sale) (Nx), or AD = C + I + G + Nx (Kenton, 2019c). Several macroeconomic factors affect aggregate demand for goods and services, including changes in interest rates, income and wealth, inflation expectations, and currency exchange rates. We'll discuss each of these ahead. For now, understand aggregate demand as capturing millions of economic transactions between millions of economic agents for a wide variety of purposes. Measured in market values (i.e., given price levels), aggregate demand captures total output for an economy and, as such, is an indicator of both consumer and business strength.

Aggregate supply represents the total number of goods produced in an economy at particular price points (Abbott & Kenton, 2019). As aggregate demand increases for a given supply of goods, consumers compete for available goods, and prices rise. As prices rise, firms are willing to produce more output. Changes in supply lag changes in demand because it takes time for firms to increase production to meet demand. Short-term changes in aggregate supply are driven by increases or decreases in aggregate demand. In the long run, however, major shifts in aggregate supply occur in response to changes in the size and quality of the labor force, technological innovations, wages, taxes, production costs, and inflation (see Sidebar 3.1: Long Run vs. Short Run).

Sidebar 3.1 Long Run vs. Short Run

(Beggs, 2018; Moffatt, 2018)

The terms *long run* and *short run* are frequently used in economics. In **microeconomics**, the short run represents a period of time when resources are relatively fixed. Examples include dependence on a certain supplier or production input. In the long run, managers have more time and opportunity to find alternative resources. These *general, contextual concepts of time* also apply to **macroeconomics** when discussing the fixed vs. flexible nature of wages, employment, fiscal and monetary policies, and technology. Adjustments in most economic variables are more feasible over the long vs. the short run. No specific timeframe is related to these terms.

Macroeconomics Principle #2: GDP is a Key Indicator of a Country's Economic Health

GDP is calculated the same way as aggregate demand (C + G + I + Nx), and, in the long run, GDP equals aggregate demand (Abbott & Kenton, 2019; Chappelow, 2019e). Policymakers, investors, and firms rely on GDP for decision-making because the metric is a snapshot of a country's economic health, growth rate, and purchasing power. These combined goods and services produced within a country during a set period of time (most commonly annually or quarterly) is measured in monetary value. The higher the value, the stronger the economy. GDP can be adjusted for inflation (see Sidebar 3.2: Nominal vs. Real Terms) and measured per capita (i.e., per person in the nation, or GDP divided by total population).

Sidebar 3.2 Nominal vs. Real Terms

(Majaski, 2020)

Numbers can be expressed in *nominal* or *real* terms. **Nominal** refers to a face value or rate that's unadjusted for inflation. **Real** refers to a value or rate that's adjusted for inflation. Real terms more accurately reflect actual purchasing power. For example, $!00, a nominal value, in 1950 has a real value of $1,081 in 2020, once adjusted for inflation. What $100 could buy in 1950 requires multiples of that nominal amount to purchase similar items in 2020. A 10% nominal rate of return on an asset you held for one year may sound like a great deal, but once you account for 4% inflation, your real return is 6%. Nominal and real terms also apply to interest rates, so always be sure you know which numbers you're looking at.

Per capita GDP provides one way to compare economic health between countries (Chappelow, 2019e). For example, GDP per capita is $1,600 in Sierra Leone, $13,500 in South Africa, $38,300 in Spain, $59,500 in the United States, and $124,500 in Qatar ("The World Factbook," n.d.). These differences are attributed not only to the value of produced goods and population counts, but also to the political economic policies of each nation that guide these economies.[13]

Balance of trade between nations is a component of the GDP equation (Chappelow, 2019e). Exports add to GDP, and imports subtract from GDP. All else being equal, a nation that exports more goods than it imports will have a higher GDP, indicating a higher demand for its goods outside of its borders relative to its dependency on foreign goods to meet its needs. *Gross National Product*, or *GNP*, an alternative measure of economic health, includes only goods provided by producers native to that country. GDP, however, includes all goods produced in-country, whether by domestic or foreign-owned entities. *Gross National Income*, or *GNI*, is the sum of all income earned by citizens of a country, whether from domestic or foreign sources.

Consumer spending is the largest component of U.S. GDP (Chappelow, 2019e). When consumers are confident about the health of the economy, their optimistic expectations lead to spending – on homes, vacations, luxury items, and so on. Businesses spend, too, when economic confidence is high, and their expenditures are closely tracked in the GDP equation. Firms will invest in major capital projects requiring machinery and other asset purchases when they expect the economy to grow. Rising business investments lead to expanded production capacity and more job opportunities. Consumer and firm reactions to economic news and predictions align with the previously mentioned notion that markets run on expectations and information. Consumer and business confidence drops in times of economic downturns, political unrest, and market uncertainties, just as it rises when economic indicators are positive.

Government spending on equipment and infrastructure is also tracked and may increase when consumer spending and business investments decline sharply, as in a *recession* (Chappelow, 2019e). Contrary to the classical economic principles explained in Chapter 2 that *minimize* the role of government, the ideas of British economist John Maynard Keynes to *increase* the role of government in the economy became popular during the Great Depression in the 1930s (Jahan, Mahmud, & Papageorgiou, 2014). In Keynes' view, aggregate demand is the most important driver of economic health and the best assurance of optimum levels of employment. To follow his reasoning, recall the components of aggregate demand: consumer spending, corporate investments, government spending, and net exports. During a significant economic downturn when optimism is diminished and expectations for economic recovery are low, economic theory tells us that consumers and businesses will spend less, not more. So, who is left to stimulate economic activity? In Keynes' view (now known as Keynesian economics), the burden of increasing output falls on the shoulders of the government to even out the booms and busts of the business cycle. Just how "active" the government should be in the U.S. economy is the subject of much political debate today. Both U.S. Republican President George W. Bush and Democrat President Barack Obama employed Keynesian-style spending policies that would make classical economists[14] uncomfortable, with mixed results (see Amadeo, 2019c).

Macroeconomic Principle #3: Fiscal Policy Dictates How the Government Taxes and Spends

The more we delve into macroeconomics, the more apparent the tie between economics and politics becomes. Pay attention to political party policy platforms, and you'll see how candidates and elected officials have philosophical differences on market principles and how best to serve their constituents. We'll keep our focus at the federal government level, where officials decide how much to tax (or how much to cut taxes) and how much to spend (and where). These tax-and-spend decisions are collectively referred to as *fiscal policy*, and they affect individuals, families, firms, and national economic conditions (Weil, 2019). They affect economic incentives and expectations, too.

Any discussion of fiscal policy must first begin with the budget *deficit*. The deficit is the amount the federal government spends over and above what it receives in tax revenues, usually over the course of a year (Amadeo, 2019d). *Deficit spending* is used by the government to address extraordinary circumstances, such as wars, military defense, and recessions, but also in attempts to create jobs and grow the economy. The accumulation of those deficits year-to-year adds to the *national debt*. A nation's ability to pay its debts is judged by the ratio of its debt relative to its GDP. The stronger the nation's economy, the more confidence foreign and other investors have in the country's ability to effectively manage its finances.[15]

When federal tax revenues exceed federal government spending in a given year, fiscal policy is described as *contractionary*, and the federal budget is in *surplus* (Weil, 2019). Note the focus is on year-to-year changes in the federal budget, even though the government is still in debt. Surpluses help to reduce the federal debt. When federal government spending exceeds federal tax revenues in a given year, fiscal policy is described as *expansionary*, and the federal budget is in *deficit*. Deficits add to the federal debt.

Stop for a moment and think what would happen if you continued to spend more than the income you earned. It wouldn't be long before you had no spending or borrowing power at all. Yet the U.S. federal government overspends *as a matter of fiscal policy practice*. Why? Recall government spending is part of the GDP equation. Government spending, in part, increases aggregate demand (Amadeo, 2019d; Weil, 2019). Expansionary fiscal policy – whether through an increase in government spending or a reduction in taxes, all else being equal – stimulates the economy. And let's not forget the self-interest of politicians. No one gets reelected on a platform of raising taxes and cutting jobs.

The U.S. federal government has accrued enormous deficits in recent years related to defense spending, tax cuts, and mandatory spending on programs like Medicaid (Amadeo, 2019d). The U.S. likewise benefits from a high level of trust from investors around the world, so incentives to reduce the national debt are relatively low. Economic theories lead some politicians to support *supply-side* or *trickle-down economic policies* that encourage tax cuts for businesses and the wealthy to increase aggregate demand and jobs. Others support direct government spending to do the same. There's no shortage of debate about how best to stimulate and support an economy.

Macroeconomic Principle #4: Monetary Policy Governs an Economy's Money Supply

Monetary policy governs the quantity of money within a country and the channels through which new money is supplied (Chappelow, 2019a). Monetary policy activities include managing money supply and interest rates, controlling inflation, buying and selling government bonds, regulating exchange rates, and mandating reserve levels for banks. We'll address each of these concepts in turn.

The U.S. authority that oversees monetary policy is the *Federal Reserve* ("Who Owns," 2017). The Federal Reserve, frequently referred to as the Fed, was created by the Federal Reserve Act in 1913 to serve as the nation's central bank. The Fed is not "owned" by anyone. Rather, it is governed by the Federal Reserve Board of Governors appointed by the President and confirmed by the Senate. The Board, in turn, reports to Congress and oversees 12 decentralized Reserve Banks located throughout the U.S. The Fed is funded by its own investments and not by Congressional funds. This structure is designed to keep the gravity of the Fed's work with the money supply as independent as possible from political maneuvering.

The Federal Reserve has a *dual mandate* from Congress to maximize employment and stabilize prices, which requires a delicate balance between economic growth and inflation (Chappelow, 2019a). Too much growth at too fast a rate in prices, supply, and production capacity can lead to an *overheated economy* and, ultimately, a recession (Chen,

2019a). Central banks use a number of tools in monetary policy, including the buying and selling of government bonds in *open market operations*, changing interest rates, and setting *reserve requirements* that require banks to retain a certain proportion of customer deposits to ensure they can cover their liabilities (Chappelow, 2019a). *Expansionary monetary policy* practices increase money supply in the market, with hopes of increasing both investments and consumer spending. If not carefully managed, however, increased money supply can lead to higher prices that begin to negatively impact cost of living and cost of doing business. In those cases, *contractionary monetary policy* practices slow the growth of the money supply with hopes of stabilizing prices. Monetary policy is a balancing act, indeed. The Fed's words and actions are closely watched, feed expectations, and move markets because of its extraordinary influence on the economy.

Nations around the world have central banks operating under their own systems of governance ("Central Banks," 2020). International finance is essential to the global economy because money is central to exchanges and can be transferred between nations at a faster rate than people, goods, or services ("How Does," 2020). The *International Monetary Fund* (IMF) was established in 1945 to ensure stability of the international monetary system ("The IMF," 2019). Today, the IMF works with 189 member nations to oversee matters of macroeconomic and financial stability on a global scale.

Macroeconomic Principle #5: Interest Rates Are a Key Component of Monetary Policy

Interest rates are charged by banks and other lenders for individuals and firms to borrow money, and they're the rates banks pay savers for depositing money into accounts ("Interest Rate," 2020). In colloquial terms, money is "cheap" when interest rates are lower. The manipulation of interest rates is a key tool used by the Federal Reserve (and other central banks around the world) to manage money supply. Let's explore exactly how this works.

Recall the Federal Reserve has a dual mandate to maximize employment and stabilize prices. To strike this balance, the Fed lowers and raises interest rates to either stimulate or slow the economy, respectively (Petroff, 2019). Lower interest rates make money "cheaper," so consumers and businesses spend less to borrow and are less incentivized to save. Essentially, lower interest rates encourage borrowing and spending over saving. With lower interest rates, consumers make more purchases on credit cards (a way of borrowing money, with an interest charge) and take out loans for home improvements, new cars, and so on. Businesses, too, are encouraged to borrow and spend to expand their operations, hire more employees, and so on. All of this assumes, of course, that expectations about the economy's health remain optimistic.

Underlying this more active use of money is the idea that money put to productive use (e.g., for growing a business or advancing one's education) is better than money earning a low interest rate sitting idle in a bank account. This increased use of money that comes with lower interest rates increases the money supply in the economy (Petroff, 2019). Raising interest rates, conversely, lowers the money supply in active use. Higher interest rates discourage borrowing and spending because money gets more "expensive." With higher rates, saving becomes more attractive so money can grow for later use.

The Fed doesn't directly set interest rates for personal, auto, and other loans, but it does take several actions to move interest rates toward desired levels (Bajpai, 2019). The

Federal Reserve sets what's known as the *federal discount rate*, or the rate at which commercial banks in the U.S. can borrow from the Fed. When banks borrow from the Fed at lower rates, they pass those savings onto customers to increase borrowing, which increases the money supply. Lower interest rates put money to work in the economy.

The Fed also uses open market operations to influence interest rates (Bajpai, 2019). This involves the Fed purchasing or selling *government bonds* in the open market. Bonds, a type of *security*, are sold by the U.S. Treasury to facilitate government spending ("Government Bond," 2020). *Treasury securities*, as they're called, are highly conservative, low-risk investments because they are backed by the full faith and confidence of the U.S. government (Cussen, 2019). The bond is a promise to repay the investor at a particular rate and time depending on the maturity of the bond. *T-Bills* have the shortest range of maturities ranging from four to 52 weeks. *T-Notes* mature in two to ten years, and *T-Bonds* (known as "long bonds") mature in 30 years. The Fed's *Federal Open Market Committee* (FOMC) decides how to use each of these securities to affect interest rates (Obringer, 2020; Petroff, 2019).

The logic behind open market operations is that when the Fed buys bonds, it increases the money supply by putting more cash in the economy in exchange for these bonds (Petroff, 2019). When the Fed buys bonds, interest rates decrease, making the newly infused cash more accessible to individuals and firms and thus stimulates the economy. When the Fed sells bonds, money is taken out of the market, and interest rates increase, thus slowing the economy.

Reserve requirements – the percentage of total bank deposits that must be kept in reserve for customer withdrawals and other obligations – are also used by the Fed to increase or decrease the money supply (Bajpai, 2019). Higher reserve requirements make less money available to circulate to bank customers. Lower reserve requirements, then, make more money available for loans and other uses. Banks with reserve levels above the required amount can lend those funds overnight at a negotiated rate to other banks (Chen, 2019b). The average of these overnight lending rates is the *federal funds rate*. The Fed uses its open market operations to affect the federal funds rate, which, in turn, affects every other interest rate in the economy, including the *prime rate*, which is the rate banks charge their customers for loans (Bajpai, 2019; Tarver, 2019).

Macroeconomic Principle #6: Inflation is a Good Thing, Until There's Too Much of It

Inflation, or rising prices, is a sign of a healthy economy (Warr, 2019). In fact, the Federal Reserve's dual mandate of stabilizing prices[16] while maximizing employment[17] is well served by rising prices, as wages tend to rise at about the same rate as inflation. The Fed likes inflation to hover around the 2% mark. If the rate drops below that, the Fed will cut interest rates to give the economy a boost. If the rate gets too high, the Fed will increase interest rates to slow the economy and keep it from overheating. An overheated economy can lead to recession when a sharp spike in prices leads to overproduction of goods and creation of excess production capacity that can later cause a slowdown in growth (Chen, 2019a).

Most commonly, the *Consumer Price Index* (CPI) is used to measure inflation over time (Warr, 2019). Each year, the Bureau of Labor Statistics prices a *basket of goods* including everyday items such as food, furniture, clothing, and a variety of services to track how the cost of the basket changes from year to year (Banton, 2019b). The resulting ratio is the CPI and indicates how consumers are experiencing inflation. Other measures, including the *Producer Price Index* and the *Employment Cost Index*, track inflation rates in production and labor markets, respectively.

The Fed is tasked with maintaining a sweet spot of inflation in the economy (Warr, 2019). *Deflation*, or falling prices, indicates demand for goods and services is lower than it should be. Deflation is troublesome, but rare, in developed economies because consumers will delay purchases when prices are falling (i.e., attempting to get the lowest price possible), stifling the economy even further. But too much inflation is a problem, too. *Stagflation* occurs when rising prices are coupled with unemployment – a double decker of a dilemma for the Fed to face.

Inflation is caused by several factors (Chen, 2019c). If demand for a particular product outpaces producers' ability to provide that product, prices will rise. Positive economic expectations combined with increased money supply can also lead to increases in demand and prices. If the cost of production inputs, such as raw materials or labor costs, rises, so, too, will prices so producers can cover those additional costs. And then there's the *wage-price spiral*: As prices of goods and services go up, workers expect and demand higher wages, too, so prices will rise as prices and wages feed off each other.

Macroeconomic Principle #7: Declining Macroeconomic Indicators Can Signal a Recession

Recessions are a normal part of the business cycle and are short-term, significant declines in economic performance across an entire economy (Chappelow, 2019b). Recessions are typically indicated by two consecutive quarters of decline in GDP and other measures, including employment. In the U.S., recessions are officially declared by the National Bureau of Economic Research.

Just because recessions are normal doesn't mean they're pleasant (Chappelow, 2019b). Recessions are marked by business failures, slow or negative growth in production, and rising unemployment. Recessions bring economic and political consequences, including shifts away from obsolete technologies, industries, or firms; dramatic policy reactions by government and monetary authorities; and social unrest resulting from job losses and related distress.

There's no single way to predict a recession is on the horizon (Chappelow, 2019b). Both *leading indicators* and *lagging indicators* provide some clues, however. Leading indicators are those that historically show changes in growth rates *before* macroeconomic indicators begin to shift and include data on purchasing, unemployment applications, labor hours, building permits, and consumer confidence measures. Lagging indicators confirm, rather than predict, when economic shifts occur, as they come *after* the fact. These include the unemployment rate, corporate profits, interest rates, and GDP, which is the primary indicator of a recession. A *depression* is a long-lasting recession, like the Great Depression of the 1930s when U.S. GDP declined more than 10% and the unemployment rate reached 25%.

There are a number of theories regarding what causes recessions (Chappelow, 2019b). Major industry changes sparked by geopolitical crises or revolutionary technologies are *negative shocks* that can have sweeping effects across an economy. Financial factors also play a role in recessions. An overextension of credit and financial risk during good economic times or overly tight, poorly timed restrictions on money supply can have negative impacts on growth. Psychological perspectives on recessions point to excessive exuberance during good times and excessive pessimism during downturns that can cause recessions to occur and even persist.

In the U.S., the *2008 financial crisis* and the *Great Recession* that followed were preceded by an overheated economy (Chen, 2019a). The unemployment rate continued to fall while inflation rose to a peak of 5.25% in 2006. A real estate *asset bubble* burst in 2007, sending shockwaves throughout the country's financial system when housing prices skyrocketed beyond sustainable demand or value, and then crashed. This perfect storm was further compounded by government spending that contributed to significant deficits.

When the onset of the financial crisis began, the Fed used conventional measures to boost the economy, including lowering the federal funds rate to nearly zero and adding $2 trillion to the money supply in three purchasing rounds of what's referred to as *quantitative easing*.[18] When these measures didn't provide the expected boost to the economy, Fed Chairman Ben Bernanke created new bank mechanisms to increase the money supply. Banks had just suffered significant losses from mortgage-backed securities and other risky financial endeavors that reflected poor management practices. As such, instead of circulating the additional cash into the economy, banks held on to it. Frustrated consumers and firms were unable to get access to this "cheap money" and lost confidence in a crisis-tainted economic environment. This unexpected clog in the banking system prohibited lower interest rates from triggering significant increases in employment or output.

No Federal Reserve plan could have anticipated the depth of the financial crisis as megabanks began to unravel. Firms central to the crisis (Lehman, Bear Stearns, and AIG) were connected to millions of households and billions of dollars, leaving them "too big to fail" if left to conventional market responses. The Fed was required to take a more active role in the unwinding and bailout of these firms while still adhering to its mandate to stabilize prices and maximize employment.

Macroeconomic Principle #8: Employment Reflects How Well an Economy is Reaching Its Potential

True *full employment* is a macroeconomic ideal in which anyone who is willing and able to work can find a job (Chappelow, 2019f). More practically, policymakers work toward low, but not zero, rates of unemployment. *Natural unemployment* is between 3.5 and 4.5 percent in the U.S., which recognizes there will always be some portion of the population out of work ("What is the Lowest," 2019).

Employment is a measure of economic efficiency (Chappelow, 2019f). That is, employment levels are high when labor resources (both skilled and unskilled[19]) are put to their best, most efficient use. High levels of employment likewise indicate the means of production in an economy, including land, labor, and capital, are optimally distributed and reaching their highest potential. In other words, nearly full employment demonstrates the economy has the right mix of doctors, teachers, workers, technology, factories, investors, and so on to meet demand for goods and services. Rising unemployment, then, indicates there are inefficiencies in the economy that need to be addressed through policy and other means.

Unemployment has a variety of causes (Chappelow, 2019f). *Cyclical unemployment* rises and falls with the business cycle. In good economic times, more jobs are available. In downturns or recessions, not so much. *Structural unemployment* occurs when major shifts in technology or other factors render a significant mismatch between what is needed and what workers are able to provide. *Frictional unemployment* comes from workers changing jobs, industries, and locations on their own accord and is a natural part of a healthy economy.

Attempts to optimize employment levels in an economy is a multi-faceted challenge. As mentioned, an economy growing too fast can lead to recession. And unemployment derives from a variety of sources, both public and private. A low rate of unemployment indicates an economy is running full speed ahead, but that progress must be balanced with price stability at the macroeconomic level to avoid overheating.

Macroeconomic Principle #9: Currency Exchange Rates Can Be Flexible or Fixed

When something is said to "have currency" it means that it has value. Whatever the "thing" is, its value can be exchanged or used to get something else of value. A college diploma has currency on the job market. So does work experience. In economic terms, currency, of course, refers to money. The true value of one unit of currency is what can be received in exchange for that currency. Ten years ago, one U.S. dollar could buy more than it can today. That decrease in *purchasing power* is attributed to inflation, or rising prices (see Sidebar 3.2: Nominal vs. Real Terms). Keep in mind, however, that wages tend to rise with prices. The same amount of work done ten years ago, generally speaking, earns a higher wage today.

The strength of a country's currency, when left to market devices, indicates global confidence in that currency. *Currency exchange rates* indicate the amount of one country's currency that can be exchanged for another country's currency (Amadeo, 2019a). The U.S. dollar and the euro are used by more people than any other currencies worldwide. As such, they are considered global currencies. Depending on the day, one U.S. dollar may convert to more than one euro (meaning a relatively stronger dollar) or less than one euro (meaning a relatively weaker dollar). When the dollar is *strong*, it has more purchasing power relative to other currencies. When the dollar is *weak*, it has less.

When left to the forces of the *foreign exchange market*,[20] or forex, the value of the U.S. dollar, or any currency, fluctuates on a moment-by-moment basis (Amadeo, 2019a). Forex traders rely on a nation's interest rates, debt levels, and economic strength to determine a currency's exchange value.[21] As such, these currency exchange rates are considered *flexible*. Both the U.S. dollar and the euro rely on flexible exchange rates.

Some countries, like China, *peg* their currencies, meaning they set a *fixed exchange rate* (Amadeo, 2019a). Countries with fixed exchange rates use the buying and selling of currencies (through their central banks) to maintain a set value of their currency compared to, say, the U.S. dollar. A pegged currency remains artificially low (Banton, 2019a). The upside of a pegged currency is that it maintains stable rates between trading nations. The downside is that it maintains an anti-competitive trading environment between countries.

China, for example, has kept its yuan lower in value than the U.S. dollar to encourage more buying and importing of Chinese products in the U.S. Large U.S. importers like Target and Wal-Mart benefit from this arrangement. However, U.S. manufacturers critical of this approach claim China pegs their currency at the cost of U.S. jobs. When the U.S. dollar can go further buying Chinese goods, demand for U.S.-produced goods drops. In extreme cases, currency crises can occur when the imbalance between the country pegging its currency and its target country's currency grows so large that it leads to what's known as a *peg break*. When a currency peg collapses, both countries can face dire circumstances, including inflation, difficulty paying debts, loss of trade markets, and investment losses on foreign assets. Peg breaks have occurred in Great Britain, Russia, and Argentina (see also, Holodny & Bobkoff, 2016).

The U.S. dollar's value on the world market depends on a number of factors (Liqudis, 2019). U.S. exports increase demand for U.S. dollars because customers must pay for U.S. goods and services in U.S. dollars. The same is true with global purchases of U.S. stocks and bonds that require buyers to exchange their currency for U.S. dollars. When demand for U.S. dollars rises, all else being equal, the supply of dollars shrinks, and the value of the U.S. dollar increases relative to that of other currencies. In times of economic downturns or pessimistic expectations related to the performance of the U.S. economy, a sell-off of U.S.-based assets can occur. Those dollars are then converted back to other currencies, thereby increasing the supply of dollars and lowering the value of the U.S. dollar relative to other currencies. It's important to note, however, that the U.S. dollar is considered a *safe haven* in times of global economic uncertainty. Because of its historical strength, the U.S. economy enjoys the faith and confidence of global investors. GDP reports, geopolitical events, and other economic news feed the global psyche about the health and stability of the U.S. economy. Once again, expectations matter and move markets. Psychological factors including sentiment toward the U.S. can often have a more powerful effect on value of the U.S. dollar than the fundamental forces of supply and demand.

Macroeconomic Principle #10: International Transactions Drive the Global Economy

Adam Smith (1776) writes how international trade provides more benefit to more people than *protectionist* policies that isolate a country from trading partners. Protectionist policies favor domestic producers at the cost of consumers having limited access to international markets. For example, when governments place sizable *tariffs* (i.e., taxes) on foreign imports, foreign manufacturers are discouraged from exporting to tariff-imposing countries because the tariffs make production too costly. Countries place tariffs on foreign goods to make them more expensive. The assumption is that consumers will (or should) prefer comparable products produced in their own country, even if they are more expensive than their foreign counterparts.[22] Tones of patriotism are used to support import tariffs, arguing that domestic production supports domestic jobs and national interests (see also, Heakal, 2019).

Rent-seeking refers to groups, like manufacturers, lobbying governments to protect their particular industry with tax breaks, tariffs, or outright import restrictions to prevent cheaper products from entering the market (Heakal, 2019). Smith (1776) opposes protectionist measures. He argues that even if jobs are lost in the short run, both consumers and more productive workers are better off in the long run with free trade. Smith vehemently defends the right of consumers to buy whatever they want from the cheapest source available. Recall from Chapter 2 the central and compelling nature of competition in Smith's writings.

International trade opens markets beyond a producer's geographical borders (Heakal, 2019). More competition leads to more competitive pricing, which ultimately benefits consumers when they have access to a broader selection of goods and services, some of which aren't available in their own country. Economic principles are at work in the global economy, too. As production costs, such as labor, rise in one part of the world, those costs are passed on as higher prices to consumers in markets around the world.

Specialization and *comparative advantage* are important concepts in world trade (Heakal, 2019). Economic theory tells us that countries are best served by producing products that make the most efficient use of their readily available resources, such as land, labor, capital, and technology. In doing so, these countries leverage their comparative advantage to produce certain products. Like firms, countries must specialize in what they do best. For example, if a country optimizes its resources by producing wine, it can trade with another country that specializes in producing the cotton it needs.

Politics and economics once again overlap in world trade matters (Heakal, 2019). Critics of comparative advantage claim smaller nations with fewer resources are disadvantaged in world trade. As discussed in Chapter 2, levels of economic and political freedoms vary greatly around the globe. These freedoms (or lack thereof) directly impact how open, protected, or restricted a nation's trading capabilities will be.

International transactions fuel the global economy ("How Does," 2020). Although no one entity owns or controls the world economy, there's no denying the widespread role mega-sized corporations and banks play in these transactions. The world's top firms, in fact, earn revenues that exceed the GDP of nations ("Comparison," 2020). Their presence drives growth, encourages competition, raises productivity and efficiency, and, in the long run, helps advance underdeveloped nations. There is much debate, however, about the effects of globalization in parts of the world where oppressive political regimes and high levels of corruption prevent the benefits of capitalism from reaching those who need them most. As discussed in Chapter 2, political and economic freedoms are fundamental for the wealth of nations to rise. Individual freedoms combined with national resources available for economic production vary significantly around the globe and impact capitalist outcomes.

Economics, Communication, and You

Goodness, we've covered a lot of territory here. Understanding the firm- and market-level implications of economic decision-making is no small undertaking, but consider what a better strategist and advisor you can be when you apply these principles to your public affairs practice. Economics acumen enables you to understand the incredibly broad reach your firm's actions and words can have on not only your company, but also entire markets. If you're feeling a bit more weight on your shoulders, then you've properly grasped the importance of how what you say, when you say it, to whom you say it, and how accurately you say it has a rippling effect far beyond the writing quality of a press release or social media post. The work of public affairs is information sharing. Information feeds expectations, and expectations move the economy – locally, nationally, and globally. Apply your knowledge of microeconomic nuances to better understand your firm and its customers. Apply your knowledge of macroeconomic shifts to better understand your industry and global markets. Realize your firm's positions on production decisions, public policies, and economic priorities will always have opponents. Economics acumen helps you to defend your positions, and, just as importantly, understand and perhaps even learn from your opposition. In doing so, public affairs maximizes its value to an organization and society.

Notes

1 Line management includes the functions of manufacturing, marketing, and sales that are directly involved in generating revenues and profits for the company. Staff functions are not directly involved in producing and selling goods or services but rather provide support for line functions that do (Woodruff, 2018).
2 See Chapter 4 The Art and Science of Financial Statements for an explanation of above the line, below the line, and the bottom line.
3 Or a share of someone's stomach, if you're in the food and beverage business. With credit to Bill Dillon, Ph.D., The Herman W. Lay Professor of Marketing and senior associate dean at the Cox School of Business at Southern Methodist University, Dallas, TX.
4 *Ceteris paribus* is the Latin phrase commonly used in economics meaning "holding other things constant." Supply and demand are affected by multiple factors other than product price. Thus, if all of these other factors are "held constant," or "all else being equal," a higher price will trigger more supply and less demand (see Kenton, 2019a).
5 *Ceteris paribus* applies to substitutes and complements, too. In this case, we assume if the price of liquid soap increases relative to the price of bar soap, consumers will switch to bar soap as an acceptable substitute – as long as the price of bar soap doesn't change. In time, prices of both liquid and bar soap can change.
6 See Chapter 8 Why You Cannot Ignore Operations Management for further discussion of factors involved in production decision-making.
7 Also known as the additional unit providing "net marginal benefit."
8 See Powers (2012) for what "making it up in volume" can mean for a business and Coren (2019) for an application of this concept to car manufacturer Tesla.
9 See Chapter 10 What is Strategy? for further discussion of barriers to entry.
10 See Chapter 5 How and Why Finance Rules the Business World for further discussion of shareholders and the regulatory and reporting requirements of publicly held firms.
11 See Chapter 2 Capitalism: Its Benefits and Discontents for further discussion of monopolies and the importance of competition in a free market.
12 See Chapter 6 Marketing Envy and Other Observations for further discussion of the importance of competing on attributes other than price in a free market.
13 See Chapter 2 Capitalism: Its Benefits and Discontents for a brief discussion of how capitalism and other means of organizing economic activity differ outside of the U.S.
14 See Chapter 2 Capitalism: Its Benefits and Discontents for a description of classical and neoclassical schools of economic thought that greatly restrict the role of the government in the economy.
15 See Amadeo (2019e) for a useful reference showing U.S. deficit, debt, GDP ratio, and related events that led to this spending since 1929.
16 Price stability for the Fed means keeping the rate of inflation relatively constant (Chen, 2019c).
17 Maximizing employment for the Fed does not mean zero unemployment. Rather, the Fed aims to keep unemployment at natural, or normal, levels based on historical data, between roughly 3.5 and 4.5 percent ("What is the Lowest," 2019).
18 This overview of the financial crisis and related Fed activities is from my 2015 MBA notes in Dr. Harvey Rosenblum's macroeconomics course at the SMU Cox School of Business in Dallas,

Texas. Dr. Rosenblum retired as executive vice president and director of research from the Federal Reserve Bank in Dallas in 2013.
19 Unskilled labor requires a high school diploma or mastering a specific skill in lieu of a high school diploma. Skilled labor requires additional skills or education (Mahuron, 2019).
20 The foreign exchange market, also referred to as FX or currency market, is the largest financial market in the world comprising banks and other financial centers operating 24 hours a day, closing only on weekends (Ganti, 2019).
21 All else being equal, fiscal policy that leads to higher interest rates, such as U.S. government borrowing to increase spending, attracts foreign capital to the U.S. and strengthens the U.S. dollar in the short run (Weil, 2019). The same is true when the Federal Reserve increases the federal funds rate, leading to higher interest rates across the economy (Tarver, 2019). In the long run, however, an increase in U.S. debt can lead to distrust of U.S. assets and can weaken the U.S. dollar relative to other currencies (Weil, 2019).
22 Campaigns to "buy local" and promoting products "made in the USA" follow this rationale.

References

Abbott, B., & Kenton, W. (2019, October 16). *Aggregate supply*. Retrieved from www.investopedia.com/terms/a/aggregatesupply.asp.

Alden, M. (2012, January 12). *7 companies with unrivaled economies of scale*. Retrieved from www.dividendmonk.com/7-companies-with-unrivaled-economies-of-scale/.

Amadeo, K. (2019a, April 22). *Exchange rates explained: The two types of exchange rates*. Retrieved from www.thebalance.com/what-are-exchange-rates-3306083.

Amadeo, K. (2019b, June 25). *Economies of scale: How to make economies of scale work for you*. Retrieved from www.thebalance.com/economies-of-scale-3305926.

Amadeo, K. (2019c, August 7). *Compare Obama versus Bush on economic policies and the debt*. Retrieved from www.thebalance.com/how-do-obama-and-bush-compare-on-their-economic-policies-3305622m.

Amadeo, K. (2019d, December 16). *Current U.S. federal budget deficit*. Retrieved from www.thebalance.com/current-u-s-federal-budget-deficit-3305783.

Amadeo, K. (2019e, December 26). *U.S. budget deficit by year compared to GDP, debt increase, and events*. Retrieved from www.thebalance.com/us-deficit-by-year-3306306.

Bajpai, P. (2019, April 3). *How central banks control the supply of money*. Retrieved from www.investopedia.com/articles/investing/053115/how-central-banks-control-supply-money.asp.

Banton, C. (2019a, April 10). *Currency peg*. Retrieved from www.investopedia.com/terms/c/currency-peg.asp.

Banton, C. (2019b, May 3). *Basket of goods*. Retrieved from www.investopedia.com/terms/b/basket_of_goods.asp.

Beggs, J. (2018, December 11). *The short run and the long run in economics*. Retrieved from www.thoughtco.com/the-short-run-versus-the-long-run-1147826.

Boyd, N. (2019). *Economic agents: Types and roles*. Retrieved from https://study.com/academy/lesson/economic-agents-types-roles.html.

Central banks of different countries. (2020). Retrieved from http://bankersdaily.in/central-banks-of-different-countries/.

Chamberlin, A. (2019, February 24). *An investor's guide to cyclical and counter-cyclical industries*. Retrieved from https://articles2.marketrealist.com/2014/02/investors-guide-cyclical-counter-cyclical-industries/.

Chappelow, J. (2019a, April 11). *Monetary policy*. Retrieved from www.investopedia.com/terms/m/monetarypolicy.asp.

Chappelow, J. (2019b, May 6). *Recession*. Retrieved from www.investopedia.com/terms/r/recession.asp.

Chappelow, J. (2019c, May 13). *Microeconomics*. Retrieved from www.investopedia.com/terms/m/microeconomics.asp.

Chappelow, J. (2019d, June 13). *Law of supply and demand.* Retrieved from www.investopedia.com/terms/l/law-of-supply-demand.asp.

Chappelow, J. (2019e, June 27). *Gross Domestic Product – GDP.* Retrieved from www.investopedia.com/terms/g/gdp.asp.

Chappelow, J. (2019f, August 29). *Full employment.* Retrieved from www.investopedia.com/terms/f/fullemployment.asp.

Chen, J. (2019a, May 24). *Overheated economy.* Retrieved from www.investopedia.com/terms/o/overheated_economy.asp.

Chen, J. (2019b, June 25). *Federal funds rate.* Retrieved from www.investopedia.com/terms/f/federalfundsrate.asp.

Chen, J. (2019c, August 7). *Inflation.* Retrieved from www.investopedia.com/terms/i/inflation.asp.

Comparison of the world's 25 largest corporations with the GDP of selected countries. (2020). Retrieved from www.globalpolicy.org/component/content/article/150-general/50950-comparison-of-the-worlds-25-largest-corporations-with-the-gdp-of-selected-countries.html.

Complementary and substitute goods. (n.d.). Retrieved from https://econprojectsd.weebly.com/complementary-and-substitute-goods.html.

Coren, M.J. (2019, July 24). *Tesla's losses are piling up despite record unit sales.* Retrieved from https://qz.com/1674199/teslas-losses-are-piling-up-despite-record-sales/.

Cross-price elasticity of demand. (n.d.) Retrieved from https://courses.lumenlearning.com/boundless-economics/chapter/other-demand-elasticities/.

Cussen, M.P. (2019, March 3). *Introduction to Treasury securities.* Retrieved from www.investopedia.com/articles/investing/073113/introduction-treasury-securities.asp.

Deans, G.K., Kroeger, F., & Zeisel, S. (2002, December). *The consolidation curve.* Retrieved from https://hbr.org/2002/12/the-consolidation-curve.

Decisions are made at the margin. (2019). Retrieved from https://certell.org/mini_lessons/decisions-are-made-at-the-margin/.

Definition of macroeconomics. (2019). Retrieved from https://economictimes.indiatimes.com/definition/macroeconomics.

Dolan, E. (2011, March 31). *Why it's obvious we are losing the war on drugs.* Retrieved from www.businessinsider.com/econ-101-hayek-and-why-we-are-losing-the-war-against-drugs-2011-3.

Ganti, A. (2019, October 10). *Foreign exchange market.* Retrieved from www.investopedia.com/terms/forex/f/foreign-exchange-markets.asp.

Garrison, S. (2018). *Types of business organization.* Retrieved from www.studyfinance.com/lessons/busorg/.

Government bond. (2020). Retrieved from www.bankrate.com/glossary/g/government-bond/.

Hall, M. (2018, January 16). *Is demand or supply more important to the economy?* Retrieved from www.investopedia.com/ask/answers/040815/demand-or-supply-more-important-economy.asp.

Hall, M. (2019a, July 1). *Marginal revenue and marginal cost of production.* Retrieved from www.investopedia.com/ask/answers/041315/how-marginal-revenue-related-marginal-cost-production.asp.

Hall, M. (2019b, September 29). *Monopoly vs. oligopoly: What's the difference?* Retrieved from www.investopedia.com/ask/answers/121514/what-are-major-differences-between-monopoly-and-oligopoly.asp.

Hayes, A. (2019a, June 25). *Marginal analysis.* Retrieved from www.investopedia.com/terms/m/marginal-analysis.asp.

Hayes, A. (2019b, June 25). *Perfect competition.* Retrieved from www.investopedia.com/terms/p/perfectcompetition.asp.

Heakal, R. (2019, August 21). *The investor's guide to global trade.* Retrieved from www.investopedia.com/insights/what-is-international-trade/.

Henderson, D. R. (2019). *Opportunity cost.* Retrieved from www.econlib.org/library/Enc/OpportunityCost.html.

Holodny, E., & Bobkoff, D. (2016, August 22). *One move almost always sets off chaos in the currency market.* Retrieved from www.businessinsider.com/what-is-a-currency-peg-2016-8.

How does the global economy work? (2020). Retrieved from www.edology.com/blog/accounting-finance/how-does-global-economy-work/.

The IMF at a glance. (2019). Retrieved from www.imf.org/en/About.

Interest rate. (2020). Retrieved from www.bankrate.com/glossary/i/interest-rate/.

Jahan, S., Mahmud, A. S., & Papageorgiou, C. (2014, September). What is Keynesian economics? *Finance & Development, 51*(3). Retrieved from www.imf.org/external/pubs/ft/fandd/2014/09/basics.htm.

Kenton, W. (2018, October 22). *Price elasticity of demand*. Retrieved from www.investopedia.com/terms/p/priceelasticity.asp.

Kenton, W. (2019a, June 25). *Ceteris paribus defined*. Retrieved from www.investopedia.com/terms/c/ceterisparibus.asp.

Kenton, W. (2019b, July 14). *Law of diminishing marginal utility*. Retrieved from www.investopedia.com/terms/l/lawofdiminishingutility.asp.

Kenton, W. (2019c, October 15). *Aggregate demand*. Retrieved from www.investopedia.com/terms/a/aggregatedemand.asp.

Liberto, D. (2019, August 26). *Imperfect competition*. Retrieved from www.investopedia.com/terms/i/imperfect_competition.asp.

Liqudis, N. K. (2019, August 23). *3 factors that drive the U.S. dollar*. Retrieved from www.investopedia.com/articles/forex/09/factors-drive-american-dollar.asp.

Mahuron, S. (2019, January 28). *Skilled labor vs. unskilled labor*. Retrieved from https://smallbusiness.chron.com/skilled-labor-vs-unskilled-labor-46154.html.

Majaski, C. (2019, July 11). *Private vs. public company: What's the difference?* Retrieved from www.investopedia.com/ask/answers/difference-between-publicly-and-privately-held-companies/.

Majaski, C. (2020, November 30). *Nominal*. Retrieved from www.investopedia.com/terms/n/nominal.asp.

Meet the 2019 CNBC Disruptor 50 companies. Retrieved from www.cnbc.com/2019/05/15/meet-the-2019-cnbc-disruptor-50-companies.html.

Merlo, Z. (2016, October 24). *How do you identify a fragmented industry?* Retrieved from https://marketplacer.com/blog/how-do-you-identify-a-fragmented-industry/.

Moffatt, M. (2018, September 20). *The short run vs. the long run in microeconomics*. Retrieved from www.thoughtco.com/the-short-run-vs-long-run-1146343.

Nikolas, S. (2019, April 25). *Variable cost vs. fixed cost: What's the difference?* Retrieved from www.investopedia.com/ask/answers/032515/what-difference-between-variable-cost-and-fixed-cost-economics.asp.

Obringer, L.A. (2020). *How the Fed works*. Retrieved from https://money.howstuffworks.com/fed10.htm.

Perfect competition and why it matters. (2019). Retrieved from www.khanacademy.org/economics-finance-domain/microeconomics/perfect-competition-topic/perfect-competition/a/perfect-competition-and-why-it-matters-cnx.

Petroff, E. (2019, October 1). *The Fed's tools for influencing the economy*. Retrieved from www.investopedia.com/articles/economics/08/monetary-policy-recession.asp.

Popik, B. (2011, February 25). *We lose money on every sale, but make it up on volume*. Retrieved from www.barrypopik.com/index.php/new_york_city/entry/we_lose_money_on_every_sale_but_make_it_up_on_volume.

Powers, E. (2012, April 25). *Losing money, but making it up on volume*. Retrieved from www.inc.com/ed-powers/losing-money-but-making-it-up-on-volume.html.

Robinson, N. (2017, September 26). *The role of expectations in economics*. Retrieved from https://bizfluent.com/info-8045196-role-expectations-economics.html.

Rogers, C. (2016, September 28). *What does it mean to be a disruptor?* Retrieved from www.marketingweek.com/what-does-it-mean-to-be-a-disruptor/.

Smith, A. (1776). *An inquiry into the nature and causes of the wealth of nations (Vol. I & II)* [1981 reprint]. Indianapolis, IN: Liberty Fund.

Sunk cost. (2018, December 29). Retrieved from www.accountingtools.com/articles/what-is-a-sunk-cost.html.

Sunk cost fallacy. (2019). Retrieved from www.behavioraleconomics.com/resources/mini-encyclopedia-of-be/sunk-cost-fallacy/.

Tarver, E. (2019, October 1). *How moves in the Fed Funds Rate affect the U.S. dollar.* Retrieved from www.investopedia.com/articles/investing/101215/how-fed-fund-rate-hikes-affect-us-dollar.asp.

Warr, R.S. (2019, June 19). *Fed's dilemma: Inflation is healthy for the economy – but too much can trigger a recession.* Retrieved from http://theconversation.com/feds-dilemma-inflation-is-healthy-for-the-economy-but-too-much-can-trigger-a-recession-118556.

Weil, D. N. (2019). *Fiscal policy.* Retrieved from www.econlib.org/library/Enc/FiscalPolicy.html.

What are barriers to entry? (2019). Retrieved from https://corporatefinanceinstitute.com/resources/knowledge/economics/barriers-to-entry/.

What is the lowest level of unemployment that the U.S. economy can sustain? (2019, December 31). Retrieved from www.federalreserve.gov/faqs/economy_14424.htm.

What is a sunk cost? (2019). Retrieved from https://corporatefinanceinstitute.com/resources/knowledge/economics/sunk-cost/.

Who owns the Federal Reserve? (2017, March 1). Retrieved from www.federalreserve.gov/faqs/about_14986.htm.

Woodruff, J. (2018, November 21). *Differences between line and staff functions.* Retrieved from https://bizfluent.com/info-8584290-differences-between-line-staff-functions.html.

The World Factbook: Country comparison – GDP per capita. (n.d.). Retrieved from www.cia.gov/library/publications/the-world-factbook/rankorder/2004rank.html.

Chapter 4
The Art and Science of Financial Statements

In Chapter 2, we covered the purpose of a business, which is to *create value* for shareholders, customers, and other stakeholders. Value, as a term, is broadly applied in business, including references to economic, monetary, shareholder, and company value. As communicators, we interpret and convey value associated with a company's products, services, and various initiatives to a number of audiences through interpersonal, print, and digital channels. But, in the financial realm, value is all about the numbers. Lots and lots of numbers.

Financial statements provide a snapshot of the value-creating activities of a firm over a specific period of time. The formulation of these statements with numerous *line items* is relatively standardized, meaning you can see how your company's financial performance varies across a quarter, or a year, or several years, depending on your company's reporting cycle. You're able, then, to compare "apples to apples" because the reported figures in your company's statements are calculated in a similar manner in each reporting period, providing you with a better feel of how your company performs over time. And you can also compare statements side-by-side to get a rough idea of how your company is performing vis-à-vis its competitors in your industry. This is important info for communicators to know.

Before we delve into the details, there are a couple of important points to make. First, context is key in financial statement analysis. "Compared to what?" is an important question to ask when reviewing entries on these statements. One standalone accounting entry, one performance indicator, or one financial ratio is just a number until we see how it compares to an industry standard, the same line item for the same company in a different time period, or against a comparable figure for a competing firm in the same industry. It's essential to compare apples to apples when it comes to financial measures, or else *the measures are not comparable*.

Second, note that the title of this chapter includes both art *and* science. As we'll discuss, there are guidelines in place to ensure a level of consistency in how reporting companies calculate entries on their financial statements. That's the science. One of the intentions behind this consistency is to allow investors, analysts, and other interested stakeholders a reasonable opportunity to compare performance within and between firms with the confidence that calculations used to compile these statements are not only similarly formulated, but also fair estimates of value. That said, so-called standardized accounting methods still allow a great deal of room for interpretation, and this room for maneuver is well within

DOI: 10.4324/9781003000600-5

the bounds of financial reporting laws. That's the art. Such maneuvers, however, if taken too far or with the intent to deceive, can have significant reputational (among many other) effects on the company, as we'll address.

Financial Reporting Standards: FASB and GAAP

FASB (pronounced "FAS-bee" in practice) stands for the Federal Accounting Standards Board, a nonprofit organization established in 1973 to govern accounting rules ("About the FASB," n.d.). FASB is recognized by the Securities and Exchange Commission as the standard-setter for financial accounting and reporting practices for public companies. The specifics of these reporting practices are known as GAAP ("gap"), or Generally Accepted Accounting Principles.[1] Many private and non-profit organizations also follow GAAP. Why? Because stakeholders familiar with the reporting methods of publicly held companies have come to expect the same reporting consistency from other types of firms. Think, too, about startup founders who launch private firms with hopes of being acquired or going public one day.[2] Following GAAP from the start makes their financials more accessible (and comparable) for potential buyers and investors. Intuitively, use of a widely accepted accounting standard lends credibility and trustworthiness to a firm's reporting methods – two attributes we communicators strive to earn and preserve for our companies.

As communicators, we thankfully don't need to master the many complexities of financial accounting, but having business acumen means grasping fundamental accounting principles that dictate not only how entries on financial statements are calculated, but also how stakeholders expect a company to communicate about its financial health. These principles underscore how businesses "think" about the accounting process, so it's important that we who are charged with communicating on the company's behalf understand this mindset, too. The ten basic standards of GAAP are as follows (Kumaran, 2015, para. 3):

- **The business as a single entity concept.** The company's assets and activities are legally separate from the assets and activities of its owners, and the life of the firm can continue long after that of its owners.
- **The specific currency principle.** U.S. companies report all figures in U.S. dollars. Any foreign transactions are converted to U.S. dollars using current exchange rates.[3] For brevity, a common notation on financial statements is "$000," meaning figures are presented in thousands of U.S. dollars. For example, a notation of $4,025.00 in thousands indicates a value of $4,025,000.00, or 4.025 million U.S. dollars.
- **The specific time period principle.** Financial statements reflect business operations conducted over a particular span of time that is clearly noted on each statement.
- **The historical cost principle.** Recorded values reflect prices at which items were bought or sold, not current values that change over time. As such, assets held at historical cost are generally *undervalued* on financial statements compared to values they would garner at current market rates.
- **The full disclosure principle.** Accounting scandals in recent years have brought increased attention to the GAAP requirement that businesses reveal every aspect of their operations in their financial statements. Footnotes, as we'll discuss, provide necessary details that support financial transparency.

- **The recognition principle.** Companies must report (i.e., *recognize*) income and expenses in the same period they were accrued. GAAP requires companies to use the *accrual*, rather than the cash, basis method of accounting. In FASB's view, accrual accounting provides a more accurate picture of financial health because transactions are recorded in the same time period in which they occur (Ross, 2015; see also "Accrual Accounting," 2017). To illustrate, under the accrual method, when a company sells a product on credit to a customer, both the sale and the forthcoming payment (known as a *receivable*) are recorded at the time of the sale. Under the cash method, the sale isn't recognized until the cash payment is received. The former reporting method gives a more complete and timely view of company transactions (see Sidebars 4.1 and 4.2: Debits and Credits and Recognizing Revenues).
- **The non-death principle of businesses.** Businesses are assumed to continue operations into perpetuity with no end date. A related term you may encounter is *going concern*, meaning the business is assumed to remain in business for the foreseeable future and not expected to suddenly stop operating and sell off assets at deeply discounted prices ("The Going Concern Principle," 2017). When the business is a going concern, it's reasonable, then, for accountants to anticipate the recognition of both income and expenses at a future date.
- **The matching principle.** The matching principle is a key element of GAAP accrual accounting that states revenues must be matched to expenses in the same period a transaction occurs, regardless of when payment is made ("Accrual Accounting," 2017). The matching principle, as you may have already realized, is closely related to the recognition principle. In essence, the matching principle focuses on recognizing expenses whereas the recognition principle focuses on recognizing revenue ("Matching Principle," 2016). By *matching* we mean that *revenues* must be matched with the *expenses* incurred by the company to generate those revenues ("Revenue Recognition," 2017). In other words, when a business recognizes revenue generated from a product sale, it also must recognize the cost of getting that product into the customer's hands.
- **The principle of materiality.** Material items are those that have a significant impact on financial statements and must be reported ("The Materiality Principle," 2017). For example, if one particular accounting entry would change a profit into a loss, regardless of its dollar amount, it is considered *material*, or essential, to include in financial statements. Without this entry, the reporting of a company profit would be misleading and inaccurate. On the other hand, if the accounting of a $100 expense for a multi-million dollar corporation would have no impact whatsoever on the presentation of financial information, it is considered immaterial. The reporting and accounting procedures used for immaterial items aren't as important. In fact, some immaterial items can even be disregarded in the accounting process. GAAP, however, does not provide definitive guidance on what constitutes materiality because materiality is situation dependent. The *effect* of an entry being included (or not) matters more than the *amount* of the entry. An immaterial item for a large company could be a material item for a smaller firm. Judgment in matters of materiality is best left to the company auditors (see Sidebar 4.3: Internal vs. External Audits).[4]
- **The principle of conservative accounting.** I liken this principle to erring on the side of caution in financial reporting. Conservatism in accounting means *recording a loss*

even when there is uncertainty about the loss actually occurring, and *not recording a gain* when there is doubt about a gain being realized ("The Conservatism Principle," 2017). The principle of recording assets at historical cost reflects a conservative approach to accounting. Conservatism directs accountants to be reasonable and prudent regarding the value of estimates and to base estimates on the best information they have at the time. As with materiality, conservatism in practice relies on the professional judgment of accountants and related experts.

Sidebar 4.1 Debits and Credits

("Debits and Credits," 2017; Schneider, 2017; "T Account," 2017; "What is a General Ledger," 2017)

In accounting lingo, for every **debit**, there must be a **credit**, and vice versa. Each business transaction that has a monetary impact on financial reporting affects at least two accounts and is recorded in a **general ledger account**. Debits *increase* an asset or expense account or *decrease* a liability or equity account. In the two-column accounting entry system, debits are always on the left. Conversely, credits *increase* a liability or equity account or *decrease* an asset or expense account. Credits are always on the right. The total amount of debits for one transaction will always equal the total amount of credits for the same transaction. This equality keeps accounts in balance and enables the creation of financial statements.

For example, if a $50,000 machine is purchased (a debit, or increase of an asset) with a part cash (a credit, or decrease of an asset), part credit (a credit, or increase of a liability) sale, the accounting entry would look like this, following the convention described, with each side equaling $50,000. **T accounts** are used to track these transactions for the general ledger account:

Equipment	50,000	
Cash		10,000
Accounts Payable		40,000

Sidebar 4.2 Recognizing Revenues

("Revenue Recognition Principle," 2016; "Why Did the FASB," n.d.)

The GAAP recognition principle dictates that revenues, and their related expenses, are recognized and reported in the same accounting period that they are accrued. A central component of accrual accounting is that revenue is recorded for financial statements when it is **earned**, not necessarily when it is **received**. Revenue is said to be **realized** when goods or services are exchanged for cash or other assets and **earned** when the company transfers ownership of the product to the buyer.

All this accounting jargon may sound tedious, but the timing of revenue recognition has a significant impact on financial reporting. In 2014, FASB issued clarifying guidance on revenue recognition to make standards more comparable across industries. Special allowances include:

- In long-term projects that take years to complete, revenue can be recognized as earned at various stages of completion.

- Manufacturers in the oil, mining, and agricultural industries may recognize revenue as goods become marketable but before they are actually sold.
- Companies that offer installment sales may recognize revenue when cash is actually received.

Sidebar 4.3 Internal vs. External Audits

("Internal Audit," 2021; Kenton, 2020)

Audits refer to the process of independently checking the accuracy of financial records.

An **internal audit** examines a company's internal controls/procedures and provides recommendations for improvements. Internal audits are conducted by employees who are independent of management and report directly to the board's audit committee.

An **external audit** examines all information, including ledgers, bank accounts, and transactions, related to a company's financial reports. External audits are conducted by third parties outside of the firm to verify whether financial statements are GAAP-compliant and free from material misstatements. External auditor reports are usually published in a company's annual report and include the auditor's opinion on the veracity of financial statements.

The Big Three: Three Statements, Three Formulas, Many Different Names

Our primary focus is on three major financial statements, and we'll review each in turn. Each of these statements – the income statement, the balance sheet, and the cash flow statement – tell their own important *part* of the story about a company's financial health, but you need to look at *all three* statements to get the full picture. These statements are also linked formulaically. That is, a transaction affecting one statement can literally ripple through one or both of the other statements, changing multiple line item values. Again, our objective here is not to crack the nuances of calculating accounting entries but rather first to understand what each statement tells us about the state of a company's operations and, secondly, how these statements work together to tell the company's financial story. Numbers shown as is on these statements are positive, or added, values. Numbers shown in parentheses are negative, or subtracted, values. A financial statement noted as *consolidated* simply means the activities of the firm and its subsidiaries are combined into one presentation as a single reporting entity ("Consolidated," 2017).

The Income Statement

The basic formula for the income statement is:

Revenue – Expenses = Income

What the company takes in through sales of products and/or services, minus the expenses related to producing those products/services and running the day-to-day business, renders what funds remain, known as net income, earnings, or profit,[5] for the stated reporting period. The income statement – also known as the statement of operations, statement of earnings, profit-and-loss (or P&L) statement, statement of operating results, or statement of income (Loth, 2017b) – no matter how intricately presented with numerous line items, *always* reduces to this simple formula. Keep this in mind, and you'll be able to decipher any income statement that crosses your desk.

Income statements come in varying lengths, formatting styles, and levels of detail, but the same basic formula underlies each: Revenue – Expenses = Income. The *single-step* income statement is the simplest form, presenting income as the difference between revenues/gains and expenses/losses ("Single-Step Income Statement," 2017). We'll instead focus on the fundamental components of the more detailed *multi-step* income statement typically used by larger organizations to distinguish operating from non-operating sources of revenues, expenses, losses, and gains ("Multi-Step Income Statement," 2017; see Figure 4.1: Income Statement Example[6]). The following list comprises the major categories of financial info you'll find on an income statement, along with explanations of how these sections fit together to calculate the firm's income for a set period of time.

Of important note is that each company has its preferred nomenclature for naming line items. Don't be thrown off if you see line items labeled differently from the categories below, or if you see numerous line items with obscure titles. With time, you'll quickly spot sections representing the three pieces of the ever present, always reliable formula: Revenue – Expenses = Income. You'll see, too, where the term "bottom line" originates – the firm's income (or profit, or earnings) is literally at the bottom of the income statement.

- *Company name, time period, and currency notation.* The income statement is clearly marked with the company name and the time period covered on the statement. The timeframe may be a (three-month) quarter, a series of quarters, a year, or a series of years. A company's *fiscal year* (noted "FY") used for accounting purposes may not match a calendar year ("Fiscal Year," 2017). Columns representing multiple quarters or fiscal years on the same income statement allow for line item comparisons between operating periods. "USD" and/or the dollar sign will designate U.S. dollars, and look, too, for whether figures are in thousands ($000) or millions ($MM). Denomination abbreviations may vary – just be sure you're quoting figures accurately, as those zeros make a difference!
- *Revenue.* Revenue, sales, sales revenue, or some other derivation of the term is the *top line* of the income statement, representing the total number of dollars brought in from sales.[7] Gross revenue is the total dollar amount. Net revenue, if included, is gross revenue minus any returns, discounts, or revenue the company doesn't expect to collect ("Beginners' Guide," 2007). Recall from our earlier discussion of GAAP-mandated accrual accounting that just because revenue is *recognized* doesn't mean cash payments have been *received* (Loth, 2017b). We'll cover more on that important caveat when we get to the cash flow statement.
- *Cost of goods sold (COGS).* In practice, you'll hear the term "cogs" used to describe this part of the income statement. The COGS line item, which may be labeled *cost of sales* or *cost of services*, captures the *direct costs* of producing the company's products

and/or services. Direct costs are those that can be traced directly to the product being sold, including manufacturing, labor, and direct material costs. Whereas financial accountants primarily focus on providing information to external stakeholders, managerial (or cost) accountants track operational metrics for internal decision-making and planning purposes, including the determination of direct (vs. indirect) costs, budgeting, and forecasting ("Managerial Accounting," 2017).

- *Gross income.* Gross Income (aka gross profit or gross margin) = Revenues − COGS. Gross profit demarcates *the line* you'll hear referenced in management discussions ("Above the Line," 2017). Specifically, revenues and COGS are *above the line* and receive a good deal of managerial attention because these line items vary more than expenses and other entries that literally appear *below the line*, that is, underneath gross profit, on the income statement.
- *Operating expenses.* This category lists expenses that are not included in COGS but incurred by the business during the reporting period ("The Income Statement," 2017). Most frequently referred to as *SG&A* (sales, general, and administrative) expenses, these are the ongoing costs of doing business and remain relatively fixed. SG&A expenses include administrative, marketing, selling, legal, and other professional support costs, including communication staff, collectively referred to as *overhead*. Unlike COGS, SG&A expenses are not directly tied to particular products or services being sold but rather support a broad range of the company's operations ("Beginners' Guide," 2007). SG&A expenses are also closely monitored by management because every expense has the effect of reducing net income, or the bottom line. You'll find line items related to *depreciation* in this section, too. Businesses *write-off* (that is, deduct from taxable income) the cost of machinery and other *tangible assets* over time as depreciation expenses ("Depreciation," 2017). If, for example, a company purchases a $100,000 piece of equipment, it can write-off the entire $100,000 in one year, or write-off a portion of the cost in each year of the usable life of the machine, which could amount to $10,000 a year for ten years, using rules for *straight-line depreciation*.[8] As we progress down the items on the income statement, it will become evident that, all else being equal, a $10,000 deduction results in a higher net income (at least on paper) than a $100,000 deduction. As such, firms generally prefer to depreciate assets over time. *Amortization* is a similar write-off process but for *intangible assets* like patents, copyrights, and trademarks and appears as a separate line item(s) on the income statement (Fontinelle, 2017; "Intangible Asset," 2017; see Sidebar 4.4: R&D, Brands, and Goodwill).

Sidebar 4.4 R&D, Brands, and Goodwill

(Hargrave, 2020; "Intangible Asset," 2017; "Research and Development," 2021)

Research and Development (R&D) expenditures are made to improve existing products and develop new products. Companies with multiple intangible assets – including patents, trademarks, and brands – generally spend more on R&D efforts. R&D includes both the acquisition and application of new knowledge. Industries with high R&D spending include technology, semiconductors, and pharmaceuticals.

> A company's **brand names** are valuable intangible assets that drive sales. **Goodwill** is an intangible asset resulting from one company buying another company. Goodwill is the purchase price premium paid over and above the fair value of the acquisition that recognizes the value of a company's brand recognition, customer service, employee talent, proprietary technology, etc.

- *Operating income.* Operating Income (aka income from operations or EBIT, Earnings Before Interest and Taxes) = Gross Income – Operating Expenses.[9] Operating income reflects how much revenue the company keeps *after* covering the costs of normal operations but *before* deductions related to interest, taxes, and other non-operating expenses that appear further down the income statement (Loth, 2017b). Industry analysts often prefer operating income over net income as a measure of company profitability because it reflects management's efficiency in managing costs.
- *Other revenues, expenses, gains, and losses.* This catch-all category captures relevant line items related to the business but not to operations per se, including *interest* earned on cash and/or paid on loans, other income and/or expenses, and *extraordinary* (that is, one-time or unusual) gains and/or losses reported for the stated accounting period ("Extraordinary Item," 2017; "The Income Statement," 2017). Depending on the individual entries, these items will be added to or subtracted from operating income to calculate taxable income.
- *Income before taxes.* Income Before Taxes (aka pre-tax income or taxable income or earnings before taxes) = Operating Income +/- Other Revenues, Expenses, Gains, and Losses. Income before taxes is the amount upon which the company's taxes owed are calculated. Pretax income is another profitability measure of interest to analysts because firms have a number of methods at their disposal to reduce taxes owed and thus impact reported income (Loth, 2017b).
- *Income taxes.* The value of this line item represents an *estimate* of what the company expects to pay in taxes, not an amount actually paid (Loth, 2017b).
- *Net income.* Net Income (aka net profit or net earnings) = Income Before Taxes – Income Taxes. Net income is the bottom line, that is, what dollars remain after all relevant deductions are taken from the top line revenue figure. A *net loss* will be reported if expenses exceed revenue (Loth, 2017b). A reference to *comprehensive income* on the income statement reflects net impacts to earnings from asset value changes (e.g., investments) explained on the cash flow statement ("Comprehensive Income," 2017). The most common measures of profitability, however, are net income and the aforementioned measures of gross income, operating income, and income before taxes (Loth, 2017b).
- *Earnings per share (or EPS):* EPS = Net Income/Number of Outstanding Shares. Many income statements include an earnings per share calculation, which indicates how much money shareholders would receive for each share of *common* stock owned *if* the company distributed all of its earnings for the reporting period ("Beginners' Guide," 2007). A *diluted earnings per share* calculation accounts for any convertible securities[10] the company may have, essentially increasing the denominator of the equation above and rendering a diluted EPS value that is *less* than the basic EPS value, hence the term "diluted" ("What is the Difference," 2015).

EXXON MOBIL CORPORATION
CONDENSED CONSOLIDATED STATEMENT OF INCOME
(millions of dollars)

	Three Months Ended March 31,	
	2020	2019
Revenues and other income		
Sales and other operating revenue	55,134	61,646
Income from equity affiliates	775	1,709
Other income	249	270
Total revenues and other income	56,158	63,625
Costs and other deductions		
Crude oil and product purchases	32,083	34,801
Production and manufacturing expenses	8,297	8,970
Selling, general and administrative expenses	2,579	2,770
Depreciation and depletion	5,819	4,571
Exploration expenses, including dry holes	288	280
Non-service pension and postretirement benefit expense	269	358
Interest expense	249	181
Other taxes and duties	6,832	7,405
Total costs and other deductions	56,416	59,336
Income (Loss) before income taxes	(258)	4,289
Income taxes	512	1,883
Net income (loss) including noncontrolling interests	(770)	2,406
Net income (loss) attributable to noncontrolling interests	(160)	56
Net income (loss) attributable to ExxonMobil	(610)	2,350
Earnings (Loss) per common share *(dollars)*	(0.14)	0.55
Earnings (Loss) per common share – assuming dilution *(dollars)*	(0.14)	0.55

Figure 4.1 Income Statement Example

The Balance Sheet

The basic formula for the balance sheet is:

Assets = Liabilities + Shareholders' Equity

Essentially, the balance sheet tells you what the company *owns* (i.e., assets) and how the company *paid* (or what it *owes*) for those assets (i.e., via liabilities or shareholders' equity) at the end of a specified accounting period ("Balance Sheet," 2017; see Figure 4.2: Balance Sheet Example). The term *statement of financial position* may be used in place of balance sheet, but the idea is the same. The balance sheet literally *balances* – it must – always, and without exception. If the company acquires an asset, the Assets side of the equation increases in value. For the equation to remain balanced, so, too, must the right side of the equation increase *by the same amount* in Liabilities and/or Shareholders' Equity. The debits and credits of accounting entries (see Sidebar 4.1: Debits and Credits) trace this balancing act for each company transaction. Our focus, however, is understanding the big picture of what's included in the balance sheet. As with the income statement, don't be concerned with differences in formatting or line item names. Just look for the three components of the formula, Assets = Liabilities + Shareholders' Equity, which are clearly marked headings on this statement. Let's dive in.

- *Company name, time period, and currency notation.* Same as on the income statement, but there's an important difference in dates on balance sheets versus dates on income statements (Way, 2017). An income statement reports earnings over a specified *range of time*, say a quarter or fiscal year. The balance sheet, however, reports financial conditions at *one specific point in time*, that is, at the *end* of a particular accounting cycle. Balance sheet information is presented "as of" a particular date provided on the statement, meaning figures reflect transactions leading up to that specified date. You may see more than one period in time reported on a balance sheet.
- *Assets.* Assets are resources owned by the company, including equipment, land, patents, and buildings ("Asset," 2017). They have economic value in that assets are expected to provide future benefit (e.g., by increasing revenues or reducing costs) to the company's operations. On the balance sheet, assets are divided into *current* and *non-current* assets (Loth, 2017a; "Reading the Balance Sheet," 2017). Current assets, such as inventory, are expected to convert into cash within one year. Cash and cash equivalents (e.g., bank accounts) are the most fundamental of current assets because they are the most *liquid* assets (see also Nickolas, 2017). Financial *liquidity* is an important measure for companies because it indicates how quickly assets can be converted into cash to pay bills and other obligations (Mueller, 2017). Non-current assets can be *tangible* (e.g., equipment and buildings, also known as *fixed assets*) or *intangible*[11] (e.g., patents, copyrights, intellectual property), but these assets have a lifespan longer than one year and are not as readily convertible into cash as current assets. Asset listings include, but are not limited to, cash, *accounts receivable* (i.e., payments due but not yet received by the company, such as credit sales), inventory, supplies, *prepaid* items (e.g., the company has paid for 12 months of insurance and 10 months of coverage still remain on the policy), investments, land, equipment, buildings, and goodwill ("Balance Sheet," 2017). Next to some asset line items, like buildings and equipment, you'll see deductions for *accumulated depreciation* (see Sidebar 4.5: Book Value). The net value of these assets, that is, their historical cost minus their accumulated depreciation charges, becomes the *carrying value* of these assets on the company's books ("What is Accumulated Depreciation," 2017).[12] The value, total assets, concludes this section of the balance sheet.

Sidebar 4.5 Book Value

(Hayes, 2020; Murray, 2020; Tuovila, 2020)

Book value of an asset is equal to the carrying cost of an asset on the balance sheet. Specifically, it's the original cost of an asset minus its accumulated depreciation (i.e., annual average depreciation multiplied by the age of the asset in years). Book value decreases over time. That is, the original cost stays the same while depreciation increases.

> **Book value of a company**, also known as net asset value (NAV), equals total assets minus intangible assets and liabilities, providing an estimated value of a company's assets that shareholders would receive if the company were liquidated.
>
> Book value is typically **lower than market value** because it is based on acquisition cost. As such, asset values shown on the balance sheet are conservatively stated.
>
> If an asset has significant **impairment** in its book value because of a substantial decrease in market price, physical condition, or other negative economic or political impact, GAAP requires the company to record a **book value reduction**, also known as an **asset write-down**. Book value reduction is considered an **unusual item** that lowers asset value on the balance sheet and results in an offsetting expense on the income statement.

- *Liabilities.* Liabilities are the company's financial obligations to outside parties, including bills and loan payments to be paid ("Reading the Balance Sheet," 2017). Like assets, liabilities fall into *current* and *long-term* categories, with the former type of liabilities due and expected to be paid within one year of the balance sheet date. Look for the term *payable* in line item names, which means these are monies owed by the company to creditors and others who have a claim on the company's assets, such as salaries, debt payments, interest, and income taxes ("Balance Sheet," 2017). Also recognized as liabilities are dollars received for services not yet rendered, which could be labeled as *unearned revenue*. For example, when the company receives a customer deposit or payment for a product not yet delivered, accountants recognize the company's obligation to complete these future transactions as liabilities on the balance sheet. *Accrued liabilities* represent goods or services received, but not yet paid for by the company ("Accrued Liability," 2017). You may see the term *deferred liabilities* used to record these accounts. As we've discussed, the labeling of line items varies by company, but the idea is the same – liabilities represent what the company owes others. A value for total liabilities completes this section.
- *Shareholders' (or stockholders' or owner's) equity.* Shareholders' equity indicates the *net worth* of the company, or the amount by which assets exceed liabilities ("Reading the Balance Sheet," 2017). Recall our base equation: Assets = Liabilities + Shareholders' Equity. If we instead solve for Shareholders' Equity, the formula becomes Shareholders' Equity = Assets − Liabilities and represents, for accounting purposes, what funds remain if the company were to sell off all of its assets and pay off all of its liabilities ("Balance Sheet," 2017). The shareholders' equity account initially holds monies invested to start the business, whether in cash, shares of stock, or some combination of the two. Common line items found in this section include common stock, preferred stock, treasury stock, and *paid-in capital*, or monies paid in exchange for shares of stock. At the end of each fiscal year, the company can transfer funds from net income (on the income statement) to *retained earnings* on the balance sheet, which indicates monies left over, or retained, in a particular accounting period after *dividends*[13] have been paid to shareholders ("Retained Earnings," 2017). Retained earnings are used by the company to reinvest in its operations. A *net loss* on the income statement would result in a reduction of the retained earnings account. A *deficit* occurs when the net loss exceeds retained earnings, rendering a negative

EXXON MOBIL CORPORATION
CONDENSED CONSOLIDATED BALANCE SHEET
(millions of dollars)

	Mar. 31, 2020	Dec. 31, 2019
Assets		
Current assets		
Cash and cash equivalents	11,412	3,089
Notes and accounts receivable – net	20,871	26,966
Inventories		
Crude oil, products and merchandise	12,067	14,010
Materials and supplies	4,434	4,518
Other current assets	1,465	1,469
Total current assets	50,249	50,052
Investments, advances and long-term receivables	42,981	43,164
Property, plant and equipment – net	248,409	253,018
Other assets, including intangibles – net	14,165	16,363
Total assets	355,804	362,597
Liabilities		
Current liabilities		
Notes and loans payable	27,755	20,578
Accounts payable and accrued liabilities	35,815	41,831
Income taxes payable	1,203	1,580
Total current liabilities	64,773	63,989
Long-term debt	31,857	26,342
Postretirement benefits reserves	21,913	22,304
Deferred income tax liabilities	24,863	25,620
Long-term obligations to equity companies	4,024	3,988
Other long-term obligations	19,631	21,416
Total liabilities	167,061	163,659
Commitments and contingencies (Note 3)		
Equity		
Common stock without par value		
(9,000 million shares authorized, 8,019 million shares issued)	15,636	15,637
Earnings reinvested	416,919	421,341
Accumulated other comprehensive income	(24,339)	(19,493)
Common stock held in treasury		
(3,791 million shares at March 31, 2020 and 3,785 million shares at December 31, 2019)	(226,137)	(225,835)
ExxonMobil share of equity	182,079	191,650
Noncontrolling interests	6,664	7,288
Total equity	188,743	198,938
Total liabilities and equity	355,804	362,597

Figure 4.2 Balance Sheet Example

figure. The retained earnings amount at the *end* of one accounting period serves as the starting balance of retained earnings for the *beginning* of the next accounting period. The company's *statement of shareholders' equity* provides supporting details for how the total value of shareholders' equity shown at the bottom of the balance sheet was calculated ("What is the Statement," 2017).
- *Total liabilities and shareholders' equity.* Here's the total value of these two sections and, lo and behold, this sum equals the total assets value, supporting the underlying formula of the balance sheet: Assets = Liabilities + Shareholders' Equity. On this one statement, you see what the company holds in assets and how, via liabilities and equity, it paid for those assets.

The Cash Flow Statement

The basic formula for the cash flow statement (or statement of cash flows) is:

Cash Inflows – Cash Outflows = Cash Remaining

Pretty simple, right? The difference between cash coming in and cash being spent equals the cash the company has on hand ("Cash Flow Statement," 2017b; see Figure 4.3: Cash Flow Statement Example). In business, cash is key. In fact, *cash is king*. It's the only asset that's ready to pay the bills, and it's difficult (but unfortunately, not impossible) to fake. All other assets have to be *converted* to cash before they can be used for payments. An income statement with a positive bottom line (i.e., net income, or profit) may give the impression that the company is doing well, but a business without cash will eventually fail ("How Can a Company," 2017). *This is why review of all three financial statements is critically important.* Otherwise, you see only part of a company's financial picture. The most common approach used for preparing the cash flow statement is the *indirect method*, meaning the statement begins with net income, followed by a series of additions and subtractions that adjust *net income* into what's *truly cash* ("Cash Flow Statement," 2017b). Firms need profits *and* cash. Net income, however, *does not equal* cash in the bank, which is why a company can *look* profitable on the income statement but be in dire straits with its cash position (Heakal, 2017; see also "Cash Flow Statement," 2017a). *Burn rate* refers to how quickly a company uses its cash (McClure, 2021). Although it's common for new firms to rely on cash supplies while building sustainable revenue streams, too much cash use, even by mature firms, can be indicative of a company relying on borrowed funds (i.e., debt) or shareholder equity instead of operations to stay afloat. However, using too little cash to reinvest in the business can hamper growth and place a firm behind its more innovative competitors. Cash management is a delicate, but important, balancing act for companies. Here are the components of the cash flow statement ("Cash Flow Statement," 2017b).

- *Company name, time period, and currency notation.* Like the income statement, the cash flow statement covers a specified interval of time.
- *Cash flows from operating activities.* The cash flow statement begins with net income – the bottom line of the income statement. Adjustments are then made to net

EXXON MOBIL CORPORATION
CONDENSED CONSOLIDATED STATEMENT OF CASH FLOWS
(millions of dollars)

	Three Months Ended March 31,	
	2020	2019
Cash flows from operating activities		
Net income (loss) including noncontrolling interests	(770)	2,406
Depreciation and depletion	5,819	4,571
Noncash inventory adjustment – lower of cost or market	2,245	-
Changes in operational working capital, excluding cash and debt	(942)	2,257
All other items – net	(78)	(896)
Net cash provided by operating activities	6,274	8,338
Cash flows from investing activities		
Additions to property, plant and equipment	(5,945)	(5,199)
Proceeds associated with sales of subsidiaries, property, plant and equipment, and sales and returns of investments	86	107
Additional investments and advances	(728)	(910)
Other investing activities including collection of advances	220	209
Net cash used in investing activities	(6,367)	(5,793)
Cash flows from financing activities		
Additions to long-term debt	8,466	-
Reductions in long-term debt	(2)	-
Reductions in short-term debt	(1,533)	(3,777)
Additions/(reductions) in commercial paper, and debt with three months or less maturity *(1)*	5,829	6,776
Cash dividends to ExxonMobil shareholders	(3,719)	(3,505)
Cash dividends to noncontrolling interests	(45)	(43)
Changes in noncontrolling interests	94	(74)
Common stock acquired	(305)	(421)
Net cash used in financing activities	8,785	(1,044)
Effects of exchange rate changes on cash	(369)	43
Increase/(decrease) in cash and cash equivalents	8,323	1,544
Cash and cash equivalents at beginning of period	3,089	3,042
Cash and cash equivalents at end of period	11,412	4,586

Figure 4.3 Cash Flow Statement Example

income based on operating activities that affect cash, such as account payments and inventory purchases,[14] to derive *net cash from operating activities*. If net cash from operations is consistently higher than net income, earnings are said to be of *high quality* because they are generating cash for the firm. Conversely, concerns are raised when net cash from operating activities is *less than* net income.
- *Cash flows from investing activities.* Cash receipts and disbursements related to investment activities, such as the purchase of a building or sale of equipment, are captured here, rendering *net cash from investing activities*. Analysts are particularly interested in changes in *capital expenditures* (i.e., investments in property, plant, and

equipment) shown in this section, more commonly referred to as "CapEx," because they are indicative of the company investing in its own operations (see also "Cash Flow Statement," 2017a).
- *Cash flows from financing activities.* Cash receipts and disbursements related to financing activities, such as additions or reductions in debt, payment of dividends, and stock purchases, are reconciled to provide *net cash from financing activities*.
- *Net increase (decrease) in cash.* Here, values of net cash from operating activities, investing activities, and financing activities are combined to calculate a net increase (or decrease) in cash over the reported period.

Those All-Important Footnotes: Read Them

We've completed our tour of the three major financial statements, which are key communication vehicles for companies. And you now have a set of go-to, basic formulas that will help you crack the "big idea" of each statement, no matter how many line items appear. By regulatory design, financial reporting is intended to be informative, transparent, and reliable for decision-making. Although the presentation of financial information is simplified for the reader, the accounting behind the numbers isn't always evident, simple, or usual. As such, line items in need of further explanation are accompanied by *footnotes* (also called *explanatory notes*, or just *notes*) to provide the details needed (Loughran, n.d.). Here is a sampling of the types of notes you may encounter – *always read them* to understand what's behind the numbers (see also "Beginners' Guide," 2007).

- **Basis for presentation.** An explanation of the business and its major accounting policies.
- **Significant accounting policies and practices.** Includes methods used for calculating depreciation, valuing inventory, paying for employee benefits, estimating tax payments, granting stock options, and accounting for intangible assets, among other entry types that require clarification. These footnotes are often used to justify management's most complex judgment calls.
- **Disclosure of subsequent events.** Notice of major events that happened after the close of the accounting period, such as the purchase or sale of part of the company. Not all events affect the accounting estimates provided, but those that do are considered material and must be disclosed.
- **Contingencies.** Acknowledgement that some event could happen (or not happen) and lead to a future loss.
- **Reporting debt.** Discloses creditor claims against company assets, along with details of how the company finances its debt obligations.

Caveats and Communication Roles for Accounting and Finance

The complexity of the financial reporting process is equally matched with the communication demands that result from this process. Sharing your company's financial profile with a number of internal and external stakeholders will naturally raise a number of questions, concerns, and, yes, challenges to your company's way of doing business. And guess who's on the front line needing to respond? That would be *you*, not the accountants. Here are some caveats and insights to guide you.

- **Proactively build your internal network.** The importance of building – and relying on – your internal network of financial contacts raised in Chapter 1 is worth revisiting here. If you haven't already, take the initiative, and get to know the go-to people in finance and accounting. Don't wait until an urgent media request or crisis erupts. Work with them early and often. The more you learn about financial reporting, the more questions you will have, and you need expert colleagues to help you communicate accurately. You're also keeping your financial colleagues aware of the types of questions and issues that are raised by the information they provide. These relationships are key to sustaining your financial literacy and credibility.
- **Realize that businesses keep two sets of books.** The financial reporting particulars we've covered are designed for investors, analysts, creditors, regulators, and other audiences to get a closer look at how a company operates. It's in the company's interest to cast the best light possible on earnings and performance indicators for these groups. But there's another financial stakeholder we've not yet mentioned, and that's the Internal Revenue Service (IRS). In the U.S. tax system, the more you earn, the more you pay, so corporations use tax laws and professional advisors to minimize taxable income and thus their tax payments, which is perfectly legal (Connolly, 2012). So, yes, businesses keep two sets of books – one set following GAAP that includes a number of estimates for investors and a second set following IRS regulations to report what actually happened in the firm for tax purposes. The particular differences between GAAP and IRS accounting aren't as important for our work as being prepared to explain this widely accepted practice when necessary.
- **Know that financial statements reflect neither economic reality nor what the company is worth.** The aforementioned GAAP principles of historical cost and conservatism provide a prudent presentation of company assets, *not* their current market values. We'll discuss more reliable ways to determine a company's value in Chapter 5.
- **Stay in your industry lane when making comparisons across firms.** This may be evident to you, but you may need to remind certain stakeholders of the need to compare apples to apples when it comes to corporate finances. Depreciation methods, sales patterns, inventory levels, fixed assets, debt, and CapEx, among other measures, *vary* depending on industry. Understand the norms in your industry, and you'll effectively rebut someone attempting to compare line items from your manufacturing firm to that of a service company.
- **Think beyond customers for revenue generation.** The top line drives the rest of the income statement, but think beyond the obvious customers when you consider how your corporate or public affairs team can help increase revenue streams. Which stakeholders are you interacting with on a regular basis? Suppliers? Regulators? Employees? Elected officials? How can the work you do help increase sales by removing obstacles, providing information, gathering feedback, improving relationships, resolving conflict, or bringing what you learn externally back inside the firm for effective action? You don't need to be directly connected to customers to have a revenue-producing mindset. Know how your firm makes money, connect those dots to what you do, and apply that knowledge to your communication strategies.

- **Keep a watchful eye on expenses.** As communicators, we are pure SG&A expense. So, while you're working to drive revenues, be mindful of reducing expenses, too. Be prepared to explain, defend, and justify cost-cutting when it affects employees and communities. Ultimately, more revenues and fewer expenses are how profits are made. And when it's time to propose spending on communication initiatives, have your business case ready to justify the expenditure. How, exactly, will your proposal contribute to the bottom line? Every manager at the table has to answer this same question, and the more *quantifiable* your response, the better.
- **Remember that the profitable firm attracts attention.** Profitable firms have the resources and autonomy needed to respond to changing market conditions, take risks, overcome barriers to entry, and forge new markets though innovation.[15] Consequently, profitable firms have imitators and critics, too, some of which are more formidable than others. Understand not only how your company creates value and differs from the competition, but also how its profits benefit more than just shareholders. When you're an industry leader (or striving to be), your profits may be called "excessive" when the economic tide turns in your favor, yet you'll get no accompanying sympathy during the rough patches. In good and bad times, steward the stakeholder relationships you are charged with managing, and you'll help your firm to accomplish its goals.
- **Help improve your firm's cash position.** How, you ask? If your corporate role interacts with customers, suppliers, partners, or other stakeholders who are slow in making payments to the company, work with your finance contacts to see if there's a need for some relationship mending or payment process repair, and then communicate accordingly to quicken those cash receipts. Too often problems go unspoken until someone takes the time to ask, "What's going on?"
- **Actively seek ways to support business objectives with communication.** When you're at the decision-making table, *actively* listen for how your team can help the firm reach goals, avoid crisis, gather intel, smooth transitions, and so on, even in ways not done before. *No one else around the table is thinking like a communicator*, so you'll need to interject your ideas. You'll take your colleagues by surprise if your usual role is an observational one, but that's OK. With practice, you'll become more effective demonstrating your ability to tie business objectives to communication objectives. And here's a hint: First bounce your thinking off your internal financial contacts (revisit the first point on this list) and get their feedback. Soon you'll have backup in those meetings, and they'll come to you for advice, too. It's a beautiful thing – for you and your company.

When Creative Accounting Leads to Crisis

The reporting of financial data may involve art and science, but when the *art* goes too far, crisis can erupt and lead to devastating damage for the firm, its employees, and its reputation. Firms are said to *cook the books* when they falsify their financial statements to bolster earnings and other measures to improve their reporting profile ("Cook the Books," 2017). This is fraud. Several firms were caught cooking the books in the early 2000s, leading to new regulations to protect investors including the Sarbanes-Oxley Act, which we'll cover in Chapter 5. Cooking the books can take several forms, including accelerating revenues, delaying expenses, and faking sales. Here's a sampling of the worst corporate accounting scandals of all time ("The 10 Worst," n.d.).

- **Waste Management (1998).** Reported $1.7 billion in fake earnings by falsely stretching depreciation time lines for property, plant, and equipment on their balance sheet. By doing so, Waste Management reduced depreciation expense on their income statement. With less expense to deduct, the company made profits look higher than they should have been.
- **Enron (2001).** Thousands of employees and investors had their retirement accounts wiped out when Enron kept enormous debts off the balance sheet, making the company look more sound than it really was.
- **WorldCom (2002).** Used fake accounting entries to boost revenues, deflate expenses, and inflate asset values by $11 billion. See below for a closer look at the WorldCom case.
- **Tyco (2002).** Inflated income by $500 million, plus the CEO and CFO used a series of false transactions, including loans, stock sales, and executive bonuses, to steal $150 million from the company.
- **HealthSouth (2003).** Pressured employees to "create" numbers and transactions across a number of years, thereby inflating earnings by $1.4 billion.
- **Freddie Mac (2003).** This government-backed mortgage financer purposely misstated $5 billion in earnings.
- **AIG (2005).** This insurance giant was caught booking loans as revenue and manipulating stock prices to the alleged tune of $3.9 billion in accounting fraud.
- **Lehman Brothers (2008).** The bankruptcy of this global financial services firm sparked the financial crisis in 2008. Books were cooked to show $50 billion more in cash and $50 billion less in *toxic*, or practically worthless, assets than actually existed.
- **Bernie Madoff (2008).** Madoff's Wall Street investment firm hoodwinked investors with a $65 billion *Ponzi scheme*[16] – the largest in history.

A Closer Look at the WorldCom Debacle

WorldCom CEO Bernie Ebbers' primary focus was building a company that would be considered number one on Wall Street (Kaplan & Kiron, 2007; see also "Teaching Note," 2005). The problem was that his vision confused cause and effect. Rather than focusing on effective leadership, talented employees, and great products, Ebbers instead created a corporate culture where managers were expected to do whatever was necessary to salvage WorldCom's fragile stock price. Those actions included threatening employees to maintain the accounting farce that eventually led to the company being caught. Here are some takeaways from the Harvard Business School case (Kaplan & Kiron, 2007; see also "Teaching Note," 2005), which I highly recommend as an applied use of the material we've discussed in this chapter.[17]

- **The pressure to succeed is real.** And this pressure to keep a short-term,[18] quick-fix view comes from a number of market sources, particularly when a company has a record-breaking start, explosive growth, and a high-riding stock price. Recall our discussion of how the profitable firm attracts attention. Every company has ups and downs, but Ebbers wanted to maintain the illusion of prosperous times even after the *dotcom bubble* burst.[19]

- **Self-interest can be misdirected.** Our coverage of the origins of capitalism in Chapter 2 makes clear that self-interest drives the economy, but self-interest taken too far can be detrimental to an organization. In the case of WorldCom, self-interest led company insiders to suppress bad news, report a more favorable picture than was the case, and focus on self-serving compensation incentives that rewarded continuation of fraudulent behavior.
- **CEO know-how matters.** Obvious, I realize, but Ebbers lacked the professional background and expertise to have a strategy beyond acquiring[20] other companies to grow WorldCom. Furthermore, he surrounded himself with business associates who personally benefited from his former acquisitions, so who would be motivated to question his leadership? WorldCom's troubles began to surface when the federal government, citing *anti-trust*[21] concerns, blocked a proposed merger with Sprint.
- **The red flag of working backwards.** By backwards, I'm referring to Ebbers' insistence on maintaining a key expense-to-revenues ratio by fudging the numbers instead of focusing on how to improve that ratio by addressing underlying drivers in the business.
- **The accounting underbelly of WorldCom's fraud.** This wouldn't be a proper ending to a chapter on financial reporting if I didn't share a bit of WorldCom's accounting shenanigans. Here are some highlights (see also Beresford, Katzenbach, & Rogers, 2003 for the full investigative report).
  - *Finagling with the line-cost expenditures to revenues (E/R) ratio.* We'll cover financial ratios more thoroughly in Chapter 5, but for WorldCom case purposes, the gist is that the company got creative with their financial statements to hold the ratio of line-cost expenses[22] to revenues (or E/R, a leading industry performance indicator for which lower values are better than higher values) at 42%, when it was actually at or above 50%. How did they do that? When you decrease the numerator (i.e., expenses in this case) and increase the denominator (i.e., revenues in this case), both reported on the income statement, the quotient/ratio gets smaller. 50% suddenly becomes 42% through some creative accounting.
  - *Releasing accruals improperly.* WorldCom first used *accrual accounts* to feign expense reduction (see also "Where Accruals Appear," 2010). Accrual accounts are created on the balance sheet (usually as current liabilities) with the intent of recording an expense on the income statement. These accounts *accrue*, or accumulate, dollars to cover expenses that haven't yet been billed. WorldCom had amounts set aside to pay anticipated bills associated with line costs and improperly *released* them to reduce expenses and boost net income. Releasing accruals is akin to the company realizing it put more money aside than it actually needs to pay bills and "releasing" those funds for similar uses. This is an allowable process, but WorldCom was found inappropriate and deceptive in its manipulation of these accounts.
  - *Capitalizing what should have been expensed.* After available accrual accounts were exhausted, WorldCom began reducing E/R ratio-related expenses by moving them *off* the income statement and *onto* the balance sheet. In accounting terms, they *capitalized* costs that should have been *expensed* (see Sidebar 4.6: Operating

vs. Capital Expenses). Recall that CapEx is the purchasing of long-term assets (i.e., property, plant, and equipment that appear on the balance sheet), whereas operating expenses support the day-to-day business (and appear on the income statement). WorldCom took expenses that should have appeared on the income statement and falsely recorded them as capital expenditures on the balance sheet. Had they correctly reported operating expenses on the income statement, per GAAP, their E/R ratio would have exceeded their targeted 42%, and their net income would have turned negative to reveal the loss they were actually experiencing. Remember the formula of the income statement: Revenue – Expenses = Income. WorldCom fraudulently cooked the books to lower expenses and thus keep reported income and earnings per share artificially high to hide what was really going on financially – that is, WorldCom was taking a hit, just like its competitors, during an economic downturn. Its strangely high stock price and ability to maintain an E/R ratio in troubled times was downright suspicious.

Sidebar 4.6 Operating Expenses vs. Capital Expenditures

("CapEx vs. OpEx," 2021; Maverick, 2017)

Operating expenses and capital expenditures describe how firms spend money. Each category is treated differently for tax and accounting purposes.

Operating expenses (OpEx) are the day-to-day costs related to running a business and are fully deductible (or "expensed") in the year incurred on corporate tax returns. OpEx appears on the income statement. **Capital expenditures**, more commonly referred to as CapEx, are major asset purchases (e.g., equipment) that enhance the company's ability to earn profits. Capital expenditures are depreciated over time. CapEx assets appear on the balance sheet, but their depreciation is expensed on the income statement.

Why do these expense nuances matter? Because a company's bottom line presentation differs depending on whether an expense is classified as OpEx or CapEx. OpEx lowers taxable income, but CapEx increases a company's balance sheet. Accurate reporting of each is essential for financial statements to be reliable.

The WorldCom fallout resulted from an amalgamation of unethical leadership, hazardous corporate culture, and a lack of internal controls to catch the early warning signs of a financial crisis. The communication implications of corporate fraud are plentiful. Our purpose here was to help you understand the numbers so that you can better inform your communication strategy – both when your firm is thriving and when it hits the inevitable bumps in the road.

Notes

1 The IFRS (International Financial Reporting Standards) Foundation develops standards for globally accepted accounting standards. Learn more at www.ifrs.org.
2 Both acquisitions and going public are discussed in Chapter 5 How and Why Finance Rules the Business World.
3 Currency exchange rates are discussed in Chapter 3 A Micro and Macro View of the Economy.

4 See also Chapter 2 Capitalism: Its Benefits and Discontents for further discussion of corporate governance and independent auditing procedures.
5 "Income," "earnings," and "profit" are often used interchangeably in financial context.
6 Financial statement examples provided in Figures 4.1, 4.2, and 4.3 are from www.sec.gov. From the website FAQ: *All government-created content on sec.gov and EDGAR public filing content are free to access and reuse. Information presented on www.sec.gov is considered public information and may be copied or further distributed by users of the web site.*
7 Business rankings like *Fortune 500* are based on a company's revenues, not profits.
8 *Accelerated depreciation* is another method of depreciating assets that allows larger write-offs early in the life of the asset, thereby initially reducing taxable income and deferring tax liabilities to later years ("Accelerated Depreciation," 2010).
9 Some, but not all, income statements include a line for EBITDA (Earnings Before Interest, Taxes, Depreciation, and Amortization).
10 See Chapter 5 How and Why Finance Rules the Business World for further discussion of financial ratios, securities, and classes of shareholders.
11 Only intangible assets that are *acquired* (not created) by a company appear on the balance sheet ("Intangible Asset," 2017).
12 You're not seeing double. *Depreciation expense* for the stated accounting period appears on the income statement. *Accumulated depreciation*, subtracted from historical cost to determine the current book value for an asset, appears on the balance sheet.
13 See Chapter 5 How and Why Finance Rules the Business World for further discussion of stocks and dividends.
14 Depreciation is added back to net income because it is a "non-cash" expense and not an actual cash reduction in net income (Parker, 2019). Working capital (aka net working capital) equals the difference between current assets and current liabilities, or the amount the firm has available to pay short-term expenses ("What Changes," 2020). Changes in working capital appear on the cash flow statement.
15 See Chapter 3 A Micro and Macro View of the Economy, Chapter 6 Marketing Envy and Other Observations, and Chapter 10 What is Strategy? for related discussions of the firm's operating environment.
16 Similar to a *pyramid scheme*, the *Ponzi scheme* uses new investors to generate returns for existing investors. Eventually, the flow of investors and money runs out, and the scheme is exposed ("Ponzi Scheme," 2017).
17 See Chapter 2 Capitalism: Its Benefits and Discontents for related discussions of corporate governance, auditing, and internal controls and Chapter 12 Last but Not Least: Business Ethics for a discussion of business ethics.
18 For an excellent discussion of the importance of a long-term view, and how it affects stakeholder prioritization, read *Conscious Capitalism* (Mackey & Sisodia, 2014).
19 A high volume of speculative investments into the "new economy" of Internet startups in the late 1990s collapsed when frenzied expectations of profitability failed to materialize ("Dotcom Bubble," 2017).
20 See Chapter 5 How and Why Finance Rules the Business World for a discussion of growth strategies, including mergers and acquisitions (M&A).
21 See Chapter 2 Capitalism: Its Benefits and Discontents for a discussion of anti-trust measures used to preserve competition.
22 Line costs are the costs incurred to carry a voice or data transmission from one point to another (Beresford, Katzenbach, & Rogers, 2003).

References

About the FASB. (n.d.). Retrieved from www.fasb.org/jsp/FASB/Page/SectionPage&cid=1176154526495.

Above the line, below the line. (2017). Retrieved from www.business-literacy.com/financial-concepts/above-line-below-line/.

Accelerated depreciation. (2010, November 14). Retrieved from www.accountingtools.com/articles/what-is-accelerated-depreciation.html.

Accrual accounting. (2017). Retrieved from www.investopedia.com/terms/a/accrualaccounting.asp.

Accrued liability. (2017). Retrieved from www.investopedia.com/terms/a/accrued-liability.asp?lgl=myfinance-layout.

Asset. (2017). Retrieved from www.investopedia.com/terms/a/asset.asp.

Balance sheet (explanation), part 1, part 2, and part 3. (2017). Retrieved from www.accountingcoach.com/balance-sheet/explanation.

Beginners' guide to financial statement [sic]. (2007, February 5). Retrieved from www.sec.gov/reportspubs/investor-publications/investorpubsbegfinstmtguidehtm.html.

Beresford, D.R., Katzenbach, N. deB., & Rogers, C.B., Jr. (2003, March 31). *Report of investigation by the Special Investigative Committee of the Board of Directors of WorldCom, Inc.* Retrieved from www.sec.gov/Archives/edgar/data/723527/000093176303001862/dex991.htm.

CapEx vs. OpEx: All you need to know. (2021). Retrieved from https://efinancemanagement.com/financial-accounting/capex-vs-opex.

Cash flow statement. (2017a). Retrieved from www.investopedia.com/terms/c/cashflowstatement.asp.

Cash flow statement (explanation), part 1 and part 2. (2017b). Retrieved from www.accountingcoach.com/cash-flow-statement/explanation/1.

Comprehensive income. (2017). Retrieved from www.investopedia.com/terms/c/comprehensiveincome.asp.

Connolly, T.P. (2012, October 2). *Is it OK to keep two sets of books? A primer on deferred tax assets.* Retrieved from https://blogs.cfainstitute.org/insideinvesting/2012/10/02/is-it-ok-to-keep-two-sets-of-books-a-primer-on-deferred-tax-assets/.

The conservatism principle. (2017, May 14). Retrieved from www.accountingtools.com/articles/2017/5/14/the-conservatism-principle.

Consolidated financial statement. (2017). Retrieved from www.businessdictionary.com/definition/consolidated-financial-statement.html.

Cook the books. (2017). Retrieved from www.investopedia.com/terms/c/cookthebooks.asp.

Debits and credits. (2017, July 13). Retrieved from www.accountingtools.com/articles/2017/5/17/debits-and-credits.

Depreciation. (2017). Retrieved from www.investopedia.com/terms/d/depreciation.asp.

Dotcom bubble. (2017). Retrieved from www.investopedia.com/terms/d/dotcom-bubble.asp.

Extraordinary item. (2017). Retrieved from www.investopedia.com/terms/e/extraordinaryitem.asp?lgl=rira-baseline-vertical.

Fiscal year. (2017). Retrieved from www.investopedia.com/terms/f/fiscalyear.asp.

Fontinelle, A. (2017). *Amortization.* Retrieved from www.investopedia.com/terms/a/amortization.asp.

The going concern principle. (2017, May 14). Retrieved from www.accountingtools.com/articles/2017/5/14/the-going-concern-principle.

Hargrave, M. (2020, April 30). *Goodwill.* Retrieved from www.investopedia.com/terms/g/goodwill.asp.

Hayes, A. (2020, November 30). *Book value.* Retrieved from www.investopedia.com/terms/b/bookvalue.asp.

Heakal, R. (2017, May 4). *What is a cash flow statement?* Retrieved from www.investopedia.com/articles/04/033104.asp.

How can a company have a profit but not have cash? (2017). Retrieved from www.accountingcoach.com/blog/how-can-a-company-have-a-profit-but-not-have-cash.

The income statement. (2017). Retrieved from www.investopedia.com/walkthrough/corporate-finance/2/financial-statements/income-statement.aspx?lgl=rira-baseline-vertical.

Intangible asset. (2017). Retrieved from www.investopedia.com/terms/i/intangibleasset.asp.

Internal audit vs. external audit. (2021). Retrieved from www.wallstreetmojo.com/internal-audit-vs-external-audit/.

Kaplan, R.S., & Kiron, D. (2007, September 14). *Accounting fraud at WorldCom.* HBS No. 9-104-071. Boston, MA: Harvard Business School Publishing.

Kenton, W. (2020, December 21). *Auditor's report.* Retrieved from www.investopedia.com/terms/a/auditorsreport.asp.

Kumaran, S. (2015, September 24). *The ten Generally Accepted Accounting Principles (GAAP).* Retrieved from www.invensis.net/blog/finance-and-accounting/ten-generally-accepted-accounting-principles-gaap/.

Loth, R. (2017a). *Breaking down the balance sheet.* Retrieved from www.investopedia.com/articles/basics/06/balancesheet.asp.

Loth, R. (2017b, May 5). *Understanding the income statement.* Retrieved from www.investopedia.com/articles/04/022504.asp?lgl=rira-baseline-vertical.

Loughran, M. (n.d.). *Ten common notes to the financial statements.* Retrieved from www.dummies.com/business/accounting/ten-common-notes-to-the-financial-statements/.

Mackey, J., & Sisodia, R. (2014). *Conscious capitalism: Liberating the heroic spirit of business.* Boston, MA: Harvard Business School Publishing.

Managerial accounting (2017). Retrieved from www.investopedia.com/terms/m/managerialaccounting.asp?lgl=rira-baseline-vertical.

Matching principle. (2016). Retrieved from www.myaccountingcourse.com/accounting-principles/matching-principle.

The materiality principle. (2017, May 14). Retrieved from www.accountingtools.com/articles/2017/5/14/the-materiality-principle.

Maverick, J.B. (2017, March 29). *What is the difference between CAPEX and OPEX?* Retrieved from www.investopedia.com/ask/answers/020915/what-difference-between-capex-and-opex.asp.

McClure, B. (2021, May 26). *How burn rate is a key factor in a company's sustainability.* Retrieved from www.investopedia.com/articles/fundamental/04/022504.asp.

Mueller, J. (2017). *Understanding financial liquidity.* Retrieved from www.investopedia.com/articles/basics/07/liquidity.asp.

Multi-step income statement. (2017). Retrieved from www.accountingcoach.com/income-statement/explanation/4.

Murray, J. (2020, July 20). *What is the book value of assets?* Retrieved from www.thebalancesmb.com/what-is-the-book-value-of-an-asset-398146.

Nickolas, S. (2017, April 9). *What items are considered liquid assets?* Retrieved from www.investopedia.com/ask/answers/032715/what-items-are-considered-liquid-assets.asp.

Parker, J. (2019, July 18). *How depreciation affects cash flow.* Retrieved from www.investopedia.com/ask/answers/080216/how-does-depreciation-affect-cash-flow.asp.

Ponzi scheme. (2017). Retrieved from www.investopedia.com/terms/p/ponzischeme.asp.

Reading the balance sheet. (2017, May 6). Retrieved from www.investopedia.com/articles/04/031004.asp.

Research and development (R&D). (2021). Retrieved from https://corporatefinanceinstitute.com/resources/knowledge/accounting/research-and-development-rd/.

Retained earnings. (2017). Retrieved from www.investopedia.com/terms/r/retainedearnings.asp.

Revenue recognition. (2017). Retrieved from www.investopedia.com/ask/answers/011315/why-does-gaap-require-accrual-basis-rather-cash-accounting.asp?lgl=rira-baseline-vertical.

Revenue recognition principle. (2016). Retrieved from www.myaccountingcourse.com/accounting-principles/revenue-recognition-principle.

Ross, S. (2015, January 13). *Why does GAAP require accrual basis rather than cash accounting?* Retrieved from www.investopedia.com/ask/answers/011315/why-does-gaap-require-accrual-basis-rather-cash-accounting.asp?lgl=rira-baseline-vertical.

Schneider, B. (2017). *Accounting basics: The basics.* Retrieved from www.investopedia.com/university/accounting/accounting3.asp?ad=dirN&qo=investopediaSiteSearch&qsrc=0&o=40186&lgl=rira-baseline-vertical.

Single-step income statement. (2017). Retrieved from www.accountingcoach.com/income-statement/explanation/3.

T account. (2017, July 10). Retrieved from www.accountingtools.com/articles/what-is-a-t-account.html.

Teaching note: Accounting fraud at WorldCom. HBS 5-105-083. (2005, June 2.). Boston, MA: Harvard Business School Publishing.

The 10 worst corporate accounting scandals of all time. (n.d.). Retrieved from www.accounting-degree.org/scandals/.

Tuovila, A. (2020, December 16). *Book value reduction.* Retrieved from www.investopedia.com/terms/b/book-value-reduction.asp.

Way, J. (2017). *The difference in dates between a balance sheet and an income sheet.* Retrieved from http://smallbusiness.chron.com/differences-dates-between-balance-sheet-income-sheet-24881.html.

What changes in working capital impact cash flow? (2020, June 8). Retrieved from https://investingplanner.com/2020/06/what-changes-in-working-capital-impact-cash-flow/.

What is a general ledger account? (2017). Retrieved from www.accountingcoach.com/blog/what-is-a-general-ledger-account.

What is accumulated depreciation? (2017). Retrieved from www.accountingcoach.com/blog/what-is-accumulated-depreciation.

What is the difference between earnings per share (EPS) and diluted EPS? (2015, May 11). Retrieved from www.investopedia.com/ask/answers/051115/what-difference-between-earnings-share-eps-and-diluted-eps.asp.

What is the statement of shareholders' equity? (2017). Retrieved from www.fool.com/knowledge-center/statement-of-shareholders-equity.aspx.

Where accruals appear on the balance sheet. (2010, August 23). Retrieved from www.accountingtools.com/articles/where-do-accruals-appear-on-the-balance-sheet.html.

Why did the FASB issue a new standard on revenue recognition? (n.d.). Retrieved from www.fasb.org/jsp/FASB/Page/BridgePage&cid=1351027207987.

Chapter 5

How and Why Finance Rules the Business World

While I was an undergraduate in business school, and even later when I was in industry and then an MBA student, I noticed something different about people in finance. Whether they were students, professors, or executives, the successful ones carried a certain mystique. They lived for numbers and analysis. They spoke a language few people understood. They were Excel wizards. They had nice clothes, nice cars, and impressive job titles. The one thing I found they frequently wrestled with, however, was making something complex understandable for a non-financial audience. I never doubted their competence. I just marveled at how many struggled to explain concepts they clearly understood but just couldn't effectively convey.

If you've ever taken a college-level finance, accounting, computer science, or statistics class, it's likely you've experienced having a brilliant expert struggle to explain something they obviously and deeply comprehend. There are exceptions, naturally, but in our line of work as communicators, it is imperative for us to effectively convey the complex to stakeholders who make decisions based on the information we provide. When you're the face and voice for an organization, you must be comfortably conversant on all of its moving parts, and, as we discussed in Chapter 1, building your internal network of expert sources is key to this learning.

Why is corporate finance so important? Because it's responsible for the company's capital structure, that is, how the firm finances its activities, chooses its investments, returns capital to investors, and balances risk and profitability ("What is Corporate Finance," 2020). Corporate finance is a commanding force, led by the *Chief Financial Officer*, or CFO. The function controls a company's purse strings, so you can understand why it's involved in every major decision a company makes. If you, too, want to be influential in company decision-making, you need to understand (and speak) finance. And that's precisely our focus in this chapter.

The Focus on Creating Value

We know from Chapter 2 that the purpose of the firm is to create value. But value for whom? And what do we mean by value? Value relates to stock price and asset value as well as to brand value, customer value, and reputation value. The overarching idea of creating value is for the firm to deliver benefits to a variety of stakeholders that exceed the costs of those benefits (Hillstrom, 2020). A firm that continuously delivers value will thrive. One

DOI: 10.4324/9781003000600-6

that fails to do so will not. A key component of value creation is identifying which activities actually drive value for a corporation and then dedicating limited resources to those activities. Can effective communication and stakeholder relationship-building contribute to value creation? Absolutely, and so can technology, innovation, management, intellectual property, and employee talent. The challenge for the firm is to figure out how to link both tangible (e.g., machinery) and intangible (e.g., knowledge) assets to value creation, which is the essence of corporate strategy.[1]

Shareholder value indicates the returns and wealth created for a company's stockholders. In Chapter 2, we addressed the difference between focusing mainly on the interests of shareholders (shareholder primacy) versus attempting to balance the varied interests of many stakeholders (stakeholder model), including employees, customers, suppliers, and, yes, investors, too. The concept of shareholder value gained dominance in the U.S. in the 1980s, following an economic downturn in the late 1970s (Heillbron, Verheul, & Quak, 2014). Firms stumbling to recover from economic setbacks became targets of *corporate raiders* – outsiders who acquired company shares in undervalued companies to gain control, reorganize, and sell off parts of the company in the name of increasing shareholder value. CEO and other C-suite executive compensation packages began shifting to include more stock so that top management would have pay "at risk" and thus have the same interests as shareholders (Denning, 2017). Under this arrangement, as stock value rises, not only investors, but also executives, benefit financially. And if stock value drops, everyone loses value. The downside of this approach is the exceeding pressure placed on executives to increase the stock *price* rather than to implement business strategies that organically enhance value, including stock price, for all stakeholders in the long run. Decades of this approach to executive compensation have shown that firms focusing primarily on stock price tend to be short-term minded, which can prove harmful for investment strategy and result in excessive risk-taking to artificially inflate just one measure of company performance: the share price of its stock.[2]

Organizational culture is likewise impacted when increasing stock price is the primary goal of the firm. Management inevitably takes the form of top-down "command-and-control" tactics because employees are rarely motivated by making money for shareholders and the C-suite (Denning, 2017). Investments in research and development, along with innovation, tend to be cast aside in favor of other opportunities with a seemingly quicker payoff in boosting share price. A short-term business mindset gets costlier over the long term when the outcomes of neglected areas of investment (e.g., employees, communities, technology) become apparent. The late, famed General Electric CEO Jack Welsh described shareholder value as an outcome, not a goal, of a business that should be run for the benefit of stakeholders beyond shareholders alone.

Although the U.S. is undoubtedly a financially driven economy, the business shift away from shareholder primacy and toward a broader stakeholder approach to value creation is gaining traction. That's good news for corporate communicators whose focus expands across multiple stakeholder groups. The Business Roundtable, a professional association for American CEOs, in 2019 issued their "redefinition" of a corporation's purpose, specifically moving away from shareholder primacy toward a focus on value creation for multiple stakeholders including customers, employees, suppliers, communities, and shareholders ("Business Roundtable Redefines," 2019). Communication is central to this evolving way of doing business and underscores the importance of communicators having business acumen.

Three Functions of Corporate Finance

Capital Investments and Budgeting

Companies have numerous opportunities to invest and grow a business, but not all are optimal. Corporate finance uses analytical techniques to determine where best to invest the firm's money in long-term assets such as manufacturing plants, machinery, and real estate (Kenton, 2019a; "What is Corporate Finance," 2020). *Capital* can mean cash provided by an individual or group (e.g., shareholder or bank) in exchange for promise of a return on the profits generated by investing that cash (e.g., dividend or interest payments). Capital also refers to *capital investments* made in physical assets (e.g., property, plant, and equipment, or PPE[3]). Any use of the term capital will refer to investments made for *long-term returns* to the business, that is, projects and equipment expected to generate profits for more than one year.[4]

How capital is used is the purview of corporate finance. *Capital budgeting* involves deciding how and where capital expenditures will be made (Kenton, 2019a). *Capital projects* are large-scale projects requiring significant commitments of financial and human capital, such as new facilities, operating systems, or machinery. Given their scale, capital investments must be carefully selected and closely managed to balance risk and reward. These are major outlays of cash that require significant resource commitments for an extended period of time, with uncertain returns ("Describe Capital Investment," n.d.). Even with the best analysis on the front end, there are no guarantees capital projects will deliver the economic benefits expected. As discussed in Chapter 3, corporate resources, including capital, are limited, even if they are relatively plentiful. As such, corporate finance managers must determine where capital investments are best made. Let's discuss how they do that, step by step (see Sidebar 5.1: Financial Lingo to Know).

Sidebar 5.1 Financial Lingo to Know

(Brown, 2019)

Financial terms — budget, forecast, projection, and pro forma — are often used interchangeably, but there are important nuances to understand.

- **Budgets** are statements of intent indicating where the business wants to go. If the company aims for a 10% growth in sales, it will prepare its annual budget based on that objective.
- **Forecasts** are management's "best guess" as to what financial outcomes *could* result if a course of action, like hiring additional sales people, occurs. Forecasts account for uncertainties. **Rolling forecasts** are updated to get a more realistic picture of how well management's expectations are aligning with the budget, or what's actually happening in the business. That way, the business knows if plans are on track, or if corrections need to be made.
- **Projections** are financial statements based on hypothetical assumptions and management asking, "What if we…?" Projections are statements about future alternatives, such as

> increasing production capacity or adding a new product line. Projections are useful for planning purposes.
>
> **Pro forma** financial statements show what the income statement, balance sheet, and cash flow statement *would look like if* an event, like a new investment in the business, took place. Pro forma statements are used for gaining access to capital and can be overly optimistic in estimating how successful a future event could be for the business. Pro forma statements should never be presented as actual financial statements.

In Chapter 3, we reviewed how the benefits of an investment must outweigh the risk of that investment. It's a basic economic principle, and one that's quantified in corporate finance. Capital projects are funded based on their ability to meet or exceed a *hurdle rate*, also known as the *minimal acceptable rate of return (MARR)*. Think of a hurdle in a track meet. The runner has to get over the hurdle to get to the finish line. It's the same with a financial hurdle rate. If a capital project doesn't at least meet a minimally accepted rate of return, it won't get funded. If a project doesn't meet or exceed a hurdle rate, the cost (and risk) outweigh the benefit, and it's not a prudent use of limited capital funds.

Companies have lots of opportunities for capital investment, but limited capital to invest. Thus, a thoughtful process is required to determine which projects get funded ("Describe Capital Investment," n.d.). The process begins by identifying and prioritizing capital improvements that need immediate attention, such as replacing worn equipment, and new projects, such as purchasing a building for expansion. Once resource requirements are quantified for each, those needs must be matched with available funding, time, and human capital to complete those projects. The outcome is a list of capital project alternatives the company could pursue.

Next, baseline criteria are used to evaluate the value-increasing potential of each project under consideration ("Describe Capital Investment," n.d.). These criteria are measurements used to rank-order alternatives not only against each other, but also against a minimal acceptable rate of return. Baseline criteria methods include the payback method, accounting rate of return (ARR), net present value (NPV), and internal rate of return (IRR). These methods allow companies to remove projects from consideration that don't meet minimal criteria for value creation. Baseline criteria are used for shortening the list of alternatives, identifying which projects have the greatest profit-making potential, and funding those. We'll cover each of these evaluation methods in turn, moving from the simplest to the more complex.

The *payback method* of evaluating capital investment alternatives simply examines the amount of time required for the company to recover its initial investment, whether through forecasted cash flows[5] from the project or cost savings that are expected as a result of the project ("Evaluate the Payback," n.d.). Capital funds tied up in one project obviously cannot be used for another project, so companies may just want to recover their initial investment as quickly as possible and then put the money to use elsewhere. For example, if the company payback requirement on an initial investment of $1 million is 5 years, and the project being evaluated has an expected payback period of 7.5 years, this project would not be further considered for funding. In this case, the firm would judge the project as taking too long to return its initial investment. If, however, cash flows from the project were expected to pay back the initial $1 million investment in four years, this payback period is faster than the company's five-year acceptable minimum and will be funded. The payback period can be any time requirement set by the company.

Whereas the payback method focuses on how rapidly cash flows from a project return an initial investment, the *accounting rate of return (ARR)* calculates the return on investment in terms of net income ("Evaluate the Payback," n.d.). As such, ARR considers expected revenues, cost savings, and expenses related to the capital investment to determine the bottom line[6] impact of the investment. The ARR is expressed as a percentage. For example, an ARR of 25% would mean the firm could expect a 25% increase to net income, or a 25-cent return on each dollar invested, as a result of investing in a capital project. The ARR would then be compared to the company's minimal accepted rate of return, or increase, to net income to determine the project's potential for capital funding. If the ARR exceeds the company's minimal return requirement, the project is funded. If, however, the ARR is less than the company's minimal return requirement, the company will use capital funds for other, more profitable options. Like the payback period, a company's minimal accepted rate of return is not a set number. Rather, these thresholds are determined by the company based on how much financial risk managers are willing to bear before making capital investments. For riskier projects – like opening a new factory – financial managers will set higher hurdle rates that must be met before investing.

The payback and ARR methods of evaluating capital investment options are informative but not optimal on their own because they do not account for the *time value of money* ("Explain the Time Value," n.d.). The basic principle of the time value of money is that the value of a dollar today is greater than the value of a dollar in the future. Why? Think about it. If you have one dollar to invest *today*, it will earn more money for you in the future. And prices generally increase over time (i.e., inflation), so today's dollar will have more buying power than it will at some future point in time. You can buy more with one dollar today than you can, say, three years from now. This is what is meant by the time value of money. If given the choice of receiving $100 today or $100 one year from now, the time value of money principle compels you to take that $100 today. If you invest it wisely, it will earn more money for you in one year. If you spend it, you can buy more with it today than you can in one year. Having that money in your hands today is less risky because the future is uncertain.

Businesses consider the time value of money when making capital investments ("Use Discounted Cash Flow," n.d.). Let's say competing potential capital projects appear to meet baseline criteria set by the company in terms of payback period and/or accounting rate of return, but the company can only fund one of the projects. How does the company decide which one? *Discounted cash flow* (DCF) models are used by financial analysts to examine the value of expected *future* cash flows generated by capital investments in *today's* dollars. This method discounts, or converts, future cash streams into today's dollars so firms have a better idea of the value generated by a project, in current terms. That value is then compared to the initial investment and a hurdle rate, or minimal acceptable rate of return, set by the company to determine whether or not the capital project will be funded. The two DCF models we'll cover are net present value (NPV) and internal rate of return (IRR).

The net present value of an investment equals the sum of the present value of expected future cash flows minus the present value of the cash invested today (Kenton, 2019b). The

Table 5.1 Capital Investment Choices

	Product A	Product B	Product C
Initial Investment	$1,000,000	$500,000	$2,500,000
Cash Flow Yr 1	$25,000	$35,000	$265,000
Cash Flow Yr 2	$35,000	$40,000	$380,000
Cash Flow Yr 3	$50,000	$85,000	$650,000
Cash Flow Yr 4	$65,000	$225,000	$800,000
Cash Flow Yr 5	$80,000	$310,000	$925,000

formula is: $NPV = TVECF - TVIC$, where net present value (NPV) equals the difference between today's value of the expected cash flows (TVECF) from the capital investment and today's value of the invested cash (TVIC) needed now to generate those future cash flows. Recall that capital investments are those that generate returns for more than one year. As such, cash flows are projected by financial analysts for each year of the project's life, *discounted* back to present day, and then summed to reflect the present value of funds expected in the future. The *discount rate* used in the NPV calculation is the company's *cost of capital*, such as the interest rate on a loan to make the investment. Or, if the company uses its own money, the discount rate represents the return the company could earn on other opportunities to invest those dollars (see also Merritt, 2018). It makes sense to compare investment alternatives using the same discount rate[7] to see which delivers the highest NPV. The higher the NPV, the more profitable the project is expected to be.

Here's an example. Say your company has the opportunity to expand your manufacturing capacity to add a new product line. You have three possible choices: Product A, Product B, and Product C. The initial investment and expected cash flows for each are shown in Table 5.1.

To calculate and compare NPV for each investment opportunity, the expected cash flows in future years are discounted back to present day. That way, analysts can compare the investment required today with the total earnings each project is expected to generate – all in present-day dollars (Kenton, 2019b; Merritt, 2018). The rule of thumb in finance is to fund projects with positive NPV values, and the higher the NPV, the better. If the project NPV is positive, the project is expected to make money. In other words, a positive NPV tells us the expected earnings from the project exceed the initial investment, so it makes sense to invest. A negative NPV indicates the initial investment will exceed the expected returns. A negative NPV project will lose money, so managers will look elsewhere for capital investment opportunities. Businesses don't have an endless supply of capital (or employees, time, production capacity, and so on), so only select capital projects will be included in the capital budget. Executives must make capital investment decisions that best align with the firm's objectives and available resources (Allen, 2015).

Here's how the math works: NPV = The summation of $R_t/(1 + i)^t$ for each period of the project's life, where R_t equals the expected cash flow, i equals the discount rate, and t equals the number of time periods, such as years, into the future when the cash flow is expected (Kenton, 2019b). Financial calculators and spreadsheets are used to calculate NPV (see, for example, "Net Present Value Calculator," 2020). Based on the numbers provided, the NPV for each product line investment with a 5% discount rate is shown in Table 5.2.

Table 5.2 Capital Investment Choices With NPV for Each

	Product A	Product B	Product C
Initial Investment	$1,000,000	$500,000	$2,500,000
Cash Flow Yr 1	$25,000	$35,000	$265,000
Cash Flow Yr 2	$35,000	$40,000	$380,000
Cash Flow Yr 3	$50,000	$85,000	$650,000
Cash Flow Yr 4	$65,000	$225,000	$800,000
Cash Flow Yr 5	$80,000	$310,000	$925,000
NPV	($785,095)	$71,042	$41,470

So, which product lines should the company pursue? Product B, with the highest NPV, is the top choice. If the company has enough funding, Product C, with a lower but still positive NPV, could also be pursued. Product A, with its negative NPV, should not, as it will lose money for the company. When NPV values are positive and fairly close, the *profitability index*, or the NPV divided by the initial investment, is a helpful way to compare how much profit is expected for each dollar invested (Merritt, 2018). In this case, the profitability index for Product B (71,042/500,000) is higher at .14 than it is for Product C (41,470/2,500,000) at .02. The company is still making money on both product lines, but it's earning 14 cents on the dollar for Product B compared to only 2 cents on the dollar for Product C. This makes intuitive sense when you see a higher NPV associated with a $500,000 investment than with a $2,500,000 investment. As a business, you want the most bang, or value, for your invested buck, which makes Product B the best choice (see also Allen, 2015).

An important caveat for NPV calculations is that they are based on assumptions – not guarantees – about future cash flows, cost of capital, project life, and forward-looking economic conditions (Woodruff, 2019). NPV is a straightforward calculation, but the challenge and risk of finance is first getting the key assumptions right. Furthermore, managers need to consider factors beyond NPV when selecting opportunities for capital investment, including the firm's competitive environment, sources of capital, and consumer trends that affect demand for the firm's products. For example, if consumers are becoming more health-conscious, is it a good idea to dedicate a major capital outlay to a product that goes against that trend? Should a firm borrow capital from a bank or instead draw from cash on hand for a capital investment? Is it better to expand into a new product line, or invest more funds in enhancing current products? NPV values alone cannot answer these questions. And NPV considerations get more complex when ranking projects with different lifespans and upfront investment amounts. Still, NPV considers the time value of money, making it a preferred investment metric over the payback method and the accounting rate of return (see also Allen, 2015).

The Internal Rate of Return, or IRR, method of investment analysis is closely related to NPV (Hayes, 2019). In fact, the equation is the same. The only difference is that instead of *providing* a discount rate, the equation is solved to *determine* the discount rate required to make the NPV of future cash flows equal to the initial investment required in today's dollars. In other words, the IRR is the discount rate that renders NPV equal to 0. If the IRR exceeds the company's hurdle rate or cost of capital, the project is expected to add value. As with NPV, the higher the value of IRR, the better. But, unlike NPV expressed in dollars, IRR is expressed as a percentage return. Firms vary in their preference of using NPV or IRR as an investment metric.[8] Both calculations tend to move in the same direction (that is, support or not support a project) most of the time (Allen, 2015).

An important note about investment metrics: NPV calculations are highly sensitive to chosen hurdle rates (Allen, 2015). Tweaking a required return (i.e., discount rate or cost of capital) just slightly higher will lower NPV, and lowering a required return will inflate NPV. Accuracy in selecting hurdle rates is paramount to realizing value from capital investments and avoiding what could be misrepresentations of a project's promise. For example, arbitrarily adding a premium to cost of capital to compensate for additional risk; failing to accurately calculate the cost of capital; not updating cost of capital when market conditions drastically change; and/or using standardized hurdle rates of 10, 15, or 20% instead of the true cost of capital can lead to investments that diminish, not enhance, firm value. Allen (2015) suggests separating analysts who forecast project cash flows from those who determine hurdle rates to avoid manipulation of either calculation. This speaks, too, to the importance of aligning stakeholder interests in financial matters. If managers are compensated based on increasing sales instead of creating value, capital projects may not get the analytical attention they require.

Capital investments and budgeting are the purview of corporate finance but can be driven by outside factors that affect corporate reputation. Volkswagen in 2015 admitted that 11 million of its diesel vehicles were equipped with software that activated equipment to reduce emissions while the vehicle was being tested but allowed emissions to increase above the legal limit while the vehicle was operating (Ewing & Mouawad, 2015; Gates, Ewing, Russell, & Watkins, 2017). The scandal forced the company to set aside $9.6 billion to make cars compliant with pollution regulations and reduce planned capital spending by $1 billion. Instead of updating its Phaeton luxury vehicle and modernizing a plant in Mexico, Volkswagen had to divert funds from capital investments and delay or cancel other projects to cover operating and legal expenses related to the emissions scam. All this was from a company with plans to become the world's largest auto maker (see also "Describe Capital Investment," n.d.). What could have been billions of dollars in added value were instead diverted to respond to a crisis of Volkswagen's own making.

Capital Access and Financing

The second function of corporate finance focuses on funding the previously described capital investments. In other words, how does the company pay for, or finance, the initial investment required for a capital project? Where does the money come from? Cash reserves[9] can be used for capital investments, but larger projects will require additional funding from external sources, namely *debt* and *equity*. We'll discuss debt and equity in turn, but, for now, let's talk about how much cash a company needs.

There's no set number when it comes to how much *cash* a business should have on hand at any given time. A general rule of thumb for small businesses is to keep three to six months of operating expenses in cash on reserve (Paniello, n.d.). For larger, and particularly publicly held, firms, strategies for maintaining cash reserves get more complex. Firms sitting on too little cash risk not being able to pay their bills. Those sitting on what investors think is too much cash give the impression that the company isn't reinvesting enough cash in its business. Cash is yet another balancing act in corporate finance: How much to stash vs. how much to spend?

Knowledge-based firms in industries like software, pharmaceuticals, entertainment, and media do not have the same level of spending requirements found in more capital-intensive industries like energy, manufacturing, and construction (McClure, 2020). As such, service firms can build up cash reserves whereas capital-intensive firms need to draw on their cash reserves more frequently. *Cyclical industries*, like manufacturing, boom when the economy expands but need to stockpile cash and then draw on those reserves to get through economic downturns when demand for their goods drops. Too much cash on the balance sheet[10] can signal to investors that management is lacking investment opportunities or a long-term view of how the money could be put to value-creating use. Holding cash carries an opportunity cost, meaning there are other, more lucrative ways to use the money. For example, a project with a 20% return on investment outweighs any return the money could earn sitting in a bank account. Business is about creating value. All else being equal, cash is best used where it delivers the greatest returns.

Let's now turn to the scenario where the firm doesn't have enough cash on hand to finance capital projects like expansions, equipment replacements, or technology upgrades. Recall that the NPV calculation used to make go/no-go decisions on available projects includes the cost of *obtaining* the capital needed to finance a project. So, yes, it absolutely makes sense for a firm to secure funds it doesn't already have to make an investment that will more than cover the cost of securing those funds. For positive NPV projects, the benefits outweigh the costs, and thus generates value for the business.

Most firms use a combination of debt and equity financing to grow a business (Maverick, 2019; see Sidebar 5.2: Understanding Securities). *Debt financing* is what it sounds like. Firms become indebted to pay back *principal* (the amount borrowed) plus interest to creditors who have confidence in the firm's ability to repay its debts (Chen, 2020a). Smaller firms rely on *installment loans* (a lump sum paid back in equal installments over time), *revolving loans* (*lines of credit* that provide money to be use, repaid, then used again), or *cash flow loans* (a lump sum paid back as revenues come in) for debt financing (Guillory, 2020). Large companies sell *bonds*,[11] also known as *debt instruments*, to individual or institutional investors.

Sidebar 5.2 Understanding Securities

(Kenton, 2020b)

A **security** is a negotiable financial instrument that holds monetary value.

Equity securities include shares of stock that represent ownership interest in a publicly held company. Shares of stock are traded on securities exchanges around the world.

Debt securities include corporate and government bonds that represent money borrowed and must be repaid. Bonds are not listed on major exchanges. Rather, bonds are traded over-the-counter (OTC) through brokers.

Bonds are fixed income instruments. If a company issues a 5% bond with a $1,000 *face* or *par value* that matures in five years, investors pay $1,000 and, at the end of five years (on the *maturity date*) get their $1,000 paid back (Chen, 2020b). In the interim, the company pays interest, or *coupon payments*, in the amount of 5%, or $50, per year for five years. Thus, the investor has a fixed income flowing from the bond purchase. Coupon payments can be made monthly, quarterly, or semiannually, depending on the terms of the debt agreement. Investors can purchase numerous bonds as part of their portfolio.

High-quality corporate bonds are considered safe, conservative investments (Chen, 2020c). Three U.S. agencies rate the creditworthiness of corporate bond issuers: Standard and Poor's Global Ratings, Moody's Investor Service, and Fitch Ratings. The highest rated bonds are referred to as *Triple-A* because they carry the lowest risk of defaulting on promised payments. The lowest rated corporate bonds have higher coupon payments to offset their higher risk of default. Firms typically hire investment banks to underwrite and market bond offerings to investors.

Whether through loans, bonds, or other debt instruments, firms using debt financing to raise capital face certain advantages and disadvantages (Maverick, 2019). A downside of debt is the need to repay the funds borrowed. The upside is that the lender has no control over the business. Debt has tax advantages, too. Interest paid by firms is tax-deductible. And fixed loan payments make it easier to forecast expenses.

For firms – just like individuals – debt can reap benefits until, well, it doesn't. What if there's a downturn in the economy? What if the capital investment doesn't provide the cash flows and related benefits expected? The debt still must be repaid. Too much debt can hamper a company's ability to grow (Maverick, 2019).

Equity financing is another way for businesses to raise capital, with its own set of advantages and disadvantages. The positive side of equity financing is that there is no debt for the company to repay. Equity financing provides needed capital, but the company sells an ownership share, or stock, in the company to get those funds (Banton, 2019). Whereas bondholders are paid in interest, *shareholders* are paid through a share of the company's profits.[12] And as owners in the company, shareholders have a say in company operations (Chen, 2020c; Maverick, 2019). The only way to remove shareholders is to buy them out, which can cost the firm much more than the capital acquired – in time, resources, and reputation risk.

Capital structure refers to the particular mix of debt and equity a firm uses for capital financing. But how does a company know just how much debt it should carry and how much equity it should share? Financial theory tells us that an *optimal capital structure* is one that maximizes a company's market value while minimizing its cost of capital (Hayes, 2020a). So, here we have another balancing act in corporate finance. Debt is cheaper. Interest payments are relatively low and tax deductible. But taking on too much debt increases risk to shareholders with equity stakes in the company.[13] If a company goes bankrupt, debtholders (including bond holders) get paid before shareholders (see Sidebar 5.3: Bankruptcy 101).

Sidebar 5.3 Bankruptcy 101

(Fried, 2018; Segal, 2020b)

When a business can no longer pay its debts, it declares **bankruptcy**. The U.S. Bankruptcy Code outlines the different legal proceedings available, referred to by their chapter name.

A business filing for **Chapter 7** bankruptcy stops operating and goes completely out of business. A trustee is appointed to liquidate, or sell, the company's assets. The proceeds are used to pay off debts. **Secured creditors** whose debts are backed by company assets, or collateral, are paid first, followed by **bondholders**, and then **shareholders**. Depending on what funding remains, shareholders may not be fully compensated for the value of their shares. Shareholders have the highest risk of not recouping their investment, but unlike creditors and bondholders, can benefit from rising share prices while the company is operating.

A business filing for **Chapter 11** bankruptcy continues to operate and is allowed to **reorganize**. Reorganizing involves restructuring debt so it can be paid and making necessary changes to the company in hopes it can be profitable again. The company is assigned to work with a committee that represents the interests of creditors and shareholders and helps get the company out of debt. If the company fails to develop a court-approved reorganization plan, its assets are liquidated to pay creditors.

For clarity, **individuals** with limited incomes and unable to pay their debts can file for Chapter 7 bankruptcy to have their assets (usually property) liquidated and debts repaid. Individuals, including those who run their own business as a sole proprietor, can file for Chapter 13 bankruptcy and follow a court-approved repayment plan without having their assets sold.

Companies, then, are challenged to strike the proper balance where the marginal benefit of debt equals its marginal cost (Hayes, 2020a).[14] One way to do this is to minimize a company's WACC (pronounced "whack"), or its *weighted average cost of capital*. Recall that higher NPV values indicate more profitable projects. And lower discount rates used in NPV calculations render higher NPV values. As explained earlier, that discount rate is the company's cost of capital. So, it makes sense that a company able to *minimize* its cost of capital can better optimize its *profits* from capital investments, thus creating more value. Finding the optimal capital structure by minimizing WACC is the focus of the corporate finance department.

Capital structure is the proportional mix between debt and equity. It follows, then, that the percentage of debt plus the percentage of equity used by a firm equals 100%. Here's the WACC formula:

$$\text{WACC} = E/V * Re + D/V * Rd * (1 - Tc)$$

where Re = cost of equity, Rd = cost of debt, E = market value of the firm's equity, D = market value of the firm's debt, V = E+D is the total market value of the firm's financing, E/V = percentage of financing that is equity, D/V = percentage of financing that is debt, and Tc = corporate tax rate. That is, the percentage of financing from equity is weighted by the cost of equity, and the percentage of financing from debt is weighted by the cost of debt and the company's tax rate to reflect the tax savings realized from incurring debt (Hargrave, 2020a).[15]

If, for example, a capital project yields returns of 20% and has a WACC of 11%, the company is generating 9% of value for every dollar invested in that project. If, however, a company has returns of 10% and a WACC of 17%, it is losing 7% of value, or 7 cents per dollar, for every dollar invested. WACC rates will differ across industries and across companies within those industries, but the big idea remains: Lower costs associated with *securing* capital enables a firm to create more value *with* that capital. The benefits of value-adding capital investments outweigh the costs of obtaining those benefits for shareholders and other stakeholders.

A well-run business with good financials, strong leadership, and a track record of success will have more options to *access capital* than firms lacking these attributes. A business with more risk associated with its operations will have a higher cost of capital and require more effort to access capital. Investors, whether individuals or large institutional lenders, will demand a higher return on their money as the risk of not getting their money back increases.

Shareholder Returns

Debt is less costly than equity for capital financing. Debt is preferable because once the borrowed funds are repaid, the firm's transaction with that particular lender is completed. After terms of the debt agreement are met, the lender has no further claim on the business. Equity financing, on the other hand, provides shares of company ownership to investors for however long those investors want to be involved with that business. The more shares an investor holds, the greater the influence the shareholder can exert on the business.

The third function of corporate finance is ensuring shareholders receive adequate returns on their investments in the firm (see Sidebar 5.4: Types and Classes of Shareholders). As previously discussed, firms today focus on creating value for stakeholders beyond shareholders alone, but make no mistake: Building *shareholder value* still matters and is a priority in corporate finance. The *investor relations (IR)* department, found in medium- to large-sized companies, is the primary information source and communication interface with shareholders, investment and equity research *analysts*,[16] and potential investors (Tarver, 2020; see also Laskin, 2017). IR's work with institutional investors is particularly important. Decisions made by these behemoths to buy, hold, or sell a particular stock – for whatever reason – can be not only newsworthy, but also exert great influence on the market, for better or worse.

Sidebar 5.4 Types and Classes of Shareholders

(Ganti, 2020a; Maverick, 2020; Palmer, 2019)

Institutional investors are the big players in the market moving large blocks of shares on behalf of pension funds, mutual funds, investment banks, and so on. Given the size of their transactions, institutional investors have access to investments not available to smaller investors. Institutional investors have tremendous influence on market shifts.

Retail, or non-institutional, investors are individual, non-professional investors. Retail investors are managing their own money to meet a personal goal, like funding a child's education or preparing for retirement. Retail investors buy and sell their shares (and other investments) through a licensed broker.

Class A shares are common stocks. Most shares issued by public companies are common stocks, meaning they represent a portion of ownership in the company and entitle the holder to a portion of the company's profits. Common shareholders are usually given at least one vote for each share they own. Shareholders vote at annual company meetings to elect board members and determine the outcome of shareholder resolutions on company policies.

> **Class B shares** – or any other class of shares offered beyond Class A – are also common stocks. Class B shares typically carry fewer voting rights compared to Class A shares, depending on how the company structures its stock. All classes of common stock provide equity ownership and rights to share in the company's profits.
>
> **Preferred stock** is not common stock, but rather a cross between a stock and a bond. Preferred stockholders have limited or no voting rights but have a higher claim on dividend payments. That is, preferred stockholders are paid dividends before any dividends are paid to common stockholders. And if the company is forced to liquidate, preferred stockholders have repayment priority over common stockholders.

Retained earnings, discussed in Chapter 4, are the monies remaining after *dividends* have been paid to shareholders. Companies draw from retained earnings for their capital investments in addition to seeking debt and equity capital. The ending balance for retained earnings in an accounting period serves as the starting balance for retained earnings in the next accounting period. Net income from the current accounting period is added to the retained earnings balance, and then dividends paid to shareholders are subtracted from that balance to update retained earnings for the current period.

Dividends are distributions of company profits paid to shareholders ("How and Why," 2020). Dividends can be paid monthly, quarterly, or annually, among other variations,[17] and are paid per share of stock owned by an investor. Not all companies pay dividends, and the corporate finance department is central in setting dividend policy for the company. Walmart, for example, has paid dividends to shareholders since it announced a 5-cents-per-share annual payment in 1974 (DelRay, 2020). Today, that annual dividend exceeds $2 per share. Multiply that amount by the number of outstanding Walmart shares, and the total exceeds $6 billion in profit distributed to shareholders in one year. Conversely, Amazon has never paid a dividend to its shareholders.

Why do corporate dividend policies vary so sharply? There are two schools of thought about dividends. Companies that don't pay dividends claim that reinvesting profits into the business – instead of distributing them to shareholders – will ultimately add more value to the business and thus increase the market value of the stock ("How and Why," 2020).[18] Companies focusing on growth typically reinvest their earnings rather than pay dividends. Instead of distributing excess cash as dividends to shareholders, these companies will invest in more projects, acquire new assets, or buyback the company's own shares.

A *share buyback*, also known as a *stock repurchase*, builds shareholder wealth by reducing the number of outstanding shares on the market (Janssen, 2020). In essence, when a company buys back its own shares, it is reinvesting in itself.[19] A buyback is generally viewed as a positive maneuver. When the company absorbs the repurchased shares, the relative share of ownership held by remaining stockholders increases, and the share price often increases when fewer shares are on the market. As such, shareholder value is enhanced (see Sidebar 5.5: Stock Splits and Dilution).

> **Sidebar 5.5 Stock Splits and Dilution**
>
> (Beers, 2020; Ganti, 2019)
>
> Whereas a share buyback, or stock repurchase, decreases the number of a company's outstanding shares, a **stock split** has the opposite effect.
>
> A stock split decision by a company's board of directors increases the number of outstanding shares by issuing more shares to current shareholders. The most common split ratios are 2-for-1 or 3-for-1, meaning the shareholder will have 2 (or 3) shares for every 1 share held before the split.
>
> The stock's price will be reduced after a spilt. In a 2-for-1 split, stock price will be halved. Market cap (see related sidebar) stays the same.
>
> Why split a stock? A company may want to make its stock more affordable for a broader base of investors. As new investors purchase the stock, the initial drop in price can turn into a price increase because of heightened demand for the stock.
>
> Conversely, a company can use a **reverse split** to increase its share price. A 1-for-10 reverse split would reduce the number of shares on the market and increase the price of each share by a factor of 10. Every 10 shares held by an investor would be replaced with one share. Market cap, again, remains constant, so company value doesn't change.
>
> Stock splits do not increase or decrease **dilution** because each shareholder's ownership percentage remains the same after the split.
>
> Dilution occurs when a company issues new shares of stock. The number of outstanding shares increases. Therefore, each shareholder's ownership percentage in the company decreases, or is diluted. The downside of dilution is the shrinking piece of the pie owned by the shareholder. The upside, however, is that the additional capital earned from issuing new shares can increase the company's value.

Other companies stand by dividend payouts as a way of providing returns to shareholders who want an income stream ("How and Why," 2020). Dividend payments – especially from companies that have a long-standing record of paying dividends – are seen by investors as a sign of financial strength. Mature companies like Walmart with decades of consistent dividend payouts are among the most stable companies in today's market. A reduction in dividend distributions would have a negative impact on their stock price. The reverse is also true: An increase in dividend distributions would likely have a positive impact on their stock price.

An increase in stock price provides investors with *capital gains,* meaning they can sell the stock for more than they paid to acquire the stock, thus providing a return on their initial investment. Whether through dividend payments and/or an increase in stock value, providing returns and increasing value for shareholders is a critical function of corporate finance.

Public vs. Private Companies

Financial management is equally important whether a company is privately or publicly held, and it's important to understand how the two types of ownership differ. *Privately held companies* are owned by founders, managers, and/or private investors, whereas *publicly held companies* have sold part of their ownership to the public via shares of stock (Majaski,

2019). A number of large firms are privately held, including Cargill, Mars, and Deloitte (Murphy, 2019). Private firms can "go public" through an *initial public offering (IPO)* of stock (see section on startups ahead), and public companies can revert back to private firms.[20]

Private companies are restricted in the number of ownership shares they can sell to raise equity capital. Like public companies, private companies can use debt financing (e.g., through a bank) to fund their investments, but they cannot access public capital markets to sell stocks or bonds to fund their growth (Majaski, 2019). Private companies must rely on their profits and private sources of equity and debt for capital financing. An advantage of remaining privately held is that management can forego the scrutiny and shareholder pressures many public companies face. And privately held firms aren't required to adhere to the financial disclosures and reporting requirements mandated by the *U.S. Securities and Exchange Commission (SEC)* for public firms.

Lastly, when it comes to valuating a company (e.g., for a sale, merger, or acquisition), analysts can access more data to determine what a publicly held company is worth ("Private vs. Public," 2020). Because of federal reporting requirements, financial metrics for public firms are readily available, including reports written by investment and research analysts who follow those companies. As discussed in Chapter 4, private firms tend to follow the same financial accounting standards as public firms, which helps potential investors and creditors assess their value in the same way they would for a public company.

The Stock Market

Let's now turn to the broader functioning of the stock market. It's an actual *exchange* where investors buy and sell ownership shares in publicly held corporations (Amadeo, 2020). Each business day, the *stock exchange* works like an auction house, running in large part on the expectations of traders, investors, and sellers. Traders who are optimistic about a company's performance will bid up the price of that stock. Sellers want stock prices as high as possible so they can widen the gap between what they paid for the stock and what they can earn when they sell that stock. Buyers, conversely, want stock prices low when they purchase shares, with the expectation that the price will continue to increase as they hold the stock. The expression "buy low, sell high" is relevant for stock market investing (see Sidebar 5.6: Reading the Market).

Sidebar 5.6 Reading the Market

(Sraders, 2019)

A number of business publications track daily moves in the market. Here are the elements to look for when following stocks:

The **ticker symbol** is the letters used to identify a company's stock on an exchange. For example, Target's ticker symbol is TGT, and Goldman Sachs' is GS.

Open price is the stock's opening price on a particular trading day. **Close price** is where the stock stopped trading at the end of normal trading hours on the same day. A close price higher than an open price indicates an upward movement in the stock. A close price lower than an open price indicates a downward movement. **Previous close** indicates the stock's closing price on the previous day.

> **Net change** is the value change in a stock's price from the close price of the day before. Net change is usually quoted both in dollars and as a percentage.
>
> **Day high and low** shows the highest and lowest prices of a company's stock reached in a day, from market open to market close. These values can differ from open and close price.
>
> **Dividend per share** is provided for those companies that pay dividends. **Dividend yield**, then, is the percentage return on that divided, or annual dividend divided by current stock price.
>
> **52-week high and low** provide the highest and lowest prices at which a company's stock traded in the prior year.

The U.S. has sophisticated financial markets bolstered by easily accessible, transparent information on public companies listed in its exchanges (Amadeo, 2020). Investors from around the world are drawn to invest in U.S. companies, making the nation an appealing market to take a company public. London, Tokyo, Shanghai, and Hong Kong each have large exchanges and financial markets of their own.

Stock Exchanges

American stocks trade primarily on two of the world's largest exchanges: the *New York Stock Exchange (NYSE)* and *NASDAQ (National Association of Securities Dealers Automated Quotations)* (Fisher, 2019). The NYSE dates back to 1792, lists 2,800 companies, trades about 1.5 billion shares per day, and is considered the world's leading stock exchange. Companies must meet strict requirements to be listed on the NYSE, which maintains a reputation of trading high-performing, high-quality securities ranging from *blue-chips* (prominent, consistently high-performing companies including Walmart, American Express, Nike, and ExxonMobil) to new, high-growth companies. There's a physical place – called the floor of the NYSE – where brokers and specialists execute trades throughout each business day. An actual bell rings at the opening and closing of each trading day ("About the NYSE Bell," 2020).

NASDAQ was founded in 1971 as the world's first electronic stock market (Fisher, 2019). Unlike the NYSE, it has no trading floor but instead relies on dealers and automated networks for trading. NASDAQ lists 3,300 companies and facilitates more than 1.8 billion trades per day. NASDAQ trades a variety of stocks but is primarily known as an exchange for high-tech firms.

Stock Indices

Three broadly followed *stock market indices* – the *Dow Jones Industrial Average (DJIA)*, the *Standard & Poor's 500 Index*, and the *NASDAQ Composite Index* – track U.S. stock performance (Banton, 2020). There are thousands of similar indices using various methodologies, but these three receive the most media attention.

The Dow Jones Industrial Average follows 30 U.S. blue-chip companies that together represent a quarter of the value of the entire U.S. stock market (Banton, 2020). These companies pay consistent dividends to their shareholders. *The Dow*, as it's often called, is a price-weighted index calculated by a complex formula. Generally speaking, if the Dow is "up," economic sentiments are optimistic, and investors are confident about the direction the economy is taking. If there's uncertainty or unrest in the market – related to politics, employment, world affairs, or any factor that can impact economic conditions – the Dow will be "down." Media occasionally report on the Dow hitting record highs and lows (see Sidebar 5.7: Bulls, Bears, and Investor Psychology).

Sidebar 5.7 Bulls, Bears, and Investor Psychology

(Kramer, 2020)

A bull market is one with share prices on the rise. Market sentiments are positive. Economic conditions are widely perceived as sound. Employment levels tend to be high. Investors want to buy securities, but fewer investors are willing to sell. Someone who is "bullish" on the market is optimistic about its outlook.

A bear market is one with share prices dropping. Market sentiments are diminishing. Economic conditions are widely perceived as declining. Unemployment levels tend to rise. Investors want to sell securities, but fewer investors are willing to buy. Someone who is "bearish" on the market is pessimistic about its outlook.

Investor perceptions drive market behavior. Stock market performance and investor sentiment are inextricably connected. A decline in stock prices rattles investor confidence, which causes investors to pull money out of the market, which causes more price declines. The opposite effect occurs when the market is trending upward.

The Standard & Poor's 500 Index, more commonly referred to as *the S&P 500*, tracks 500 top U.S. companies comprising about 80% of the total value of the U.S. stock market (Banton, 2020). The S&P 500 is a market-weighted (also known as capitalization-weighted) index. *Market capitalization* (also known as *market* cap) for a firm equals its outstanding number of shares multiplied by its share price. Companies in the S&P 500 are selected primarily by the size of their market cap and give a broader view of economic health compared to the just 30 firms listed in the Dow Jones Industrial Average.

Like the S&P 500, the NASDAQ Composite is a market cap-based index, but it includes all of the stocks traded on the NASDAQ exchange, including *large-cap, mid-cap,* and *small-cap* stocks (see Sidebar 5.8: Market Cap and Volatility Defined). Although heavily tech-based, NASDAQ companies span a number of other industries, including insurance, finance, and transportation. It, too, gives an overall indicator of economic expectations, particularly for the technology sector.

Sidebar 5.8 Market Cap and Volatility Defined

(Ross, 2020)

Market capitalization, more often referred to as market cap, is the number of a company's outstanding shares multiplied by its current share price. A company with 5 million shares selling for $100 each would have a market cap of $500 million. Market cap is a popular way of segmenting publicly traded companies.

Large-cap corporations have market capitalizations of $10 billion and greater.
Mid-cap corporations have market capitalizations between $2 billion and $10 billion.
Small-cap corporations have market capitalizations between $300 million and $2 billion.

> These are general guidelines that have shifted over time. The guidelines matter most to firms on the borderlines.
> **Volatility** is a measure of the range the price of the stock can vary. Higher volatility means higher potential variance in price and more risk for the investor.
> Large caps are more mature companies and typically less volatile during market shifts. Risk-averse investors are drawn to the perceived quality and stability associated with large cap companies. Small cap and midcap stocks are more affordable for investors but also more volatile as investments.

Shareholder Activism

As company owners, shareholders have not only a right to a proportionate share of the company's profits, but also a voice in the company's business. The degree of power exerted by a particular shareholder depends on the size of the ownership share and the ability to recruit support from other shareholders. Shareholders seek change when they are dissatisfied with how management is running the company. Their level of activism in seeking change can take a variety of forms, with varying levels of intensity. Here, we'll walk through several methods of shareholder activism.

Shareholder Resolution

The U.S. Securities and Exchange Commission (SEC) regulates the *shareholder resolution* process, through which shareholders make non-binding suggestions for changes to company policies ("What is Shareholder Resolution," 2020). Shareholder resolutions are presented and voted on during the company's *annual shareholder meeting* ("Annual Meeting Handbook," 2018).[21] Annual meetings of shareholders are required by state law and outlined in a company's articles of incorporation and bylaws. Public companies registered under the *Securities Exchange Act of 1934* and listed on a stock exchange must follow federal rules requiring the production and distribution of a *proxy statement* to shareholders before the required annual meeting. Proxy statements include proposals submitted to shareholders for a vote at the annual meeting, along with other disclosures including management and executive compensation when electing members to the board of directors ("Annual Meetings," 2017).[22] Shareholders complete a *proxy card* (see Figure 5.1: Sample Proxy Card[23]) online or via phone, which gives the company authority to vote their shares as indicated on their proxy card. Alternatively, shareholders have the option of attending the annual meeting in person and casting their votes by ballot.

Annual meetings can be short, simple procedures held in a company conference room or as elaborate as hosting thousands of shareholders in a physical space with multi-media management presentations and provisions for virtual participation ("Annual Meeting Handbook," 2018). What's key is that shareholders must be able to fully participate in annual meetings. Shareholders owning at least $2,000 of common stock they've held for at least one year may file a shareholder resolution proposing change in a company policy or raising concern about an environmental, social, or corporate governance issue ("What is Shareholder Resolution," 2020).

Annual Meeting Proxy Card 1234 5678 9012 345

▼IF YOU HAVE NOT VOTED VIA THE INTERNET OR TELEPHONE, FOLD ALONG THE PERFORATION, DETACH AND RETURN THE BOTTOM PORTION IN THE ENCLOSED ENVELOPE.▼

A Proposals — The Board of Directors recommends a vote FOR all the nominees listed and FOR Proposal 2.

1. Election of Directors:

	For	Against	Abstain		For	Against	Abstain		For	Against	Abstain
01 - William D. Aaron, Jr.	☐	☐	☐	02 - William M. Carrouche	☐	☐	☐	03 - Leander J. Foley, III	☐	☐	☐
04 - John F. French	☐	☐	☐	05 - Leon L. Giorgio, Jr.	☐	☐	☐	06 - Shivan Govindan	☐	☐	☐
07 - L. Blake Jones	☐	☐	☐	08 - Louis V. Lauricella	☐	☐	☐	09 - Mark G. Merlo	☐	☐	☐
10 - Ashton J. Ryan, Jr.	☐	☐	☐	11 - Dr. Charles C. Teamer	☐	☐	☐	12 - Joseph F. Toomy	☐	☐	☐

+

	For	Against	Abstain
2. Ratification of appointment of Emst & Young LLP as the Company's independent registered public accounting firm for 2015.	☐	☐	☐

B Non-Voting Items

Change of Address — Please print your new address below.

Comments — Please print your comments below.

Annual Report
Mark here if you no longer wish to receive paper annual meeting materials and instead view them online. ☐

Meeting Attendance
Mark the box to the right if you plan to attend the Annual Meeting. ☐

C Authorized Signatures — This section must be completed for your vote to be counted. — Date and Sign Below

When shares are held by joint tenants, both should sign, Executors, administrators, trustees, etc. should give full title as such. If the signer is a corporation, please sign full corporate name by duty authorized officer.

Date (mm/dd/yyyy) — Please print date below. / /

Signature 1 — Please keep signature within the box.

Signature 2 — Please keep signature within the box.

Figure 5.1 Sample Proxy Card

Resolutions must be submitted to the company 120 days prior to the release of the annual proxy statement and are limited to 500 words. Aside from being relevant to the company's operations and of significant public concern,[24] shareholder resolutions must also be actionable by the board. Companies can attempt to omit any shareholder resolutions from the proxy statement by filing a *notice of omission* with the SEC at least 60 days prior to the proxy release. The SEC mediates any conflicts between the shareholder and the company over the proposed resolution and has the final say. If a resolution is found to meet SEC criteria, it is included in the proxy statement for a shareholder vote (see Figure 5.2: Sample Shareholder Resolution). It is not unusual for the company to recommend a vote against a shareholder resolution, as shown in Figure 5.2, yet recommend a vote for a resolution put forth by the company.

The shareholder who successfully proposes a resolution for the proxy statement then presents the resolution at the annual meeting according to rules governing who can speak, and for how long ("What is Shareholder Resolution," 2020). The challenge of getting a shareholder resolution passed with a majority vote can be daunting, particularly when the company recommends a vote against the resolution. Most shareholder votes are cast via proxy before the meeting, so there's little opportunity to influence the vote at the meeting. The SEC will allow some, but not all, resolutions to be reconsidered in subsequent years, particularly if votes in favor of the resolution continue to rise over time. Once a resolution passes, the company is obligated to implement it.

Activist groups, like Greenpeace, will purchase shares in companies they oppose. Doing so provides access to the shareholder resolution process and the opportunity to address shareholders at the annual meeting. Activist organizations (and individuals) potentially have the opportunity to bring their case for change in company policy for a number of years, particularly if shareholder votes increase in favor of their resolution.[25] I've seen firsthand how effective these groups can be by professionally, steadily, and patiently influencing shareholder votes over time.

Activist individuals and organizations can attempt to influence company policies or disclosure practices (e.g., lobbying expenses) through shareholder resolutions and requested meetings with executives. Their proportion of ownership in the company, however, is likely to pale in comparison to that of institutional investors. As discussed, institutional investors are the major players comprising pension funds, mutual funds, insurance companies, and asset managers that have corporate stocks in their massive investment portfolios (Loop, Bromilow, & Malone, 2018). Institutional investors are estimated to account for at least 70% of stock trading volume, and the percentage of corporate shares held by institutional investors has continued to rise over several decades (Josephson, 2019). This influential group of investors, including BlackRock, Vanguard Group, and Fidelity Investments, may begin by requesting meetings with company officials to express concerns about governance practices, executive compensation, or social issues related to business operations. If those interactions aren't satisfactory, institutional investors can begin the shareholder resolution process while encouraging other investors to join in their support. Institutional investors can likewise lead "vote no" campaigns against company-endorsed directors to highlight the need for more diversity or other qualifications among board members. Institutional investors readily attract media attention for their efforts.

Items 5-6. Shareholder Proposals

We are committed to active engagement with our shareholders. If you would like to speak with us, please contact our Investor Relations team at gs-investor-relations@gs.com.

Proposal Snapshot – Items 5-6. Shareholder Proposals

What is being voted on. In accordance with SEC rules, we have set forth below certain shareholder proposals, along with the supporting statements of the respective shareholder proponents, for which we and our Board accept no responsibility. These shareholder proposals are required to be voted upon at our Annual Meeting only if properly presented at our Annual Meeting.

Board recommendation. As explained below, our Board unanimously recommends that you vote AGAINST each shareholder proposal.

For detailed information on the vote required with respect to these shareholder proposals and the choices available for casting your vote, please see *Frequently Asked Questions*.

Item 5. Shareholder Proposal Requesting Report on Lobbying

The Unitarian Universalist Association, 24 Farnsworth Street, Boston, Massachusetts 00210, beneficial owner of 25 shares of Common Stock, the Benedictine Sisters of Monasterio Pan de Vida, Calle Tenochtitlan No. 501, Col. Las Carolinas, Torreón, Coahuila, Mexico, beneficial owner of 51 shares of Common Stock, and the OIP Investment Trust, 391 Michigan Avenue, NE, Washington D.C. 20017, beneficial owner of 50 shares of Common Stock, are the proponents of the following shareholder proposal. The proponents have advised us that a representative will present the proposal and related supporting statement at our Annual Meeting.

PROPONENTS' STATEMENT

Whereas, we believe in full disclosure of Goldman Sachs's ("Goldman") direct and indirect lobbying activities and expenditures to assess whether its lobbying is consistent with its expressed goals and in the best interests of shareholders.

Resolved, the shareholders of Goldman request the preparation of a report, updated annually, disclosing:

1. Company policy and procedures governing lobbying, both direct and indirect, and grassroots lobbying communications.
2. Payments by Goldman used for (a) direct or indirect lobbying or (b) grassroots lobbying communications, in each case including the amount of the payment and the recipient.
3. Goldman's membership in and payments to any tax-exempt organization that writes and endorses model legislation.
4. Description of management's and the Board's decision making process and oversight for making payments described in sections 2 and 3 above.

For purposes of this proposal, a "grassroots lobbying communication" is a communication directed to the general public that (a) refers to specific legislation or regulation, (b) reflects a view on the legislation or regulation and (c) encourages the recipient of the communication to take action with respect to the legislation or regulation. "Indirect lobbying" is lobbying engaged in by a trade association or other organization of which Goldman is a member.

Both "direct and indirect lobbying" and "grassroots lobbying communications" include efforts at the local, state and federal levels.

The report shall be presented to the Public Responsibilities Committee and posted on Goldman's website.

Figure 5.2 Sample Shareholder Resolution
Reprinted with permission from Goldman Sachs

Proxy Fight

A *proxy fight* is an aggressive action taken by company outsiders seeking support from other shareholders to vote out all or most of a company's senior management (Chen, 2019a).[26] The aim of the proxy fight is for activist investors to seize control of, or takeover, the company. Their strategy is to replace inflexible directors with those more willing to take the company in the direction the activists want to go. To be successful, activists leading the proxy fight must convince a large enough portion of shareholders to vote with them. A third-party *proxy solicitor* is usually hired to contact shareholders, share the activists' plans to turnaround the company, and request supporting votes on shareholder proxy cards.

Most proxy battles fail, and the most common targets are companies with market caps less than $1 billion (Chen, 2019a). Companies stagger board appointments and put other restrictive measures in their bylaws to diminish the likelihood of successful proxy challenges ("What is a Proxy Fight," 2020). Companies, may, however, negotiate with activist investors under threat of a proxy fight. Occidental Petroleum (Oxy) agreed to add three associates of billionaire activist investor Carl Icahn as directors and appoint a new board chairman Icahn favored after he publicly criticized the Oxy board over its acquisition of Andarko Petroleum and actively pursued a heated proxy fight ("Occidental Ends Proxy Fight," 2020).

Hostile Takeover

The heightened aggression of a *hostile takeover* occurs when an offer from Company A to acquire Company B is rejected by the Company B board of directors ("What is a Hostile Takeover," 2020). Company A, then, turns directly to Company B shareholders to pursue a takeover of the company, despite having the initial offer rejected by the board. What differentiates a "friendly" takeover (see Mergers and Acquisitions discussion ahead) from a hostile one is Company A's disregard for the initial rejection and determination to acquire the company by circumventing the board. A proxy fight, as we've discussed, is one option. The other option is a *tender offer*, which is an offer made by Company A to purchase Company B shares at an above-market price, thus allowing Company A to gather enough voting shares (more than 50%) to have controlling interest in Company B. The tender offer is typically contingent on Company A getting the number of shares it needs to gain control of the company.

You may be wondering at this point what motivates acquirers to pursue a hostile takeover and how companies can protect themselves. Takeover targets are companies perceived as underperforming and undervalued. As such, activist shareholders with a seemingly better plan to run the company see a takeover as a value-adding opportunity. That is, if they can acquire the company for less than it's potentially worth, there's more money to be made for shareholders. Takeover targets have redeeming qualities, such as valuable assets, access to desirable markets, or proprietary technology, that the acquirer finds enticing but underutilized under current management. There are several interestingly named strategies companies can take to protect themselves from a hostile takeover ("What is a Hostile Takeover," 2020):

- *Poison pill.* Companies targeted for a hostile takeover can issue a *poison pill* by allowing their shareholders to purchase additional shares at a deeply discounted price. Doing so forces the hostile acquirer to purchase even more shares to gain a controlling interest. A poison pill is issued to discourage the likelihood of a successful tender offer.

- *Crown jewels defense.* Target companies may sell off their most valuable assets (i.e., their *crown jewels*) to lessen their attractiveness for a hostile takeover.
- *Supermajority amendment.* The board can approve an amendment requiring a *supermajority* between 67% and 90% (instead of 51%) to approve a merger, making it even more difficult for a tender offer to be successful.
- *Golden parachute.* Hostile takeovers can be made even more expensive by the target company guaranteeing outlandish benefits are paid to executives removed because of a takeover – the so-called *golden parachute* for exiting the company.
- *Greenmail. Greenmail* is a battle for controlling shares. The target company can respond to a tender offer by offering shareholders an even higher price for their shares.
- *Pac-Man defense.* The *Pac-Man defense* applies only to those target companies with the resources to fight back by issuing its own tender offer to attempt to take control of the company attempting to take control of it.

Dealing with shareholders, activist and otherwise, is a time-consuming task for publicly held companies. Even more demanding is adhering to the multiple and expensive reporting requirements, which we'll cover next.

Regulatory and Reporting Requirements

U.S. Senator Paul Sarbanes and U.S. Representative Michael Oxley in 2002 sponsored passage of the *Sarbanes-Oxley Act*, commonly known as SOX, to usher in an extensive array of reporting and recordkeeping requirements for publicly held companies, including stricter rules for accountants, auditors, and corporate officers, in the wake of corporate financial scandals at Enron, Tyco, and WorldCom[27] (Kenton, 2020a). SOX was a major overhaul of corporate regulations, adding prison terms for corporate officers who knowingly certify false financial statements. SOX further requires managers and auditors to implement sufficient internal controls to ensure accuracy in financial reporting, including the proper handling and storage of company records. Costs related to annual SOX compliance are significant, ranging from tens of thousands to more than $1 million depending on company size (McDonald, 2018).

Public companies are required by the Securities and Exchange Commission (SEC) to disclose certain business and financial information to the public on a regular basis ("Public Companies," n.d.). These disclosures are mandated to protect current and potential investors from incomplete, false, or misleading information. Reporting requirements to the SEC include the following:

- **Annual Reports on Form 10-K:** The *10-K* includes the company's audited financial statements and a discussion of business results, risk factors, legal proceedings, internal controls, and executive compensation (see also, "How to Read," 2011). The *Management's Discussion and Analysis of Financial Condition and Results of Operations*, commonly known as the *MD&A*, provides the company an opportunity to tell its own story of how the year progressed. A company's *annual report* is a shorter and much more stylized version of the 10-K, including pictures, graphics, a CEO letter, and an overview of the company's activities ("Annual Report," 2019). Like the 10-K, the annual report includes financial statements and business results but in a much more appealing format for shareholders to read (see Box 5.1: 10-K vs. Annual Report).

- **Quarterly Reports on Form 10-Q:** The *10-Q* is filed for each of the first three quarters of a company's fiscal year. The annual report follows in the fourth quarter. Quarterly reports include unaudited financial statements and a discussion of business results for the prior three months and the year to date. The 10-Q also compares company performance in the current quarter to that of the same period in the previous year.
- **Current Reports on Form 8-K:** The *8-K* is filed to announce *material* information to shareholders, including changes in senior corporate leadership and other major events such as bankruptcy proceedings or preliminary earnings announcements.
- **Proxy Statements:** As discussed, *proxy statements* describe matters for shareholder voting and disclose executive compensation practices.
- **Additional Disclosures:** Major events including proposed mergers, acquisitions, tender offers, large stock transactions by executives, and other activities affecting the company must also be disclosed.

Box 5.1 10-K vs. Annual Report

The 10-K is a compilation of financial information required by the SEC in a specified format that can be cumbersome to read. 10-Ks are posted on the SEC website.

The annual report is a shorter, much more marketable, user-friendly format for shareholders and other audiences interested in the company's performance. Annual reports are posted on company websites.

UNITED STATES
SECURITIES AND EXCHANGE COMMISSION
WASHINGTON, D.C. 20549

FORM 10-K

(Mark One)

☒ Annual report pursuant to Section 13 or 15(d) of the Securities Exchange Act of 1934
For the fiscal year ended December 31, 2017

or

☐ Transition report pursuant to Section 13 or 15(d) of the Securities Exchange Act of 1934
For the transition period from _____ to _____

Commission file number 0-16125

FASTENAL COMPANY
(Exact name of registrant as specified in its charter)

Minnesota
(State or other jurisdiction of incorporation or organization)

41-0948415
(I.R.S. Employer Identification No.)

2001 Theurer Boulevard
Winona, Minnesota
(Address of principal executive offices)

55987-0978
(Zip Code)

(507) 454-5374
(Registrant's telephone number, including area code)

Securities registered pursuant to Section 12(b) of the Act:

Figure 5.3a Form 10-K

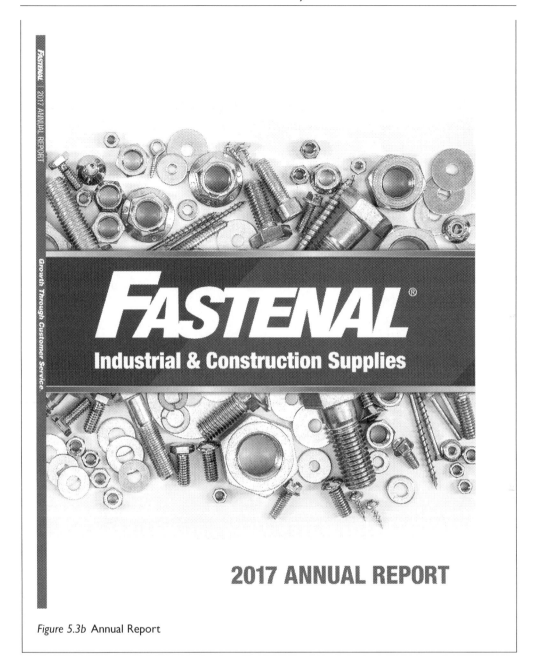

Figure 5.3b Annual Report

- **Quarterly Earnings Reports:** To ensure company information is widely and publicly available, the SEC enforces a *quiet period* between the end of a financial quarter and the scheduled time a company will announce its financial results (Cabi, 2019). The company must avoid selective disclosure of material information that could affect its stock performance during the quiet period, particularly when interacting with investors, media, and analysts. Most companies post earnings announcement dates on their websites and issue press releases summarizing their quarterly and annual SEC earnings filings in a timeframe that follows SEC guidelines ("When Must," 2020). *Earnings season* refers to the flurry of corporate announcements after the end of each quarter. Corporate earnings announcements receive a great deal of attention from the financial press and investment/research analysts. Analysts make pre-announcement predictions about company earnings. Depending on the actual numbers announced, companies are said to *meet the street* (or not) or *beat the street* if actual earnings meet or exceed analyst expectations. When a company announces strong performance, its stock price usually rises. Following an earnings announcement, companies host an *earnings call* during which executives discuss the company's performance and answer questions for investors, analysts, and business journalists when they are no longer under quiet period restrictions. Any *forward-looking statements* about the company's future plans or anticipated performance made to investor or financial audiences, orally or in writing, must be clearly identified as forward-looking and accompanied by extensive cautionary language[28] explaining the risk of actual results not meeting expectations (Hoang, 2020). The SEC provides *safe harbor* liability protection to companies that adhere to forward-looking communication requirements.

Ratio and Margin Analysis

Quarterly earnings reports, analyst presentations, financial media, creditors, and managers focus on key business indicators that demonstrate how well a company is performing over time as well as how it performs vis-à-vis its competitors. We'll cover the key financial ratios and margins to know here. Keep in mind, however, that ratio and margin expectations vary across industries. It's important to compare a company's financial performance against itself or against companies in its specific industry, across similar periods of time. Otherwise, you're comparing apples to oranges and diminishing the validity of your analysis.[29]

Financial ratios are grouped in five general categories regarding a company's performance: liquidity ratios, leverage ratios, efficiency ratios, profitability ratios, and market value ratios ("What are Financial Ratios," 2020). See Table 5.3: Key Financial Ratios for a description of each.

Quick Case Study: Wendy's and ROE

Wendy's Old Fashioned Hamburgers opened its first restaurant in Columbus, Ohio on November 15, 1969 ("The Wendy's Story," 2020). It wasn't long before founder Dave Thomas made Wendy's famous for its square beef patties, and the rest, as they say, is business history. We'll use The Wendy's Company (NASDAQ:WEN) as an example to better understand an important financial ratio: Return on Equity, or ROE.

ROE is a common measure of profitability that reflects how well (or not) companies are putting shareholder capital to work ("Why The Wendy's Company," 2020). In other words, ROE reveals the company's ability to turn shareholder equity into profits. Wouldn't you be curious as an investor to know how the company is using your money? ROE is one good indication.

Table 5.3 Key Financial Ratios

Ratio Type	Purpose	Ratios, Calculation, and Use
Liquidity Ratios	Liquidity ratios measure a company's ability to repay its liabilities with assets on its balance sheet. Higher values indicate better ability to repay liabilities with company assets if the company were forced to liquidate those assets.	**Current Ratio, aka Working Capital Ratio = Current assets/Current liabilities** Measures a company's ability to pay off current liabilities with current assets. **Quick Ratio, aka Acid-Test Ratio = (Current assets – Inventories)/Current liabilities** "Quick" assets refer to those net of inventory on hand that can be quickly liquidated if needed to pay off current liabilities. **Cash Ratio = Cash and cash equivalents/ Current liabilities** Measures a company's ability to pay off current liabilities with cash on hand and easily accessible cash (e.g., bank accounts). **Operating Cash Flow Ratio = Operating cash flow/Current liabilities** Measures the number of times a company could pay off its current liabilities with cash generated in a given period.
Leverage Ratios	Leverage ratios measure the proportion of a company's capital that comes from debt. The "right" level of debt depends on industry standards, but too much debt can put a company at risk for default on its debts. When total liabilities is the numerator, lower ratio values indicate less reliance on debt. When operating income is the numerator, higher values indicate a company's ability to cover its debt obligations.	**Debt Ratio = Total liabilities/Total assets** Measures the proportion of assets provided by debt. **Debt to Equity (D/E) Ratio = Total liabilities/ Shareholders' equity** Measures the proportion of debt weighted against equity from investors. **Interest Coverage Ratio = Operating income/Interest expenses** Measures a company's ability to pay its interest expenses. **Debt Service Coverage Ratio = Operating income/Total debt service** Measures a company's ability to pay all of its debt obligations.
Efficiency Ratios	Efficiency ratios measure how well a company is using its assets and resources.	**Asset Turnover Ratio = Net sales/total assets** Measures how well a company is generating sales from its assets. Higher values are better. **Inventory Turnover Ratio = Cost of goods sold/Average inventory** Measures how well a company is turning over, or selling, and replacing its inventory. Higher values are better. **Receivables Turnover Ratio = Net credit sales/Average accounts receivable** Measures how well a company is collecting on its receivables, that is, converting credit sales into cash. Higher values are better. **Days Sales in Inventory Ratio = 365 days/ Inventory Turnover Ratio** Measures the average number of days a company holds inventory before selling it to customers. Lower values are better.

(continued)

Table 5.3 Cont.

Ratio Type	Purpose	Ratios, Calculation, and Use
Profitability Ratios	Profitability ratios measure a company's ability to turn a profit. Higher values indicate more profitability.	**Gross Margin Ratio = Gross profit/Net sales** Measures how much profit a company is earning after paying its cost of goods sold (COGS). **Operating Margin Ratio = Operating income/Net sales** Measures how much profit a company is earning after paying COGS plus other operating expenses. **Return on Assets (ROA) Ratio = Net income/Total assets** Measures how well a company is leveraging its assets to make a profit. **Return on Equity (ROE) Ratio = Net income/Shareholders' equity** Measures how well a company is using equity from its investors to make a profit.
Market Value Ratios	Market value ratios measure the value of a company's stock. Higher values are better, but the P/E (price-earnings) ratio walks a finer line. A high P/E ratio could indicate a stock is overvalued. A low P/E ratio could indicate the stock is undervalued in light of company earnings. As with all ratios, P/E needs to be reviewed in the context of a company, its history, and its industry.	**Book Value per Share Ratio = Shareholders' equity/Total shares outstanding** Measures how much book, or accounting, value is attributed to each share of stock. **Dividend Yield Ratio = Dividend per share/Share price** Measures how much dividend is paid per dollar of share price. **Earnings per Share (EPS) Ratio = Net earnings/Total shares outstanding** Measures how much of the company's earnings (i.e., net income) can be attributed to each share of stock. **Diluted EPS** is a "what if" scenario that assumes all potential shares – such as stock options awarded but not yet exercised – have been converted to shares, thus increasing total shares outstanding (aka float) and diluting, or lowering, EPS (Ganti, 2019). **Price-Earnings (P/E) Ratio = Share price/Earnings per Share (EPS)** Measures share price relative to the earnings per share ratio.

ROE equals net income divided by shareholders' equity. At the time of this writing, Wendy's ROE is $119m/$451m, or 26% ("Why The Wendy's Company," 2020). That means that for every dollar of shareholder equity, the company earned a 26% return (i.e., 26 cents per dollar), or profit, over the past year. Is that good or bad? To answer that question, we need to look at how the hospitality industry overall performs on ROE. Keep in mind a category as broad as the hospitality industry is going to include *lots* of different types of businesses. Nevertheless, we can get a rough idea of how to put Wendy's ROE in context by looking at the industry average.

Yahoo Finance (yahoo.finance.com; "Why The Wendy's Company," 2020) reports the average ROE for the hospitality industry is 14%, so Wendy's looks superior with an ROE of 26%. But before you run out and invest your life savings in The Wendy's Company, think back to our discussion of capital structure. Capital structure includes debt *and* equity. If a company has much more debt than equity, it's going to have a high ROE. Why? As the denominator in the ROE equation – shareholders' equity – gets smaller in the capital structure mix, all else being equal, ROE gets larger. A lot of debt can put a company at great risk. Wendy's Debt to Equity (D/E) ratio, calculated by Total Liabilities divided by Shareholders' Equity, is 5.31. The D/E ratio tells us that Wendy's has 5.31 times the amount of debt on its books than it has in shareholder equity. Yahoo Finance ranks Wendy's D/E ratio as "extremely high." Wendy's has a terrific ROE, but it appears to be boosted by a lot of debt. ROE tells only the equity side of the story. You need to look at D/E to get the debt perspective.

Several lessons are learned in this quick case study. First, a standalone ratio means nothing until you have a point of comparison for it. *Compared to what?* is an important question to ask. What was the ratio value three years ago? One year ago? What ratio values do competitors have? What's the industry average for this metric? And even if you have a point of comparison, one ratio isn't enough to give a full picture of a company's performance over time. Multiple ratios are needed to draw meaningful conclusions about a company's financial health and investment potential.

The Journey from Startup to IPO

Now that we've covered the terrain of corporate finance for mature companies, let's step back to see what financing looks like when a company is first founded. A *startup* is the entrepreneurial endeavor of creating demand for a product or service in its first stages of operation (Grant, 2020). Startups are a popular idea. Since 2010, growth in the number of startups in the U.S. has steadily increased ("Quarterly Number," 2020). In just the third quarter of 2019, there were 250,000 business started in the U.S. That's quite a number of startups, but here's the stark reality: 90% of startups fail, and here are the reasons why (Patel, 2016):

- **Making a product no one wants.** Market research is a must. You can analyze anything too much, but you really, truly need a market for whatever it is you're trying to sell.
- **Segmenting roles and responsibilities.** In startup phase, everyone needs to do a bit of everything. Founders, especially, need to work *on* their business, not just *in* it.
- **Growing too slowly.** Here's the catch: You need to have rapid growth to attract more cash. No (or slow) growth means no cash, and no more business.
- **Adapting too slowly.** Changes occur rapidly in the early stages of a business. The founding team needs not only multiple skillsets, but also the ability to step back, reconfigure, and, sometimes, start over entirely from scratch when conditions demand.

Startups are typically financed by their founders but need to attract outside capital if they're going to succeed (Grant, 2020). *Seed capital* from family, friends, and other startup sources can be used for market research, prototyping, and business planning. *Angel investors* are high-worth individuals who provide early-stage funding for startups, typically in exchange for ownership equity in the company (Ganti, 2020b). It's important for startups to gain traction with these initial funds, else the business ends when the money runs out. Seed funding ranges between $500,000 and $2 million, depending on the company ("How Startup Funding," 2019). For some startups, seed funding is enough to get the business running without additional investment.

For startups looking for additional cash, *series funding* comes next. As series funding progresses, *venture capital (VC) firms, crowdfunding, private equity (PE) firms,* and *investment banks* get involved in the process. And guess what's essential throughout the startup journey: effective communication. Startups need a *pitch deck* for investor presentations to capture what the company does, what problem it solves, and why it's different than other companies with similar objectives (Patel, 2020). Real data, an engaging story, a convincing *business model* (i.e., how the business will earn revenue), and a solid team are must-haves when raising thousands, even millions, of dollars. Just like in any other transaction, people do business with people they like, trust, and perceive as motivated to succeed. Skilled communicators get entrepreneurs funded. Table 5.4 describes each step of series funding ("How Startup Funding," 2019; Marks 2018; "Private Equity," 2020).

Taking a company public is a major communication feat, so it's worthwhile to take a closer look at the Initial Public Offering (IPO). An IPO is a *primary market* offering of stock because investors are purchasing shares directly from the company (Fuhrmann, 2019). Thereafter, shares are bought and sold between traders in the *secondary market*. The road to an IPO is expensive and laden with regulatory requirements. By going public, companies agree to adhere to SEC regulations and make their financials open to public scrutiny. An investment bank, or *underwriter*, guides the firm through the process, preparing a *preliminary prospectus* (also known as a *red herring*[30] and part of the *S-1 registration statement*) for SEC review. Once finalized, the prospectus provides business and financial information for potential investors, including details of the share offering.

In the months leading up to the IPO, company executives and their underwriters conduct *roadshows* in major cities to generate enthusiasm, answer questions, and promote the company to analysts, media, and potential investors (Murphy, 2019b). Not every roadshow involves an IPO. *Non-deal roadshows* (NDRs) are held by new and mature companies to update investors on the company's current and future plans, but no equity or debt security is offered.

The quiet period for an IPO begins when the S-1 registration statement is filed with the SEC (Cabi, 2019). Once the IPO becomes public and the initial price for the issued shares is set, management must be cautious to discuss only information that is in the S-1 with investors. Media interviews or other attempts to increase demand for the IPO can violate quiet period regulations and delay the IPO timeline. Quiet period restrictions continue for a period of days after trading begins to avoid having any new information affect the market.

Float refers to the numbers of shares in the initial offering (Ganti, 2019). If management issues more shares in a *secondary offering*, they dilute the share of ownership held by those who purchased the first round of shares. Dilution reduces earnings per share (EPS; see Table 5.3: Key Financial Ratios), which can lower stock prices. Although increasing float may not initially benefit current shareholders, the additional capital can increase company value and benefit shareholders in the long run. New companies focused on growth, including those rallying from a recent IPO, may, for the same reason, choose reinvestment of retained earnings in the business over dividend payments to increase shareholder wealth.

Table 5.4 Startup Series Funding

Funding Stage	Funding Amount	Notes
Series A	$2 million–$15 million	Getting the first committed investor is paramount, after whom others are more likely to follow. Proof of concept that an entrepreneurial idea will make a great company is required. Because debt can be harder to access at this early stage, funding typically comes from venture capital (VC) firms and/or crowdfunding that raises capital by selling equity shares online. Less than half of seeded startups are likely to complete a Series A round of funding, and many startups end here.
Series B	$7 million–$10 million	This round of financing is focused on expanding both the team and the customer base for a proven market fit. No longer are founders able to work across multiple positions, so hiring great talent is a necessity. VCs and re-investors from Series A are common sources of Series B financing.
Series C	Around $25 million	Companies are now looking to expand internationally, enter new markets, develop new products, and/or acquire other businesses. Focus is on increasing the value of the company for an initial public offering (IPO) or acquisition. Private equity (PE) firms will show interest at this point of the funding cycle when the company and the product are proven. Many companies finish raising money at this stage.
Series D	Varies widely because few companies reach this stage	Series D can mean good or bad news for a company. On the upside, companies can seek a Series D round of funding to get one more boost before going public or to stay private longer and build more value. The downside is when Series D is the *down round* of financing, meaning the company hasn't met expectations set in Series C. A down round erodes trust, dilutes equity, and demoralizes employees.
Series E	Varies widely because even fewer companies reach this stage	Rationale for a rare round of Series E funding is similar to that for Series D funding.
Mezzanine Financing, aka Bridge Loans	Varies depending on need	Bridge loans are a hybrid of loans and equity financing. Investors charge a higher interest rate than a bank loan and expect the loan to convert to equity if the company defaults. This form of financing is used for the final push toward IPO or acquisition.
Initial Public Offering (IPO)	Varies depending on strategy	A company "going public" will hire an investment bank to sell a certain amount of shares, for a certain amount of money, on a stock exchange to fund the now publicly traded company.

Focusing on Growth

Whether private, public, new, or mature, companies focus on growth. But an important question is, what *kind* of growth? We'll explore two categories of growth most relevant to corporate finance here.

Top-Line vs. Bottom-Line Growth

Recall the income statement from Chapter 4. The term *top line* refers to the first line on the income statement, which is gross revenue or sales. The term *bottom line* refers to the last line of the income statement, which is net income, or net earnings, or profit. Remember that line item names may differ across companies, but the accounting principle remains the same. Gross sales, or revenues, is what the firm takes in from sales. Net income, or profit, is what is left over after deducting all expenses related to making those sales.

A focus on *top-line growth*, then, means the firm wants to increase revenues or sales (Murphy, 2019a). Top-line growth indicates how well a company is generating interest in its products and driving sales of those products. Top-line growth also flows from expanding production, increasing customer satisfaction to lower product returns, adding new product lines, and increasing prices. A focus on *bottom-line growth*, however, requires a company to identify efficiencies that can lower expenses deducted from the top line, including the cost of input goods, facilities, and personnel. Bottom-line growth means increasing profits by decreasing expenses.

The most profitable companies effectively manage both top-line, or revenue, growth as well as bottom-line, or profit, growth (Murphy, 2019a). More mature companies (or certain product lines) may experience flattening in sales over time, putting more pressure on the need to cut expenses to increase profits. Companies will also focus heavily on *cost cutting* during recessions or other economic downturns when sales are slowed. There are only two ways to increase profits: increase revenues or reduce expenses. The most successful companies figure out how to do both.

Organic vs. Inorganic Growth

Organic growth originates from the company's ongoing activities (Vance, 2020; "What is Organic," 2020). An organic growth strategy draws on the company's existing resources to grow the business and may require reconfiguration of those resources to expand the business. Companies that increase production, sales, and/or cash flow without the need to borrow funds are growing organically. Because organic growth depends on using limited resources already at the company's disposal, organic growth strategies need to be prioritized. *Inorganic growth*, conversely, relies on borrowing funds or securing capital. Inorganic growth is frequently associated with acquisitions and mergers, discussed in more detail ahead, to purchase what the business needs rather than develop it internally. Inorganic growth is often faster for introducing a new line of business, but with some tradeoffs.

The pros of organic growth include (Vance, 2020):

- Management has in-depth knowledge of the company's operations and maintains control of where the business is headed.
- Internal integrations and changes required for new business are within the same company culture.
- Sustainable, organic growth makes the company more attractive for investment or acquisition.

The pros of inorganic growth include (Vance, 2020):

- Growing much faster with an acute infusion of new resources at the company's disposal.
- Immediate increase in market share, customer base, knowledge, and experience.
- Quicker access to a competitive edge.

Let's take a closer look at mergers and acquisitions to learn how inorganic growth can both advance and challenge a business.

Mergers and Acquisitions

Commonly referred to as *M&A*, *mergers and acquisitions* are central to inorganic growth. A *merger* is a consolidation to two equally sized companies, also known as a *merger of equals* (Hayes, 2020b). When two companies merge, each of their shares are surrendered, and newly merged company shares are issued in their place. For example, in late 2019, CBS Corp and Viacom completed their merger and became ViacomCBS Inc (Shivdas, 2019). Typically, when CEOs agree that joining two entities is in the best interest of both, the deal is referred to as a merger.

Mergers can be structured in a variety of ways (Hayes, 2020b):

- **Horizontal mergers** combine two competitors that share the same product line and markets, such as two energy companies;
- **Vertical mergers** combine two complementary firms, such as a home builder and a brick manufacturer;
- **Congeneric mergers** combine two firms that serve the same customers, but in different ways, such as a bank and a brokerage firm;
- **Market-extension mergers** combine two firms that sell the same product but in different markets, such as a U.S. winery and an Australian winery;
- **Product-extension mergers** combine two firms that sell different, but related, products in the same market, such as beverage company and a food company; and
- **Conglomeration mergers** combine two companies in different business areas, such as food and toys.

An *acquisition*, on the other hand, indicates that one company has purchased and taken control of another company (Hayes, 2020b). The acquired company ceases to exist as a separate legal entity, and its stock is no longer traded. Instead, the controlling company absorbs the acquired company, and its stock continues to trade. Global cloud computing company Salesforce (2020; "Salesforce Completes Acquisition," 2019) has made more than 60 acquisitions since its founding in 1999, including data software company Tableau in 2019. An acquisition can be friendly or hostile, depending on the circumstances. Take note of how companies announce and describe their M&A activity, and you'll get some insight into how the deal occurred[31] (see Sidebar 5.9: M&A Deal at a Glance).

> **Sidebar 5.9 M&A Deal at a Glance**
>
> (Allen, 2015)
>
> M&A deals follow a general chronological sequence. Effective communication and information sharing with relevant stakeholders are essential throughout. And note: The bigger the deal, the more regulatory restrictions are imposed throughout this process.

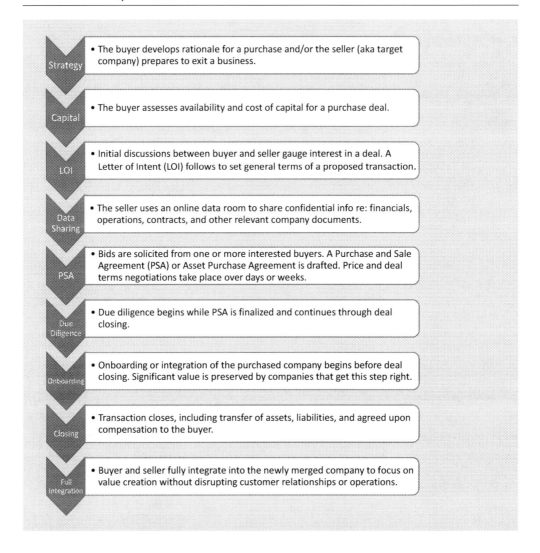

The Sherman Antitrust Act of 1890, discussed in Chapter 2, outlawed monopolies (see also Segal, 2020a). The Clayton Antitrust Act of 1914 was passed to extend the regulatory arm of the Sherman Act by making business activities intended to form a monopoly illegal, among other provisions regarding price-fixing and labor rights. Of interest here is the Clayton Act's prohibition of anticompetitive mergers and acquisitions that, given their potential size and reach, could dominate the market with monopolistic characteristics. Both the Federal Trade Commission (FTC) and the Antitrust Division of the U.S. Department of Justice (DOJ) enforce provisions of the Clayton Act and the related Hart-Scott-Rodino Act, which requires companies to seek federal review of any deal valued at more than $94 million ("Merger Review," n.d.). The FTC and/or DOJ has blocked M&A deals from proceeding when the combining of two companies would "substantially reduce competition" in an industry (e.g., see Lane, 2019).

Navigating the regulatory, financial, and communication nuances of an M&A deal are challenging enough, but add to that the pressure of creating lasting value from the combination of two companies. Ideally, a merger or acquisition should produce more value for shareholders (and other stakeholders) than either company could have done alone.

Extensive *due diligence* investigations and audits are conducted before deals are finalized to confirm buyers are getting what they think they are purchasing. But even if the financials are well aligned, an M&A deal can fail to deliver its promised value for cultural and/or integration reasons. In fact, most M&A deals – more than 50% – fail for one or more of the following reasons (Seth, 2020):

- **Limited owner involvement:** Leaving too much of the due diligence process to outside advisors can prevent owners from gaining important insights through this arduous process that could benefit the merged entity in the long run.
- **Poor integration process:** Post-merger integration is a major hurdle for organizations to conquer – culturally and organizationally. Too often these "softer sides" of the deal are overlooked and under-planned before the deal closes, which can significantly delay realization of promised *synergies* and increased profitability. By synergies, we're referring to value-creating opportunities that only the combination of two firms could bring, including new cash flows, lower production and capital costs, and streamlining of business processes (Allen, 2015).
- **Unforeseen external changes:** If the market that made an M&A deal look attractive takes a negative turn, the newly merged company can face significant, costly challenges while it's getting up and running.
- **Lack of proper due diligence:** If an M&A deal seems too good to be true, it may just be. Enthusiasm cannot overshadow the importance of due diligence, which should reveal strengths, weaknesses, and concerns about the deal. Bank of America brought more than $50 billion in devastating losses to employees, homeowners, and shareholders after acquiring Countrywide Financial in 2008 and turning a blind eye to its questionable lending practices (Rothacker, 2014).
- **Misvaluation:** Valuation sets the bid price for the M&A deal, which is best determined by a detailed discounted cash flow (DCF) valuation analysis of expected future cash flows of the acquired company (Allen, 2015). An incorrect valuation can lead to a host of other problems that further complicate a deal. A bid that's too low brings negotiations to a halt. Paying too much for an acquisition significantly reduces the value owners expect to realize and gives too much of that value to the seller. Read ahead to learn more about the valuation process.

Company Valuation

I was fortunate to study M&A with a finance PhD who spent most of his time outside of the classroom turning millions of dollars in deals in the energy sector. In Jeff Allen's (see Allen, 2015) advanced course, he required us to propose and conduct due diligence on a deal of our choosing, even a hypothetical one. My two study group members and I pursued an actual acquisition deal that required us to secure millions in capital, maintain confidentiality, meet with the current owners, and run the numbers on a company we had to learn a lot about. We saw tremendous value in our potential acquisition, got excited about our plans to realize that value, set aside our own funds to invest in it, and made plans on how we were going to run this business alongside everything else we had on our collective plates. We knew we had to replace the current management team who didn't share our vision and, from our perspective, was only draining value from the business.

In the end, we were outbid, but what an education it was. Our professor and expert guide was right: Once you're involved with a M&A deal, it's easy to get lured into doing another one.

Thousands of M&A transactions reveal a consistent theme over time (Allen, 2015). When an M&A transaction is announced, the *target company* being purchased, on average, gains sizable stock returns. Investors expect the company to gain significant value, purchase its stock, and up goes the price, further widening the gap between what investors paid for the stock and the price they expect it to reach. The *operating company*, or strategic buyer, on average gets no quantifiable bump in value when an M&A transaction is announced. Interesting, isn't it? And therefore, all the more important for the buyer to gain value from a well-structured deal.

Valuation techniques critical to an M&A deal are additionally used for investing in securities, lending and credit situations, repurchasing stock, and determining whether a potential partnership or *joint venture (JV)*[32] is a good business decision (Allen, 2015). Ultimately, the value of a company is what someone is willing to pay for it, which explains why many startups focus on building value and, instead of going public, look for a buyer with an attractive offer as their *exit strategy*. They cash out and go to beach, or stay with the buyer, or move on to their next entrepreneurial adventure (aka *serial entrepreneurs*). It's great to be the seller of an overvalued company, but not so great to be the buyer.

Public Company Valuation

Placing a value on any company is a complex task, but valuing a public company has the advantage of access to publicly available information about that company. Let's take a look at three methods used to value public companies (Allen, 2015).

- *Valuation multiples based on similar public companies.* The simplest approach to valuation is to use financial data from at least five similar companies as a guideline.[33] In this method, valuation is estimated as *multiples* of key financial measures, including earnings per share (EPS); price-earnings ratio (P/E); operating income, or *earnings before interest and taxes (EBIT)*; *earnings before interest, taxes, depreciation, and amortization (EBITDA*, or EBIT + Depreciation + Amortization); and revenue. Multiples are derived by calculating averages of financial measures across comparable companies, or *comps*, to estimate an *enterprise value*, or today's value of all future cash flows expected to be generated by the target company.[34]

    For example, if a review of comps reveals an EBITDA multiplier of 16.04, enterprise value is calculated as 16.04 multiplied by the target company's expected EBITDA in the coming year. If EBITDA is estimated to be $95 million (M), the value of the company is estimated as:

    $95M x 16.04 = $1,524M, or $1.524 billion

    Pretty simple, right? Multiples are a useful point of reference, but they should not be the only technique used to determine the value of a company. This method of valuation depends on the performance of other companies, none of which are an exact match to the target company of interest. And results will vary depending on which companies are selected as comps.

- *Discounted Cash Flow (DCF) valuation.* DCF valuation uses information drawn from target company financial data, including cash flows, historical performance, cost of capital, and forecasts. From these data, an estimate of the present value of all future expected cash flows is calculated, with one exception from our previous discussion of calculating NPV. Estimating present value for a *project* involves a finite life of that project, which could be three to ten years. Calculating the present value of a target *company* must account for its *continuing value* into perpetuity, also known as its *terminal value*.

   In DCF valuation, the forecasting of target company cash flows will typically extend five years beyond the expected closing date. But what about the many years thereafter? A single calculation, known as continuing value, provides the present value of cash flows beyond the forecasted years into perpetuity based on an assumed, constant required rate of return and constant rate of growth. Conservative estimates of constant growth rates are generally below 5% and can even be zero or negative if cash flows are expected to decline over time.

- *Adjusted Present Value (APV) valuation.* APV valuation looks very similar to the DCF method but separates present value of the investment from its associated debt tax shields (i.e., savings derived from tax-deductible interest charges). Instead of including debt tax shields in the Weighted Average Cost of Capital (WACC) calculation previously discussed, APV determines the value of debt tax shields separately.

   Certain situations favor APV over DCF calculations. If the target company's capital structure is expected to change over time, APV will provide a more accurate valuation than DCF. Further, separating operating cash flows from the effects of debt financing more clearly distinguishes the value-adding contribution of each. And lastly, an APV approach can break out other value-adding components offered by the target company and use a different rate of return to account for the risk associated with each (e.g., using a higher rate of return for a new vs. an established line of business).

Private Company Valuation

Private company valuation uses DCF and APV calculations, but there are several limitations on applying public company valuation methods to private companies (Allen, 2015). First, multiples derived from seemingly similar public companies should not be used to value private companies. Private companies have higher costs of capital compared to public companies with access to public capital markets. And the market value of a private company is unknown until a transaction occurs, such as going public or being sold. Without concrete data regarding recent, private company transactions in the same industry, valuation based on public comps is mostly speculation, or wishful thinking.

Some analysts propose calculating a publicly derived enterprise value and then discounting it in the range of 7% to 40% for a private company valuation (Allen, 2015). This approach sounds reasonable in theory, but, in practice, the range is wide, highly subjective, and unlikely to have the precision required for a multi-million dollar deal. Consider this: If the use of public comps and multiples derives an enterprise value of $320 million, discounting that value by 7% to 40% means the value of the private company lies somewhere between $192 million and $298 million. Do you really want a range in estimated value to exceed $100 million? Would you be comfortable as a buyer or seller with a value range of that size? Likely not. Valuation multiples based on public companies should not be used for private company valuation.

DCF and APV methods are appropriate for private company valuation and based on audited financial statements provided by the target company (Allen, 2015). Recall from Chapter 4 that many private companies use U.S. Generally Accepted Accounting Principles (GAAP) so their financial reporting is comparable to public companies, thus making their own valuation more straightforward. Cash flow is cash flow, whether the company is privately held or publicly traded. After cost of capital adjustments are made for a private company, DCF and APV methods will render the most accurate enterprise value estimates.

Once the value of a public or private target company is confidently established using DCF or APV, the buyer must decide on a bid price that reasonably aligns with the estimated value of the merger or acquisition (Allen, 2015). Bidding too low can end negotiations, and bidding too high can transfer too much value to the seller.[35] Once a deal closes, the buyer doesn't receive hypothetical EBITDA multiples but rather actual assets and cash flows upon which DCF and APV analyses are based. Getting valuation right is key.

Increasing Your Value to an Organization

Companies exist to create value. So should your career as a communicator. There is no shortage of brilliant people in finance, and the corporate world has plenty of outstanding communicators. There are relatively few, however, who understand finance *and* communication. Our shared aim is to get you not only comfortable, but thriving, in both of these areas. Finance isn't easy, but it's not insurmountable. The more you learn about finance (fair warning: repetition is required), the more its underlying principles will become part of the questions you ask, the strategies you develop, and the successes you help your company achieve. You'll distinguish your contributions from others who don't know, or don't care, how financial parameters drive a business.

No one is going to ask you to update a balance sheet or file the 10-K. But begin to understand finance, and you'll respond with confidence to media and analyst inquiries about your company's operations. Work on the annual report, where finance and marketing communication combine to tell the company's story for an investing audience. Build your financial acumen, and you'll have opportunities to work on IPOs and M&A deals, and you may even decide to dive in and work with a startup from the ground up.

Be sure you have finance professionals in your personal support network we discussed in Chapter 1. They'll serve as your sounding board, answer your questions, and then turn to you and ask, "So how do we *communicate* all this stuff?" That's nirvana to a business-wise communicator. Find an organization you believe in, and help it soar by increasing its value. You won't be an outsider looking in but instead part of a committed team that makes good things happen for countless stakeholders you'll never meet. It's exhausting, exhilarating, and important work.

Notes

1 See Chapter 10 What is Strategy? for further discussion.
2 See WorldCom case in Chapter 4 The Art and Science of Financial Statements as an example of what can happen when executives focus on boosting a particular measure instead of improving overall company performance.

3 See Chapter 4 The Art and Science of Financial Statements for how PPE appears on the balance sheet.
4 Capital expenditures differ from ongoing operating expenses in that operating expenses are regularly occurring to support the business whereas capital expenditures are used to grow the business and provide a future economic benefit ("Describe Capital Investment Decisions," n.d.).
5 Financial analysis involves forecasting future cash flows that a project is expected to deliver. See Chapter 4 The Art and Science of Financial Statements for an explanation of cash flow and how it differs from net income.
6 See Chapter 4 The Art and Science of Financial Statements for an explanation of the bottom line, or net income, on the income statement.
7 The discount rate will be increased for riskier projects with less certain outcomes, such as investments in areas of geopolitical instability or first-time expansions into new markets. Higher discount rates lower NPVs, making the hurdle rate on riskier projects higher to cross before a company will fund them (Gorton, 2016).
8 Modified IRR is generally preferred in financial practice. It's a conservative (i.e., lower) estimate of IRR that more accurately reflects a reinvestment rate for expected future cash flows. For example, a conventional calculation may provide an IRR of 21% that will be realized only if all cash flows from a project are reinvested at a 21% rate. A more realistic modified IRR may be 14%, which has a greater chance of being realized. NPV, IRR, and Modified IRR can be calculated in Excel (Allen, 2015).
9 See Chapter 4 The Art and Science of Financial Statements for discussion of how the statement of cash flows is calculated and the importance of cash reserves for a business.
10 See Chapter 4 The Art and Science of Financial Statements for an explanation of the balance sheet.
11 Alternatively, firms can issue notes or bills to raise capital (Guillory, 2020; "What is the Difference," 2016)
12 Companies may also issue convertible bonds, a hybrid security that converts a bond into a predetermined share of equity or stocks (Chen, 2020c).
13 Generally speaking, companies with consistent cash flows can take on more debt and have a larger proportion of debt in their capital structure. Those with more volatile cash flows will rely more on equity in their capital structures (Hayes, 2020a).
14 See Chapter 3 A Micro and Macro View of the Economy for an explanation of marginal benefit.
15 Calculating cost of equity is more complicated than calculating cost of debt and thus left to financial experts. See Hargrave, 2020a for an example calculating Walmart's WACC. See Allen, 2015 for an explanation of the mechanics and complications associated with the Capital Asset Pricing Model (CAPM) most frequently used to calculate cost of equity in practice.
16 Research analysts make recommendations on whether to buy, sell, or hold the stocks of publicly held companies. Analysts typically focus on a particular industry and base recommendations on their ongoing review of company operations, finances, and related news that can affect market performance of the company's stock (Thangavelu, 2020).
17 Variations include a *special dividend*, also known as an extra dividend, which is a non-recurring payment often associated with exceptionally strong earnings or a special event like an asset sale (Chen, 2019b).
18 An added benefit for investors is that, at the time of this writing, taxation is higher on dividends than on capital gains realized when a stock is sold for a price higher than was paid for it.
19 Share buybacks are also used to boost a share price the company believes has been too deeply discounted by the market. A more questionable motive for a stock repurchase is to improve the company's ratios for valuation purposes, which could indicate a problem with management. Higher company valuations more reliably result from good performance and good decision making. Better financial ratios are a byproduct of a well-run business (Janssen, 2020).
20 Interesting cases include Dell going from public, to private, to public again (Welch, 2018) and Zoom's successful rise one year after its IPO (Wilhelm & Miller, 2020).
21 *Annual Meeting Handbook* (2018) provides a comprehensive review of planning and executing the many details of a shareholder meeting.

22 Read more about the board of directors and corporate governance in Chapter 2 Capitalism: Its Benefits and Discontents.
23 Document examples provided in Figure 5.1 and Box 5.1 are from www.sec.gov. From the website FAQ: *All government-created content on sec.gov and EDGAR public filing content are free to access and reuse. Information presented on* www.sec.gov *is considered public information and may be copied or further distributed by users of the web site.*
24 "Significant public concern" prohibits shareholder resolutions from addressing day-to-day business operations, such as personnel changes or employee benefits. Social, governance, and ethical concerns are more likely to meet the standard required by the SEC ("What is Shareholder Resolution," 2020).
25 See "Oil Majors" (2019) article for an account of how environmentally charged shareholder resolutions have fared in the energy industry.
26 In addition to outside directors, senior corporate executives also serve as directors.
27 See Chapter 4 The Art and Science of Financial Statements for a discussion of the Worldcom scandal.
28 Legal counsel prepares the accompanying cautionary language, which must be specific to the risks and uncertainties related to the forward-looking statement. Courts have denied safe harbor protection where risk disclosures are boilerplate, incomplete, or irrelevant (Hoang, 2020).
29 See Chapter 4 The Art and Science of Financial Statements for accounting-based measures used to measure a company's performance, such as net income and total assets. Ratios and margins are calculated using figures from financial statements.
30 The preliminary prospectus is often called a *red herring*. This means it's been filed with the SEC but is incomplete and subject to change prior to SEC approval for its release (Hargrave, 2019).
31 See the press release announcing Salesforce's acquisition of Tableau ("Salesforce Completes Acquisition," 2019). The word "merger" appears nowhere in the document.
32 A joint venture, or JV, is a business arrangement in which two or more parties pool their resources for a particular business activity. The JV is its own business entity, separate from the parties' other business interests (Hargrave, 2020b).
33 A reliable source for selecting similar companies is the company's most recent 10-K filing, which frequently includes a list of the company's key competitors. Companies used for value comparisons should be of similar size and in similar lines of business per NAICS or SIC industry classification codes (Allen, 2015).
34 With some financial maneuverings, enterprise value can be converted to a bid price per share of target company stock (see Allen, 2015).
35 A target company may demand a *control premium* be paid above the estimated value of the company for relinquishing control of operations to the buyer. Executives on either side of the deal may also expect additional compensation or incentives in an M&A deal. These are negotiable points, as long as parties realize that value creation from M&A depends on contributing to shareholder wealth, not disregarding it to favor the self-interests of buyers or sellers (Allen, 2015).

References

About the NYSE bell. (2020). Retrieved from www.nyse.com/bell/history.
Allen, J.W. (2015). *Essentials of financial practice: Valuation, analysis, and M&A.* AFS Voyager Press.
Amadeo, K. (2020, May 15). *How the stock market works.* Retrieved from www.thebalance.com/how-does-the-stock-market-work-3306244.
Annual meeting handbook: A step-by-step guide for planning and running your event. (2018). Retrieved from www.broadridge.com/_assets/pdf/broadridge-annual-meeting-handbook.pdf.
Annual meetings and proxy requirements. (2017, November 28). Retrieved from www.sec.gov/smallbusiness/goingpublic/annualmeetings.
Annual report vs. 10-K: What's the difference? (2019, August 5). Retrieved from www.investopedia.com/ask/answers/102714/what-are-differences-between-10k-report-and-firms-own-annual-report.asp.

Banton, C. (2019, September 10). *Equity financing*. Retrieved from www.investopedia.com/terms/e/equityfinancing.asp.

Banton, C. (2020, April 13). *An introduction to U.S. stock market indexes*. Retrieved from www.investopedia.com/insights/introduction-to-stock-market-indices/.

Beers, B. (2020, April 15). *Understand the what and why of stock splits*. Retrieved from www.investopedia.com/ask/answers/what-stock-split-why-do-stocks-split/.

Brown, M. (2019, October 9). *Budget vs forecast vs projection vs pro forma*. Retrieved from www.planprojections.com/projections/budget-vs-forecast-vs-projection-vs-pro-forma/.

Business Roundtable redefines the purpose of a corporation to promote "an economy that serves all Americans" (2019, August 19). Retrieved from www.businessroundtable.org/business-roundtable-redefines-the-purpose-of-a-corporation-to-promote-an-economy-that-serves-all-americans.

Cabi, H. (2019, September 19). *Quiet period: What it means for public and private companies*. Retrieved from https://gilmartinir.com/what-is-a-quiet-period/.

Chen, J. (2019a, April 29). *Proxy fight definition*. Retrieved from www.investopedia.com/terms/p/proxyfight.asp.

Chen, J. (2019b, May 28). *Special dividend*. Retrieved from www.investopedia.com/terms/s/specialdividend.asp.

Chen, J. (2020a, March 9). *Debt financing*. Retrieved from www.investopedia.com/terms/d/debtfinancing.asp.

Chen, J. (2020b, April 10). *Guide to fixed income*. Retrieved from www.investopedia.com/terms/f/fixedincome.asp.

Chen, J. (2020c, April 11). *Corporate bond*. Retrieved from www.investopedia.com/terms/c/corporatebond.asp.

DelRay, J. (2020, February 18). *Walmart paid Wall Street investors $12 billion last year to keep them happy. Amazon paid $0*. Retrieved from www.vox.com/recode/2020/2/18/21142153/amazon-walmart-dividend-stock-buyback-wall-street-investors.

Denning, S. (2017, July 17). *Making sense of shareholder value: "The world's dumbest idea."* Retrieved from www.forbes.com/sites/stevedenning/2017/07/17/making-sense-of-shareholder-value-the-worlds-dumbest-idea/#355cb6382a7e.

Describe capital investment decisions and how they are applied. (n.d.). Retrieved from https://opentextbc.ca/principlesofaccountingv2openstax/chapter/describe-capital-investment-decisions-and-how-they-are-applied/.

Evaluate the payback and accounting rate of return in capital investment decisions. (n.d.). Retrieved from https://opentextbc.ca/principlesofaccountingv2openstax/chapter/evaluate-the-payback-and-accounting-rate-of-return-in-capital-investment-decisions.

Ewing, J., & Mouawad, J. (2015, November 20). *VW cuts its R.&D. budget in face of costly emissions scandal*. Retrieved from www.nytimes.com/2015/11/21/business/international/volkswagen-emissions-scandal.html.

Explain the time value of money and calculate present and future values of lump sums and annuities. (n.d.). Retrieved from https://opentextbc.ca/principlesofaccountingv2openstax/chapter/explain-the-time-value-of-money-and-calculate-present-and-future-values-of-lump-sums-and-annuities/.

Fisher, S. (2019, December 31). *NASDAQ vs. NYSE: Key differences*. Retrieved from https://finance.yahoo.com/news/nasdaq-vs-nyse-key-differences-200641822.html.

Fried, C. (2018, March 28). *Bankruptcy: Chapter 7 vs. Chapter 13*. Retrieved from www.experian.com/blogs/ask-experian/bankruptcy-chapter-7-vs-chapter-13/.

Fuhrmann, R. (2019, June 25). *The road to creating an IPO*. Retrieved from www.investopedia.com/articles/investing/080613/road-creating-ipo.asp.

Ganti, A. (2019, October 8). *Dilution*. Retrieved from www.investopedia.com/terms/d/dilution.asp.

Ganti, A. (2020a, February 1). *Preferred stock*. Retrieved from www.investopedia.com/terms/p/preferredstock.asp.

Ganti, A. (2020b, March 5). *What is an angel investor?* Retrieved from www.investopedia.com/terms/a/angelinvestor.asp.

Gates, G., Ewing, J., Russell, K., & Watkins, D. (2017, March 16). *How Volkswagen's "defeat devices" worked*. Retrieved from www.nytimes.com/interactive/2015/business/international/vw-diesel-emissions-scandal-explained.html.

Gorton, D. (2016, August 31). *A guide on the risk-adjusted discount rate*. Retrieved from www.investopedia.com/articles/budgeting-savings/083116/guide-riskadjusted-discount-rate.asp.

Grant, M. (2020, March 10). *Startup*. Retrieved from www.investopedia.com/terms/s/startup.asp.

Guillory, S. (2020, November 12). *What to know about debt financing*. Retrieved from www.nav.com/blog/debt-financing-189629/.

Hargrave, M. (2019, July 11). *Red herring*. Retrieved from www.investopedia.com/terms/r/redherring.asp.

Hargrave, M. (2020a, April 20). *Weighted average cost of capital – WACC*. Retrieved from www.investopedia.com/terms/w/wacc.asp.

Hargrave, M. (2020b, July 7). *Joint venture (JV)*. Retrieved from www.investopedia.com/terms/j/jointventure.asp.

Hayes, A. (2019, June 25). *Internal Rate of Return – IRR*. Retrieved from www.investopedia.com/terms/i/irr.asp.

Hayes, A. (2020a, March 11). *Optimal capital structure*. Retrieved from www.investopedia.com/terms/o/optimal-capital-structure.asp.

Hayes, A. (2020b, July 1). *Mergers and acquisitions – M&A*. Retrieved from www.investopedia.com/terms/m/mergersandacquisitions.asp.

Heillbron, J., Verheul, J., & Quak, S. (2014). The origins and early diffusion of "shareholder value" in the United States. *Theory and Society, 43*, 10–22.

Hillstrom, L.C. (2020). *Value creation*. Retrieved from www.referenceforbusiness.com/management/Tr-Z/Value-Creation.html.

Hoang, C.C. (2020, April 14). *Some thoughts on preparing forward-looking statements during the COVID-19 pandemic*. Retrieved from https://governancecomplianceinsider.com/some-thoughts-on-preparing-forward-looking-statements-during-the-covid-10-pandemic/.

How and why do companies pay dividends? (2020, May 18). Retrieved from www.investopedia.com/articles/03/011703.asp.

How startup funding stages work. (2019, April 29). Retrieved from www.startups.com/library/expert-advice/startup-funding-stages.

How to read a 10-K. (2011, July 1). Retrieved from www.sec.gov/fast-answers/answersreada10khtm.html.

Janssen, C. (2020, March 19). *Stock buybacks: A breakdown*. Retrieved from www.investopedia.com/articles/02/041702.asp.

Josephson, A. (2019, July 24). *What is an institutional investor?* Retrieved from https://smartasset.com/investing/what-is-an-institutional-investor.

Kenton, W. (2019a, April 25). *Capital investment*. Retrieved from www.investopedia.com/terms/c/capital-investment.asp.

Kenton, W. (2019b, June 25). *Net Present Value (NPV)*. Retrieved from www.investopedia.com/terms/n/npv.asp.

Kenton, W. (2020a, February 4). *Sarbanes-Oxley (SOX) Act of 2002*. Retrieved from www.investopedia.com/terms/s/sarbanesoxleyact.asp.

Kenton, W. (2020b, February 27). *Security*. Retrieved from www.investopedia.com/terms/s/security.asp.

Kramer, L. (2020, March 23). *An overview of bull and bear markets*. Retrieved from www.investopedia.com/insights/digging-deeper-bull-and-bear-markets/.

Lane, B. (2019, September 9). *FTC moves to block $1.2 billion merger of Fidelity National and Stewart*. Retrieved from www.housingwire.com/articles/50114-ftc-moves-to-block-12-billion-merger-of-fidelity-national-and-stewart/.

Laskin, A.V. (2017). *The handbook of financial communication and investor relations*. Hoboken, NJ: John Wiley & Sons.

Loop, P., Bromilow, C., & Malone, L. (2018, February 1). *The changing face of shareholder activism*. Retrieved from https://corpgov.law.harvard.edu/2018/02/01/the-changing-face-of-shareholder-activism/.

Majaski, C. (2019, July 11). *Private vs. public company: What's the difference?* Retrieved from www.investopedia.com/ask/answers/difference-between-publicly-and-privately-held-companies/.

Marks, H. (2018, December 19). *What is equity crowdfunding?* Retrieved from www.forbes.com/sites/howardmarks/2018/12/19/what-is-equity-crowdfunding/#31d196d73b5d.

Maverick, J.B. (2019, April 19). *Equity financing vs. debt financing: What's the difference?* Retrieved from www.investopedia.com/ask/answers/042215/what-are-benefits-company-using-equity-financing-vs-debt-financing.asp.

Maverick, J.B. (2020, April 17). *Class A shares vs. Class B shares: What's the difference?* Retrieved from www.investopedia.com/ask/answers/062215/what-difference-between-class-shares-and-other-common-shares-companys-stock.asp.

McClure, B. (2020, February 8). *Can a company have too much cash?* Retrieved from www.investopedia.com/articles/fundamental/03/062503.asp.

McDonald, C. (2018, October 1). *Costs of SOX compliance.* Retrieved from www.rmmagazine.com/2018/10/01/costs-of-sox-compliance/.

Merger review. (n.d.). Retrieved from www.ftc.gov/news-events/media-resources/mergers-and-competition/merger-review.

Merritt, C. (2018, April 20). *How to evaluate two projects by evaluating the Net Present Value.* Retrieved from https://yourbusiness.azcentral.com/evaluate-two-projects-evaluating-net-present-value-23323.html.

Murphy, A. (2019, December 17). *America's largest private companies 2019.* Retrieved from www.forbes.com/sites/andreamurphy/2019/12/17/americas-largest-private-companies-2019/#1b1384155261.

Murphy, C.B. (2019a, April 14). *Bottom-line vs. top-line growth: What's the difference?* Retrieved from www.investopedia.com/ask/answers/difference-between-bottom-line-and-top-line-growth/.

Murphy, C.B. (2019b, April 22). *Roadshow.* Retrieved from www.investopedia.com/terms/r/roadshow.asp.

Net Present Value (NPV) calculator. (2020). Retrieved from www.calculatestuff.com/financial/npv-calculator.

Occidental ends proxy fight with activist investor Carl Icahn. (2020, March 25). Retrieved from www.hartenergy.com/news/occidental-ends-proxy-fight-activist-investor-carl-icahn-186699.

Oil majors face shareholder resolutions on climate change. (2019, May 30). Retrieved from www.economist.com/business/2019/05/30/oil-majors-face-shareholder-resolutions-on-climate-change.

Palmer, B. (2019, June 25). *Institutional vs. retail investors: What's the difference?* Retrieved from www.investopedia.com/ask/answers/06/institutionalinvestor.asp.

Paniello, A. (n.d.). *How much cash should a business have on hand.* Retrieved from https://capitalwithstrategy.com/how-much-cash-should-a-business-have-on-hand/.

Patel, N. (2016, January 16). *90% of startups fail: Here's what you need to know about the 10%.* Retrieved from www.forbes.com/sites/neilpatel/2015/01/16/90-of-startups-will-fail-heres-what-you-need-to-know-about-the-10/#508bf47a6679.

Patel, N. (2020). *How to pitch an idea to investors with total confidence.* Retrieved from https://neilpatel.com/blog/pitch-to-investors/.

Private equity vs. venture capital: What's the difference? (2020, March 19). Retrieved from www.investopedia.com/ask/answers/020415/what-difference-between-private-equity-and-venture-capital.asp.

Private vs. public company. (2020). Retrieved from https://corporatefinanceinstitute.com/resources/knowledge/finance/private-vs-public-company/.

Public companies. (n.d.) Retrieved from www.investor.gov/introduction-investing/investing-basics/how-stock-markets-work/public-companies.

Quarterly number of business starts in the United States from Q1 2010 to Q3 2019. (2020). Retrieved from www.statista.com/statistics/771207/quarterly-business-starts-us/.

Rothacker, R. (2014, August 16). *The deal that cost Bank of America $50 billion – and counting.* Retrieved from www.charlotteobserver.com/news/business/banking/article9151889.html.

Ross, S. (2020, March 20). *Small cap stocks vs. large cap stocks: What's the difference?* Retrieved from www.investopedia.com/articles/markets/022316/small-cap-vs-mid-cap-vs-large-cap-stocks-2016.asp.

Salesforce. (2020). Retrieved from www.crunchbase.com/organization/salesforce#section-overview.

Salesforce completes acquisition of Tableau. (2019, August 1). Retrieved from www.tableau.com/about/press-releases/2019/salesforce-completes-acquisition-tableau.

Segal, T. (2020a, February 4). *Clayton Antitrust Act.* Retrieved from www.investopedia.com/terms/c/clayton-antitrust-act.asp.

Segal, T. (2020b, May 15). *Corporate bankruptcy: An overview.* Retrieved from www.investopedia.com/articles/01/120501.asp.

Seth, S. (2020, March 8). *Top reasons why M&A deals fail.* Retrieved from www.investopedia.com/articles/investing/111014/top-reasons-why-ma-deals-fail.asp.

Shivdas, S. (2019, December 4). *CBS, Viacom complete merger in a win for Shari Redstone.* Retrieved from www.reuters.com/article/us-viacom-m-a-cbs/cbs-viacom-complete-merger-in-a-win-for-shari-redstone-idUSKBN1Y82ZF.

Sraders, A. (2019, May 8). *How to read stocks: Charts, basics and what to look for.* Retrieved from www.thestreet.com/how-to/read-stocks-14948162.

Tarver, E. (2020, March 26). *Investor relations (IR).* Retrieved from www.investopedia.com/terms/i/investorrelations.asp.

Thangavelu, P. (2020, July 4). *A day in the life of an equity research analyst.* Retrieved from www.investopedia.com/articles/personal-finance/082815/day-life-equity-research-analyst.asp.

Use discounted cash flow models to make capital investment decisions. (n.d.) Retrieved from https://opentextbc.ca/principlesofaccountingv2openstax/chapter/use-discounted-cash-flow-models-to-make-capital-investment-decisions./

Vance, J. (2020, March 2). *Organic vs. inorganic growth – and becoming the acquisition target.* Retrieved from www.preferredcfo.com/organic-vs-inorganic-growth/.

Welch, C. (2018, December 28). *Dell returns to public stock market after years as private company.* Retrieved from www.theverge.com/2018/12/28/18159305/dell-stock-market-return-public-nyse.

The Wendy's story. (2020). Retrieved from www.wendys.com/wendys-story.

What are financial ratios? (2020). Retrieved from https://corporatefinanceinstitute.com/resources/knowledge/finance/financial-ratios/.

What is corporate finance? (2020). Retrieved from https://corporatefinanceinstitute.com/resources/knowledge/finance/corporate-finance-industry/.

What is the difference between a bond vs. note payable? (2016, January 21). Retrieved from www.fool.com/knowledge-center/bond-vs-note-payable.aspx.

What is a hostile takeover? (2020). Retrieved from https://corporatefinanceinstitute.com/resources/knowledge/deals/hostile-takeover/.

What is organic growth? (2020). Retrieved from https://corporatefinanceinstitute.com/resources/knowledge/strategy/organic-growth/.

What is a proxy fight? (2020). Retrieved from https://corporatefinanceinstitute.com/resources/knowledge/finance/proxy-fight/.

What is shareholder resolution? (2020). Retrieved from www.upcounsel.com/shareholder-resolution.

When must a company announce earnings? (2020, June 8). Retrieved from www.investopedia.com/ask/answers/04/050604.asp.

Why the Wendy's company (NASDAQ:WEN) looks like a quality company. (2020, June 27). Retrieved from https://finance.yahoo.com/news/why-wendys-company-nasdaq-wen-133958770.html.

Wilhelm, A., & Miller, R. (2020, March 24). *Looking back at Zoom's ascent a year after it filed to go public.* Retrieved from https://techcrunch.com/2020/03/24/looking-back-at-zooms-ascent-a-year-after-it-filed-to-go-public/.

Woodruff, J. (2019, January 25). *Advantages and disadvantages of Net Present Value in project selection.* Retrieved from https://smallbusiness.chron.com/advantages-disadvantages-net-present-value-project-selection-54753.html.

Chapter 6

Marketing Envy and Other Observations

Ah, marketing. Why am I envious? Because unlike those in corporate communications, or public affairs, or public relations (or any functional variant thereof), marketing professionals can readily demonstrate how their work contributes to a company's profitability. As we covered in Chapters 4 and 5, increasing sales contributes to higher profits. And that's what marketers do. Those of us on the public affairs side of the business have a more difficult time showing how our work with government officials, media, investors, communities, activists, employees, and even customers makes a company more profitable. The difference is starkly reflected in our respective budgets. But instead of harping on why marketing typically gets a (much) bigger budget than we do, let's dig into some key marketing principles that add to our business acumen.

Marketing Beyond the Customer

What is marketing? What may seem like too basic of a question to begin our discussion of marketing really isn't. I always thought of marketing as product sales and customer promotions, period. But I noticed a stark difference in how marketing was taught to me as an undergraduate versus how it was taught to me many years later as an MBA student. My more recent education in marketing revealed a practice that looks far beyond just the customer to create value for a business. Admittedly, I felt a bit defensive hearing this, thinking stakeholders beyond customers is "our" territory in public affairs. Why, I thought, are marketers concerned with anyone other than customers? I've since come to understand marketing's broader perspective, making it even more important that we understand – and work with – marketing to increase a company's value.

Apparently, I'm not alone in observing a shift in how marketing is defined. Marketing professors Sheth and Uslay (2007) describe how the word "exchange" was central to the American Marketing Association's (AMA) 1983 definition of marketing. Back then, the field focused on creating exchanges to help individuals and organizations meet their goals. These *quid pro quo* exchanges translated into "this for that," or a certain price for a certain good. The AMA revisits its definition of marketing every three years ("Definitions," 2020). Here is its most recent version:

DOI: 10.4324/9781003000600-7

Marketing is the activity, set of institutions, and processes for creating, communicating, delivering, and exchanging offerings that have value for customers, clients, partners, and society at large.

("Definitions," 2020, para. 2)

The idea of creating value permeates the marketing function and takes a system-wide, rather than an exchange or transaction, perspective. Beyond the organization, marketing aims to bring value to society by increasing product choices, economic growth, competition, and new product development. That's a much broader scope than quid pro quo exchanges between a business and its customers. This wider approach to marketing is reminiscent of the stakeholder model discussed in Chapter 2, in which management's challenge is to balance the interests of multiple stakeholders, not just shareholders or customers. Public affairs is in that balancing act, too, so include marketing among the functions in your internal network we discussed in Chapter 1.

Marketing is headed by the *Chief Marketing Officer*, or *CMO*. Increasingly, the CMO is expected to not only lead branding and marketing activities, but also business growth and highly connected *customer experiences* (*CXs*) (Brenner, 2019; see Sidebar 6.1: Market Share and Market Growth Strategies). Marketing is moving away from products and traditional marketing campaigns toward customer engagement and continuous storytelling. Consumer research and online tracking of consumer behaviors and social media posts are prevalent in the practice. Sound familiar to your own work? If you're not already collaborating with your marketing colleagues, you should be.

Sidebar 6.1 Market Share and Market Growth Strategies

("How to Calculate," 2020; Izquierdo, 2020)

Marketing is central to effective growth strategies, especially when revenue growth is a priority. Here are four ways companies can expand their market reach.

Market Development
Taking existing products to a new market, such as a new geography, customer base, or distribution channel.

Diversification
Creating new products for new markets. Carries the greatest risk of failure.

Market Penetration
Increasing market share in an existing market. Methods include lowering prices or increasing brand awareness.

Product Development
Creating new products for existing markets.

Market share is the company's share of sales in an entire market. If a market has $200 million in annual sales, and a company has $20 million in annual sales, that company has a 10% share of the market. Companies with large market shares and low cost structures are most likely to be price leaders as well, leaving competitors to follow their pricing strategy.

The Business of Branding

Much of marketing's work is done through brands, which the AMA defines as "a name, term, design, symbol or any other feature that identifies one seller's good or service as distinct from those of other sellers" ("Definitions," 2020, para. 4). From an accounting perspective, brands are intangible assets designed to create economic benefits and business value. In order to maintain their value, however, brands must be well managed, protected, and differentiated. Legal costs associated with protecting a brand can range from thousands to millions of dollars to prevent brands from being used by, or confused with, that of competing firms.

Common branding terms are often used interchangeably, and incorrectly. Let's make sure you have a solid grasp of branding terminology (Sharma, 2015):

- *Brand identity* relates to the logos, visuals, and text associated with a brand. This is the realm of the "logo cops" in your company who will insist you adhere to specific clear space rules around the use of your logo, match colors precisely, and use only company-approved marks and vendors. Be patient with these people – their rules may be frustrating, but they're critically important to protecting how your brand is presented in every venue it appears.
- *Brand image* is the image of your brand that people develop in their minds. Ultimately, it's up to them what they think of your brand. Your company is much more than your logo, and many aspects of your brand are outside of your control (see also Yu, 2018). Brands are co-created based on how customers and stakeholders experience brands. A luxury goods maker like Rolex would have a difficult time making a $15 plastic-band watch, even if there were a market for it. Customers who paid thousands for their Rolex would scoff at the dilution of the Rolex brand image.
- *Brand positioning* is how a product is presented in the market and targeted to a particular type of customer. Rugged deodorants are targeted at active men who want to maintain their physical appeal, and comfortable heels are aimed at professional women who are on the go before and after work hours. *Market segmentation* enables companies to identify and reach various categories of consumers who have different perceptions of the value delivered by certain products and services (Tarver, 2020).
- *Brand personality* conveys certain emotional or personal qualities of a brand, much like a human being. Colors, styling, and related verbiage convey whether the brand is youthful, expensive, fun, or any number of other traits normally associated with people.
- *Brand equity* is the brand's value, including both tangible and intangible elements. Brands that are unique, familiar, relevant, high-quality, and popular will render higher market values in M&A deals and IPOs discussed in Chapter 5 (see also Yu, 2018).
- *Brand experience* is the interaction customers have purchasing and using your brand. Apple, Starbucks, and Louis Vuitton ensure the customer's purchasing experience is just as notable as using their products on a daily basis. Breakfast cereal and candy bar manufacturers, on the other hand, make their purchases widely available, easily accessible on any budget, and part of daily life.
- *Brand differentiation* is how the brand sets itself apart from its competitors. Shopping at Wal-Mart is a different experience from shopping at Target. Each brand offers distinct benefits, aesthetics, and psychological appeal to customers by design.

- *Brand communication* relates to how the brand is advertised, promoted, and represented in a variety of communication channels. To be effective, communication must align with other brand attributes.
- *Brand gap* is an element of branding to be avoided. It's the difference between what the brand promises and what it actually delivers. Customers are vocal about these disconnects. No amount of brand communication can overcome a bad product.
- *Brand extension* is just that – expanding a brand beyond its original base. An athleisure company may branch out and offer vitamins and other supplements to complement its approach to a healthy lifestyle. Believe it or not, Amazon began as an online bookseller in 1995 (Easter & Dave, 2017).
- *Corporate vs. product branding* is the difference between promoting attributes of a company and promoting specific products made by that company (LaMarco, 2019). Corporate branding is generally directed toward current and potential shareholders, governments, and consumers. Product branding, however, is all about reaching customers and encouraging a purchase. Whereas corporate brand messages will differ from product brand messages, they need to complement each other, or else confusion arises among consumers. Whether consciously or subconsciously, inconsistent brand messaging diminishes customer trust.

The value-generating power of brands flows in large part from their psychological underpinnings (Pathare, 2020; "What is Emotional," 2020). Marketing principles tell us that humans buy on emotion but justify their purchases with logic. Consumers who feel an emotional connection to a brand view that brand as an extension of themselves. And they're more likely to be loyal customers as long as that emotional bond is intact. What solidifies this connection, and keeps customers coming back for more, you ask? Colors (yes, colors[1]), customer experience, social influence/identity (online and offline), transparency, keeping promises, and visual storytelling contribute to *emotional branding*. *Switching costs* play a role in customers sticking with a brand, too (Grant, 2019). If the cost of switching brands is high, customers are likely not to switch. Companies impart switching costs through mechanisms like early cancellation fees as well as psychological costs of no longer being associated with the brand community. Emotional brands contribute to a customer's perceived quality of life, especially when the company does a deep data dive to understand their customer base and engages with customers accordingly.[2] Strong emotional ties to a brand can command premium pricing, too.

Seven Ps of Marketing

The four Ps of marketing I learned as an undergraduate has grown to five Ps, and I've recently encountered seven words beginning with the letter P that describe the framework of marketing practice. I've opted to provide all seven Ps for you here (Tracy, 2004).

- *Product* is having the right product, for the right customer, at the right time. Product preferences obviously change over time, so staying on top of how and why customers are using your product – or not – is essential for success. No product, no business.

- *Price* must reflect current economic conditions[3] and is a tradeoff calculus for the business. If price must be lowered, is the product still profitable enough to warrant production? Or, are limited resources best applied elsewhere? If there's an opportunity to raise price, how many customers can you expect and afford to lose? Pricing is a sophisticated and complex function, particularly for large firms in rapidly changing pricing environments, like airlines.
- *Promotion* is how the business communicates its products (and how to get them) to customers. Promotional strategies stale quickly. What works well to drive sales in the first quarter can have little or no impact in the second quarter. New offerings, strategies, and advertising approaches are constantly needed.
- *Place* is where you're selling your product, also known as *distribution channels*. Are you in a retail space? Direct sales? Trade shows? Mail order? Catalogs? Websites? Place can contribute to or detract from how the customer experiences interacting with your product.
- *Packaging* has become increasingly innovative and part of brand strategy. It's extraordinary how much design thinking goes into packaging, particularly for luxury brands. Recyclable or biodegradable packaging is important to some brands, not so much for others. Interestingly, packaging also relates to a customer's surroundings in your place of business. What's their experience at your sales counter, in your waiting room, or on your website? Each element of packaging is part of your brand.
- *Positioning* is a brand term we covered earlier about going after a particular type of customer, such as working mothers, college students, or newly retired professionals. Brand image comes into play with positioning. That is, once you reach and retain your ideal customer, what thoughts or images do you want foremost in their mind when they think of your brand? How do they describe your products to others? How would you *like* them to describe your products?
- *People* is as important as product. And people includes every individual who has contact with your customers, from how emails are answered to how returns are handled, and every point in between. The most recognizable and valuable brands ensure their customer-facing people are aligned with their brand strategy.[4] If not, they don't hire them.

Types of Marketing

Marketing puts these seven Ps to work in a variety of ways. The practice is continuously evolving to adapt to new distribution channels, technology, and communication platforms. See Table 6.1: A Seriously Long List of Types of Marketing for just how many ways marketing can help companies drive revenue growth.

Key Marketing Concepts

Several key principles drive marketing practice. We'll begin by sorting the differences between *business-to-business* (B2B) and *business-to-consumer* (B2C) marketing and then look at the *types of goods* a firm can offer, perceptions of *value*, the *sales funnel*, *lifecycles*, and *commodities*. Understand these, and you'll have a working vocabulary to enrich and complement your communication practice.

Table 6.1 A Seriously Long List of Types of Marketing

Interested in marketing? Here's a list of the field's many varieties, some of which are overlapping. Many can be used together to increase revenues.

Account-based marketing (ABM) treats individual prospects and customers as though they are their own market with highly personalized events and promotions.	**Influencer marketing** uses recognized experts in a field who know a particular audience and can be instrumental in marketing to that audience.
Acquisition marketing focuses on lead generation provided through inbound, content, social media, and search engine marketing to convert prospects into customers.	**Informative marketing** focuses more on facts than emotions in explaining how a product solves a problem.
Affiliate marketing involves an online retailer paying a website owner, known as an affiliate, a commission for promoting its product and generating a sale.	**Interactive marketing** allows audiences to interact with infographics, videos, or other visuals within the sponsor's content.
Brand marketing is creating an emotional connection with customers through creativity, humor, inspiration, and storytelling.	**Multicultural marketing** is designing campaigns specifically for target audiences of particular ethnicities and cultures.
Buzz marketing is a viral strategy that uses creative content or events to generate word-of-mouth buzz for a product. Social listening software can track audience response.	**Native marketing** is paying a reputable publisher to collaborate and post a sponsored article that looks like the publisher's regular content.
Campus marketing is hiring college students as ambassadors to market a brand to other college students.	**Neuromarketing** gauges physiological and emotional reactions to interacting with a product.
Cause marketing is dedicating some portion of gross revenues to a cause the business deems worthwhile.	**Outbound marketing** includes cold calling, email blasts, and TV ads designed to reach as many customers as possible without regard for who on the receiving end may actually need the product.
Content marketing is a key element of inbound and digital marketing that involves creating, publishing, and distributing helpful content to a target audience.	**Partner marketing** is recruiting new business partners to sell a company's product to their customers.
Contextual marketing targets online users with ads based on their browsing behavior.	**Personalized marketing** is matching tactics with a deep understanding of buyer persona and what matters to them.
Controversial marketing takes the risk of stating a bold claim about a sensitive social issue in hopes of attracting customers who agree with the company's stance.	**Persuasive marketing** focuses more on emotions than facts to drive action.
Conversational marketing enables the ability to have one-on-one conversations where, how, and when customers want.	**Product marketing** is bringing a product to market and generating demand for that product using many of the tactics described in this table.
Customer marketing focuses on retaining and delighting customers so they turn into advocates for the brand.	**Proximity marketing** is using Bluetooth Beacons to alert smartphone users that they are in close proximity to a retail outlet.
Digital marketing is using search engines, social media, email, blogs, and other web-based tools to connect with current and prospective customers.	**Relationship marketing** focuses on deepening customer relationships to create long-term brand advocates and referrals.
Email marketing sends personalized messages to a subscriber base. Customer relationship management (CRM) and related software can track the effectiveness of emails.	**Search engine marketing**, or SEM, includes search engine optimization (SEO) and pay-per-click (PPC) advertising used to ensure a product is visible on search engine results pages (SERPs).

Table 6.1 Cont.

Event marketing is a product-based event, either in-person or online, that may include a purchase pitch.	**Social media marketing** is creating and posting content on social media platforms and tailoring content for audiences who use those platforms.
Experiential marketing is an in-person immersive experience with a product that goes beyond event marketing to have a lasting impact on potential customers.	**Stealth marketing** is using actors, influencers, fake viral videos, and/or movie product placements as marketing tactics to audiences unaware of their marketing intent.
Field marketing is designing and sharing case studies, product overviews, and competitor comparisons to help close a deal.	**Traditional marketing** refers to outbound tactics using channels that pre-date the Internet, like print, television ads, and billboards.
Global marketing is localizing a brand to reflect community preferences in other countries.	**User-generated marketing** is requesting input or sponsoring contests on social media to get new product ideas.
Guerilla marketing uses high-traffic physical locations to reach audiences in creative ways and perhaps without permission.	**Video marketing** is using video postings on websites, YouTube, or social media to boost awareness and attract customers.
Inbound marketing is a strategy for attracting or *pulling* prospective customers with digital content that provides an opening for further engagement.	**Voice marketing** is optimizing websites for voice search and using smart speakers like Amazon Alexa to provide relevant information to consumers.
	**Word-of-mouth marketing** focuses on delivering outstanding customer service to drive customer recommendations.

(Chi, 2020)

B2B vs. B2C

Products are sold to people, whether the receiving end of the products is a business or a consumer (Lake, 2019). B2B, or business-to-business marketing, is when one business, like an office supply store, promotes and sells its products to another business, like a gym, or a dentist office, or a steel pipe manufacturer. Business customers want a streamlined, hassle-free, low-cost solution for buying paper to fill their copy machines, filing cabinets for their records, and chairs for their employees and clients. Recall from Chapters 4 and 5 the importance of expense reduction. The only way to increase profits is to increase revenues or reduce expenses. Why, then, would businesses pay more for office supplies than necessary?

Businesses make purchases based on logic (Lake, 2019). B2B marketing strategies are time consuming because a successful sale depends on developing multiple relationships on the client side to reach decision makers. The bigger the business, the more layers of approval required to place an order (yes, even for office supplies), and the more intense the competition for every office supplier to get that company's account. B2B marketers focus on how their products and services save time and money and solve a company's problems. Ultimately, B2B marketers need to demonstrate how they can make a business more profitable. And won't the decision maker on the company side look good for making that happen? You bet.

Let's now switch to the B2C, or business-to-consumer, perspective of marketing. Consumers, as we've discussed, base purchases more on emotion than logic (Lake, 2019). So, too, must marketing strategies for consumers accommodate this difference. Consumer marketing requires focusing on product and service benefits. Because consumers can make purchases in minutes (much faster than a business client), messages regarding benefits or problems solved must be direct and to the point. Whereas businesses may favor in-depth promotions from their suppliers, customers aren't nearly as patient. For B2C, marketers must still offer solutions to customer problems but with simple messages and emotional appeals.

Types of Goods

Normal goods experience an increase in demand when consumer wages rise and a drop in demand when wages fall (Kenton, 2019). Also known as *necessary goods*, normal goods include food staples, clothing, and household appliances. *Inferior goods* are just the opposite. As incomes rise, demand for inferior goods, like public transportation, declines. As people are able to afford cars, they switch from taking the bus to having a car of their own. Inferior doesn't imply a lack of quality. Rather, it indicates less preference for a good as one's personal wealth increases. *Luxury goods* are what the name implies – vacations, sports cars, fine dining, high-end consumer goods, gym memberships, and so on. As incomes rise, consumers spend a larger proportion of their income on luxury goods but about the same (or less) proportion on normal and inferior goods. There is, however, an important catch to classifying goods: Luxury is in the eye of the beholder. Something considered a luxury good for one person could be regarded as a normal or even inferior good by another.

Perceptions of Value

You're likely familiar with the term *value proposition*. A value proposition, also known as a *brand promise*, succinctly describes the value a company promises to deliver to customers (Twin, 2020). It's shared with customers in a variety of venues. The best value propositions are customer-centered and differentiate a product from its competitors. Uber's "the smartest way to get around" and Slack's "be more productive at work with less effort" are good examples (Shewan, 2020). Value propositions are designed for external use. Getting to a brand promise by first specifying a company's vision, core values, and core purpose[5] is important for employees and management to remember why the company does what it does and why it's worthwhile to get out of bed for work each morning. That said, the fact remains that actual value is in the mind of consumers, also known as *perceived value* – not in the verbiage of a value proposition.

Perceived value is the customer's evaluation of the merits, benefits, and problem-solving ability of a product or service (Kopp, 2020). Marketers work to influence perceived value, which is measured by the maximum price consumers are willing to pay. Emotions contribute to a consumer's *willingness to pay* (WTP) and so does design, time/effort/money savings, convenience, and prestige. Whether products are marketed as smart bargains or luxury goods, WTP is the best indicator of perceived value. Willingness to pay is generally calculated as a narrow price range based on consumer and market research.[6] The ultimate test of WTP is to charge a price, watch what happens, and then reevaluate and adjust pricing strategy as market conditions dictate.

Figure 6.1 The Sales Funnel

The Sales Funnel

If customer relationships, connectivity, and engagement are so important in marketing, it's vital to deeply understand the process a consumer goes through to get to a product or service purchase ("What is a Sales Funnel," 2020; see Figure 6.1: The Sales Funnel). This process is referred to as the *sales funnel*, also known as the *buyer's journey*. The funnel begins with awareness – when a company first catches a prospective customer's attention. It could be someone walking by a retail space and deciding to walk in, or a social media post, or a recommendation from a friend, that leads them to learn more. Then comes research when consumers are comparison shopping, looking at reviews, and searching for deals. At the decision stage, the customer is ready to buy. As we know, emotions play an important role in the purchase decision. In the last stage of the sales funnel – action – the customer completes the transaction. Action is required on the seller's part, too, to cultivate and retain a customer relationship for the long term. The best marketers have a thorough understanding of how their prospective customers move through the funnel, including how they use the company's website and click on (or ignore) ads. Good marketers also know which parts of the funnel experience contribute to their *conversion rate*, that is, the number of prospects who actually become customers.

Life Cycle: Products, Businesses, and Markets

Like many things in life, products, businesses, and markets have a beginning, a middle, and an end. The "end" of a product, business, or market can mean finality, but it can also trigger an innovative start of something new.[7] Relevant to our marketing discussion is the *product life cycle*. Conveniently, the same idea of a product going through various phases in its lifetime also applies to businesses and markets. It's important for businesses to know where products are in this life cycle. Let's look at how marketing strategies differ for each life cycle phase ("The Product Life Cycle," 2010; see Figure 6.2: Product Life Cycle).

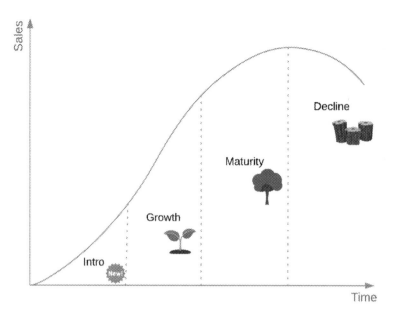

Figure 6.2 The Product Life Cycle

- In the ***introduction stage***, firms focus on building awareness and a market for a product. Pricing may be low to build market share. Distribution is limited. Promotion focuses on educating potential customers about the product.
- In the ***growth stage***, building market share is critical and focuses on building brand preference for the product. Product quality remains important, and new features may be added. Pricing remains steady as demand increases. Distribution channels are added. Promotion expands to a broader audience likely to adopt the product.
- In the ***maturity stage***, the strong growth in sales begins to peak or plateau, and even decline. Competition increases after other firms jump with similar products into a proven market. Defending market share while maximizing profit becomes a priority. New features are added to help further differentiate the product. Pricing will likely decrease because of increased competition. Distribution broadens to attract new users. Promotion focuses on differentiation.
- In the ***decline stage***, the firm can redesign, rejuvenate, or repurpose the product; continue offering it to loyal customers as a niche market; or discontinue the product by liquidating inventory or selling it to another firm willing to continue the product.

Cash Cows and Other Product Categories

Related to the product life cycle are four product categories developed in 1968 by Boston Consulting Group (BCG) and presented in the Growth-Share Matrix ("What is the Growth," 2020; see Figure 6.3: The BCG Growth-Share Matrix). This juxtaposition of market growth and relative market share has (really) stood the test of time helping companies decide if they should keep, sell, or invest more in certain lines of business. As with the product life cycle, marketing strategies differ for each product type in the Growth-Share Matrix. Let's dive into its thought-provoking elements.

The x-axis of the matrix represents relative market share, and the y-axis represents the rate of market growth. Inside, the area is divided into quadrants, each representing a product category ("What is the Growth," 2020):

- *Pets*, originally referred to as Dogs, are in the lower right quadrant. No offense to canine lovers, but dogs represent products that have low relative market share and low market growth. This is not a good combination for profitability or generating cash. Dogs, therefore, should be significantly repositioned, sold (i.e. divested), or liquidated. If left unattended, dogs can turn into cash traps and tie up resources that are better invested elsewhere.
- *Question marks* are in the upper right quadrant. These are somewhat mysterious products because they are in a high-growth market, yet the company has only a small relative market share. Question marks warrant further analysis to determine whether changes in strategy and/or increased investment could transform Question Marks into Stars.
- *Stars* are in the upper left quadrant. They're called stars for a reason – they are in a high growth market, and the company enjoys a sizable share of that market. Stars are superior candidates for further investment. If stars can maintain market leadership, they eventually become cash cows.
- *Cash cows* are in the lower left quadrant. These are products in the mature stage of their life cycle. Market growth has slowed considerably, but the company still holds a large relative market share. They're called cows because companies "milk" them for as long as they can, all the way to the bank. Cash flows from cash cows are highly predictable and should be reinvested in stars.

Cost-benefit analysis applies throughout the BCG Growth-Share Matrix. Companies must ensure additional product investment, or even divestiture, results in benefits (i.e., value creation) exceeding their costs.

Figure 6.3 The BCG Growth-Share Matrix

Adapted from The BCG Portfolio Matrix from the Product Portfolio Matrix, ©1970, Boston Consulting Group (BCG)

Competing on Something Other Than Price

Commodity is a bad word in marketing. Commodity products are fungible, that is, they are interchangeable. Think about selling sand, concrete, sugar, or soybeans. Just as importantly, think about needing to buy these fungible products. Why would you pay anything higher than the absolute lowest price you could find? Sand is sand, right?

Now think about marketing commodities. How do you convince a customer that your 5-pound bag of sugar is worth $1 more than the 5-pound bag of sugar next to it on the store shelf? If you cannot offer the lowest price for a commodity, you must differentiate it in another way, such as quality, design, packaging, benefits, or other characteristics (Hill, McGrath, & Dayal 1998; Kimmons, 2019). In other words, you differentiate your otherwise fungible product with branding.

If a company can only compete on price, it's going to face some tough challenges. The constant lowering of prices (aka *price wars*) eventually has a detrimental effect on all competitors (Kimmons, 2019). Cutting expenses is one thing. The more a company can lower its cost of goods sold (COGS),[8] the more of its revenues it can retain while still passing savings on to customers via lower prices. But if a firm is constantly cutting price, revenues are constantly declining, too. At some point, neither increased sales volume nor reduced expenses can make up for lost revenues. Competing on price puts the firm in a defensive position. It's hard to be strategic when your pricing is at the whim of your market.

To be clear, there are hundreds of commodity markets (e.g., agricultural products) upon which world economies depend. But our focus here is on consumer products, where branding is key to differentiating products like coffee (McDonald's vs. Starbucks), gasoline (regular vs. premium), and flour (store brand vs. King Arthur). Truth be told, products like coffee, gasoline, and flour are interchangeable until you differentiate them based on branding characteristics like sourcing (free and fair trade), additives (for cleaner engines), and performance (higher-rising cakes). Those points of differentiation allow for premium pricing. Remember the emotional drivers of branding? You're not alone in paying more because of them. Reason tells me that the cheaper generic flour is going to perform just as well as the King Arthur brand, but I'm not risking embarrassment by serving mediocre holiday cakes to my family and friends. Emotion wins the day and takes a bit more out of my wallet, too.

ROI and Other Nifty Marketing Metrics

After getting through Chapters 4 and 5, you may be wondering how we got this far into Chapter 6 without any number crunching. Now that we've covered some guiding principles in marketing, it's time to turn to a few numbers to demonstrate just how effectively marketing can quantify its value contribution to management. *ROI*, or *return on investment*, is the overarching metric for marketing. Before we uncover the variety of ways marketing can show how it converts its spending into revenues, let's look at the ROI formula (Cronstedt, 2018):

$$ROI = (Revenue - Investment)/Investment$$

ROI is not just for marketing. Far from it. It's one of the most popular formulas available for measuring how an investment in stocks, property, equipment, or even personnel pays off in the revenues it brings in. If you spent $1,000 on a company's shares and then later sold those shares for $1,500, your ROI is ($1,500-$1,000)/$1,000 = 0.50, or 50%. For every dollar you invested, you got your dollar plus another 50 cents back in return. Not bad, right? If you bought a piece of land for $250,000 and later sold it for $300,000, your ROI is 0.20, or a 20% return on your initial investment. You've got an extra $50,000 in the bank.

ROI is a handy calculation you can use to compare the returns from different investments, but some caveats are in order (Chen, 2020). First, the ROI formula doesn't account for the time span between investment and return. If I told you the property ROI was realized in six months, and the company shares ROI was realized in ten years, which investment would you be more excited about?[9] ROI, ideally, should be a positive value. If it's negative, the investment lost money. But again, timing matters – sometimes it's better to "cut and run" before losses get too steep. Sometimes, however, a product line or other investment is exited too quickly, just before significant returns kick in. No one has a crystal ball in business.

Applying ROI to marketing requires an in-depth accounting of spend, customer experiences, channels, and sales (Cronstedt, 2018). If you're going to brag on your ROI, you need to make sure you have the right numbers in the equation that apply only to a particular investment, project, etc. It's misleading to diminish the spend or overstate the returns. How much, precisely, did you spend and how much, precisely, did that spend deliver in revenues? Tracking these figures is also important so you're not throwing good money after bad. If you're buying the wrong ads, for example, a negative ROI will tell you it's time to call it quits and shift your ad dollars elsewhere. A high ROI will encourage you to invest more in what's working well.

Marketing metrics quantify marketing results (Ellering, 2020). Marketers can set *Key Performance Indicators*, known as KPIs, using any number of metrics to track and report their contribution to sales revenue and other indicators of marketing outcomes. Tables 6.2–6.7 list marketing metrics by category: General Marketing Metrics, Website and Blogging Metrics, SEO Metrics, Social Media Marketing Metrics, Email Marketing Metrics, and Pay-Per-Click Metrics.

Table 6.2 General Marketing Metrics

Brand Awareness measures an audience's level of familiarity with a brand or product.	**Incremental Sales** tracks sales growth over time.
Conversion Rate is the percentage of prospects who completed a desired action, such as making a purchase, with the company.	**Leads Generated** is how many sales leads, or prospects, the company brought in.
Customer Acquisition Cost totals the expense incurred to earn one customer.	**Market Share** is the percentage of sales a company has in total market sales.
Customer Lifetime Value estimates the revenue generated per customer over a customer's lifetime.	**Net Promoter Score** is a measure of customer loyalty, sentiment, and likelihood of recommending a brand.

(Ellering, 2020)

Table 6.3 Website and Blogging Metrics

Bounce Rate tracks the number of visitors who view only one page and exit.	**Referral Traffic** is traffic driven to the site by another source.
Click-Through Rate is the percentage of search engine queries that lead to a click to the company's site.	**Returning Visits** tracks repeat visitors.
Customer Attrition/Churn is how many customers are lost over time.	**Sessions by Device Type** indicates number of visits by each type of device, such as a PC or an iPhone.
Downloads tracks how many times content is downloaded.	**Time on Page** is average visitor time spent on page before exiting.
First Visit tracks the number of first-time visitors.	**Top Pages** is the best performing pages for traffic or conversion rates.
Organic Traffic is unpaid, search-engine driven traffic.	**Total Visits** is the total hits over a set period of time.
Pageviews is the total number of pages viewed.	**Traffic Sources** is other sources driving/referring traffic to the company.
Pageviews Per Session is the number of pages an average visitor will view before exiting.	**Unique Visitors** is the number of different individuals who visit.

(Ellering, 2020)

Table 6.4 SEO Metrics

Domain Authority assesses how search engines view an entire website. **Page Authority assesses** how search engines view a single webpage.	**Page Load Speed** is the time required for a site to load, which may impact search engine rankings.
Keyword Rankings is how high a page ranks in search engines for a given keyword.	**Search Traffic** indicates how much traffic is sent via a search engine.
Organic Click-Through Rate indicates how often a website is clicked when it appears in search engine results.	**Total Backlinks** is the number of links on other sites pointing to the company's site.

(Ellering, 2020)

Table 6.5 Social Media Marketing Metrics

Comments, Likes, and Shares track how often these functions are used.	**New Followers** is how many new followers are earned in a set amount of time.
Engagement Rate tracks level of interaction with audiences.	**Social Media Conversions** tracks how many social media referrals convert to website or blog sales.
Follower Growth Rate is how quickly a profile is gaining new followers.	**Social Media Traffic** tracks how much website or blog traffic originates from social media.

(Ellering, 2020)

Each of these marketing metrics is an adaptation of ROI. Specifically, metrics track what the company is getting in exchange for its investment in customer interactions – whether in person or virtually. Analytics, social listening, and tracking software can help convert each of these metrics into a number and combine them in various ways to quantify marketing's impact.

Table 6.6 Email Marketing Metrics

Email Bounce Rate is the number of undeliverable emails.	**Email Subscribers** is the number of mailing list subscribers.
Email Clicks, Forwards, and Opens are the frequencies of these actions.	**Email Traffic** tracks how much website or blog traffic originates from email.
Email Engagement also measures clicks, opens, and similar activities.	**Newsletter Signups** is the number opting into a newsletter list.

(Ellering, 2020)

Table 6.7 Pay-Per-Click (PPC) Metrics

Call Tracking is the number of calls placed after clicking an ad.	**Impression Share** is the share of ads that appeared on a viewer's screen compared to the total ads that had the potential to do so.
Click-Through Rate tracks number of ad clicks.	**Quality Score** assesses an ad's relevancy and quality of the destination page based on keywords and search intent.
Cost-Per-Click calculates the cost incurred to get one click on an ad.	**Return on Ad Spend** is the amount of revenue generated compared to the advertising spend.

(Ellering, 2020)

Learn from Marketing

I'm a numbers person, which makes my envy of marketing's ability to demonstrate their impact on the bottom line all the more frustrating. The good news, however, is how much overlap there continues to be between corporate communication, public affairs, and marketing. As a communicator, you've been in sales your entire career. You've sold ideas, proposals, and points of view. Each day, you promote your personal brand every time you interact with a colleague, boss, or stakeholder. You "get" marketing at a corporate and product level. Your work with external stakeholders makes you a vital part of branding. We've now added some terminology and a bit of number crunching to your understanding. Much of this terminology you already know.

My challenge to you is to begin quantifying your work and your results. Marketing has provided corporate communicators with a plethora of tools we can apply to public affairs practice. Sure, some require a bit more tweaking than others, but consider this: You spend time, money, and effort establishing stakeholder relationships. Have you preserved a relationship that would have otherwise ended? Have you intervened and offset the likelihood of a lawsuit? Have you established new relationships for the company that bring added value? What outcomes can you quantify from your digital practices? How are you complementing, even enhancing, marketing activities? Draw on marketing metrics and begin assigning values to your contributions. It will take some practice and internal vetting to make sure you're on point, but begin thinking like a marketer, particularly when you're discussing your work and asking for additional budget from decision-makers. Accurately speaking in terms decision-makers understand will advance your goals and increase both the value of your contributions and your business acumen.

Notes

1. Take the company color quiz at https://grasshopper.com/resources/tools/branding-color-quiz/ and learn more about the psychology behind colors in branding.
2. See Chapter 7 Getting Comfortable with the Quants for a discussion of data-driven communication strategy.
3. See Chapter 3 A Micro and Macro View of the Economy for coverage of changing economic conditions that affect business operations.
4. *Built to Last: Successful Habits of Visionary Companies* (2004) by Jim Collins and Jerry Porras is a must-read book for understanding the practices that separate good companies from great companies.
5. See my Institute for Public Relations essay on conscious capitalism at https://instituteforpr.org/part-i-the-role-of-public-relations-in-conscious-capitalism/ for what comprises a company's vision, core values, core purpose, and positioning statement.
6. See Campbell, 2020 for an informative discussion of calculating WTP for online subscription services.
7. See Chapter 10 What is Strategy? for discussion of the S Curve.
8. See related discussion of COGS in Chapter 4 The Art and Science of Financial Statements.
9. See Chapter 5 Why and How Finance Rules the Business World for a discussion of the time value of money.

References

Brenner, M. (2019, July 21). *The future of marketing and the changing role of the CMO*. Retrieved from https://marketinginsidergroup.com/strategy/the-future-of-marketing-and-the-changing-role-of-the-cmo/.

Campbell, P. (2020, June 9). *How to calculate willingness to pay and use it to inform subscription pricing*. Retrieved from www.priceintelligently.com/blog/willingness-to-pay.

Chen, J. (2020, April 27). *Return on Investment (ROI)*. Retrieved from www.investopedia.com/terms/r/returnoninvestment.asp.

Chi, C. (2020). *The ultimate list of types of marketing [41 and counting]*. Retrieved from https://blog.hubspot.com/marketing/marketing-types.

Collins, J., & Porras, J.I. (2004). *Built to last: Successful habits of visionary companies*. New York, NY: Harper Collins.

Cronstedt, J. (2018, January 8). *ROI: What is it, formula, and 5 ways to measure your marketing ROI*. Retrieved from https://medium.com/@jcron_89878/roi-what-is-it-formula-5-ways-to-measure-your-marketing-roi-9e67903e9cbf.

Definitions of marketing. (2020). Retrieved from www.ama.org/the-definition-of-marketing-what-is-marketing/.

Easter, M., & Dave, P. (2017, June 18). *Remember when Amazon only sold books?* Retrieved from www.latimes.com/business/la-fi-amazon-history-20170618-htmlstory.html.

Ellering, N. (2020). *How to select marketing metrics and KPIs to monitor*. Retrieved from https://coschedule.com/marketing-strategy/marketing-metrics-kpis/.

Grant, M. (2019, June 25). *Switching cost*. Retrieved from www.investopedia.com/terms/s/switchingcosts.asp.

Hill, S. I., McGrath, J., & Dayal, S. (1998, April 1). *How to brand sand*. Retrieved from www.strategy-business.com/article/16333?gko=658fc.

How to calculate market share. (2020, June 28). Retrieved from www.accountingtools.com/articles/how-to-calculate-market-share.html.

Izquierdo, R. (2020, May 12). *Successful growth strategy examples from real-world companies*. Retrieved from www.fool.com/the-blueprint/growth-strategy/.

Kenton, W. (2019, July 8). *Normal good*. Retrieved from www.investopedia.com/terms/n/normal-good.asp.

Kimmons, R. (2019, March 1). *Advantages and disadvantages of non-price competition.* Retrieved from https://smallbusiness.chron.com/advantages-disadvantages-nonprice-competition-10048.html.

Kopp, C.M. (2020, July 26). *Perceived value.* Retrieved from www.investopedia.com/terms/p/perceived-value.asp.

Lake, L. (2019, October 8). *Understanding the difference between B2B and B2C marketing.* Retrieved from www.thebalancesmb.com/b2b-vs-b2c-marketing-2295828.

LaMarco, N. (2019, February 5). *Corporate branding vs. product branding.* Retrieved from https://smallbusiness.chron.com/corporate-branding-vs-product-branding-37269.html.

Pathare, S. (2020). *Brand management: The psychology behind brands we love.* Retrieved from www.bynder.com/en/blog/psychology-behind-brands/.

The product life cycle. (2010). Retrieved from www.quickmba.com/marketing/product/lifecycle/.

Sharma, E. (2015, July 11). *10 branding elements and what they mean.* Retrieved from www.brandanew.co/10-branding-elements-and-what-they-mean/.

Sheth, J. N., & Uslay, C. (2007, September 1). Implications of the revised definition of marketing: From exchange to value creation. *Journal of Public Policy & Marketing, 26*(2), 302–307.

Shewan, D. (2020, February 25). *7 of the best value proposition examples we've ever seen.* Retrieved from www.wordstream.com/blog/ws/2016/04/27/value-proposition-examples.

Tarver, E. (2020, July 28). *Market segmentation.* Retrieved from www.investopedia.com/terms/m/marketsegmentation.asp.

Tracy, B. (2004, May 17). *The 7 Ps of marketing.* Retrieved from www.entrepreneur.com/article/70824.

Twin, A. (2020, July 5). *Value proposition.* Retrieved from www.investopedia.com/terms/v/valueproposition.asp.

What is emotional branding and how is it effective? (2020). Retrieved from https://digitalmarketinginstitute.com/en-us/blog/what-is-emotional-branding-and-how-is-it-effective.

What is the Growth Share Matrix? (2020). Retrieved from www.bcg.com/en-us/about/our-history/growth-share-matrix.

What is a sales funnel, examples, and how to create one. (2020, March 24). Retrieved from www.crazyegg.com/blog/sales-funnel/.

Yu, S. (2018, March 18). *Who really owns your brand?* Retrieved from https://chiefexecutive.net/really-owns-brand/.

Chapter 7

Getting Comfortable with the Quants

I admit it. I'm a stats nerd. I love working with data – gathering, cleaning, and analyzing data. Finding new insights through data makes me giddy. For me, there's nothing quite like uncovering a gold mine of findings for clients and then watching them react with delight (or, sometimes shock) at what my team and I have discovered. Perhaps the best part of data analysis is transforming those findings into communication strategy. Data-driven strategy is good stuff. When I have data on my side, I have an increased level of confidence in sharing both the good and bad news that in-depth analysis can bring. Data excites, challenges, and inspires me. I don't mind when my consulting and academic colleagues poke fun at my nerdiness. I have super powers being able to communicate, work with data, and understand business. And my friends, so will you. Read on.

The Need for Unicorns

There are great communicators. There are great business people. And there are great data scientists. But here's the catch: As complex as business and data can be, it is effective communication that stumps a lot of smart people. They understand their field, and they're deep in their expertise. But when it's time to explain dividend strategy to a journalist or convey to employees how consumer behavior in a storefront can predict how many winter coats the company needs to order, they come to us. No one has ever pulled me aside and said, "No, really – I'll do that media interview for you." Or, "Please – let me address that crisis instead of you." No one. Ever.

But I've also seen the flipside. A communicator gets sent to do a big presentation for a VIP audience, and it goes swimmingly. Until the Q&A, when it becomes immediately apparent that the communicator lacks business acumen and hasn't a clue about the data informing the presentation. I cringe in my chair out of discomfort, wishing I could help the now frazzled communicator. But it's too late. Don't be that communicator.

I get it. Not everyone loves, or even likes, stats or anything that sounds remotely mathematical or quantitatively complex. I'm convinced we have experiences along our educational journeys that either turn us toward all things analytical or lead us to run like mad in the opposite direction. Few people are neutral about number crunching. I've taught data analytics to college students for more than a decade, and each semester begins the same. "I don't do math," I commonly hear. "I'm not good with numbers," or, my perennial favorite (not), "I got into communication to get away from numbers." Once I get these students to

DOI: 10.4324/9781003000600-8

open their minds and begin to experience the magical aspects of data, many become data heads, too. Not all, but many.

So, now I turn to you with all the encouragement I can muster. Businesses need unicorns. Businesses value, reward, and promote unicorns. Unicorns are rarely handing out their resumes looking for work. You already possess a skill most people find daunting: public communication. You're well on your way to building your business acumen. And now, we're going to dive into data. As with every topic we've covered, you do not need to become an accountant, or a finance PhD, or a data scientist to be a unicorn. But if you're a great communicator who knows enough about business and data to ask the right questions, have confidence in applying your knowledge, and can help advance a business using all three skillsets, you're a unicorn. Let's begin by learning more about data science and those who practice this valuable craft.

Data Science and Data Scientists

Companies have warehouses of products in inventory, waiting to be sold. Along those same lines, companies have *enterprise data warehouses* where data from numerous sources are gathered, stored, and analyzed to create business value (Lo, 2020). *Data mining* is the analysis that uncovers insights, trends, and solutions for a business. *Data science* has two primary components:

- **Discovery of data insights** that are hidden within unfathomable volumes of data and applied to make smarter business decisions. Netflix produces new series based on movie viewing patterns. Target identifies unique shopping habits of different customer segments and then tailors messages for each segment based on their behaviors. Data scientists are part detective, part strategist. Business acumen is required to put data insights to work.
- **Development of data products**, or technical assets, that take input data and transform them via algorithms into results-based production systems. Amazon's recommendation engine and Gmail's spam filters are examples. Data scientists are not only math experts, but also coding masters. There's a culture of *hacking* among data scientists that's not about breaking into computers but rather about using creativity and ingenuity to find clever solutions to problems.

Data scientists can use data to explain something that has occurred, but *predictive modeling* is the currency of the practice. Predictive models are fueled by algorithms and fall into five general categories (Parthasarathy, 2020):

- **Classification models** are the simplest of the predictive models and best answer yes/no questions, like "Is this customer about to churn?" or "Will this loan applicant be approved?"
- **Clustering models** sort data into clusters, or groups, based on similar characteristics. Think of dividing online shoe shoppers into style preference groups, and then having the ability to send them promotions based on their personal preferences.
- **Forecasting models** are among the most widely used and can predict value-based responses to questions such as, "How many prospects are likely to convert this month?" or "How many support calls can we expect per hour?"

- **Outlier models** look for anomalies, or out-of-the-ordinary events, that pinpoint pattern disruptions like how a drop in sales correlated with a crisis or identify fraudulent claims against an insurance company.
- **Time series models** use historical data to predict future occurrences, such as the number of patients expected to visit an emergency room in the next two weeks or the number of online orders expected in the next three months. Time series models are particularly helpful because they can account for additional variables that affect outcomes over time, like weather, trends, and economic conditions.

Artificial Intelligence, Machine Learning, and Deep Learning

Figure 7.1: Data Science Illustrated shows the relationship between data science and its close cousins *Artificial Intelligence* (AI), *Machine Learning* (ML), and *Deep Learning* (DL). These terms are increasingly relevant to business practices, so let's explore the meaning of each. AI research dates back to the 1950s, so it's not as new as it may seem (Thakur, 2020). AI has evolved over time. For many decades, AI research was limited to supercomputing labs. What began as attempts to create machines that mimicked neural networks in the human brain (i.e., "thinking machines") evolved into machine learning and, most recently, deep learning. ML and DL are subsets of AI.

AI is enabling a machine to interpret and learn from data so it can make "intelligent" decisions based on patterns drawn from that data (Thakur, 2020). AI is a collection of algorithms that allows computers to draw inferences from the correlation of, or relationship between, data points. For example, a machine can be programmed to detect traffic violations based on camera feeds and traffic violation tickets.

Machine learning enables machines to learn from huge volumes of data (Thakur, 2020). In ML, a machine is first "trained" on a known dataset so programmers can finetune their predictive models and ensure their accuracy. Then new datasets are given to the machine to analyze and build on its past learning. A machine that is "learning" doesn't need explicit instructions on how to handle data. Instead, it renders findings from data based on its own experience. Streaming music services use machine learning (Grossfeld, 2020). The more users indicate preferences, the better the service gets at selecting music the listener will like.

Deep learning is an advancement of ML. It draws on artificial neuron networks that imitate how a human brain draws conclusions based on certain cues (Grossfeld, 2020). DL is preferred for the largest of datasets when an even higher level of accuracy is required

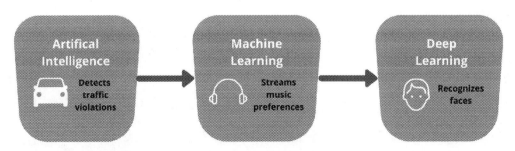

Figure 7.1 Data Science Illustrated

(Thakur, 2020). DL can solve more complex problems than ML, but its programming is more complex, too. Siri, Alexa, and Google Assistant are examples of DL applications. DL recognizes faces on Facebook, recommends movies on Netflix, aggregates news stories, and detects fake news stories. DL is a branch of artificial intelligence.

Data Big and Small: Use and Privacy

Artificial intelligence, machine learning, deep learning, and other data science methods yet to be developed will continue to interface with the mind-blowing amount of data we humans generate on a daily basis. Each day, 95 million photos and videos are shared on Instagram, 306 billion emails are sent, and 500 million Tweets are posted (Bulao, 2020; "60 Incredible," 2020). You've heard of gigabytes (GB), but data are now spoken of in terms of zettabytes (ZB), which equals about one trillion gigabytes. The entire digital universe at the time of this writing is estimated to be 44ZB. That's 40 times more bytes than there are stars in the known universe (Desjardins, 2019). Wow.

Big data are created through transactions, sensors, and other connected devices ("Use Big Data," 2019). *Small data* are collected through primary research methods including focus groups, surveys, and online communities. Big data are described by three Vs: volume, velocity, and variety. Big data are, well, really big in volume and require advanced computer processing to manage. Small data can be processed on a single computer. Big data have high velocity, or speed, and are collected in seconds, minutes, and hours. Small data are collected over days, weeks, or months. Big data have a high level of variety. Some data points are structured (e.g., numbers), some are semi-structured, (e.g., clickstream data, like mouse clicks), and others are unstructured (e.g., video) or even unknown. The structure of small data are known, certain, and much more comprehensible for human analysis.

It's likely you've done some form of primary research and gathered small data. Here's the good news: The combination of big data and small data lead to powerful insights about your company, your products, and your customers ("Use Big Data," 2019). Big data explain the "what" of consumer behavior, that is, navigating websites, making purchases, and deciding what they're having for dinner and where they're going to vacation. Small data explain the "why," or the motivations, attitudes, and emotions behind those actions. Each type of data provides valuable insights that are applicable to a company's operations. Combining the two gets you closer to the full customer story.

Companies daily capture, store, and analyze four types of customer data using direct and indirect collection methods (Freedman, 2020):

- **Personal data** include personally identifiable information, like gender, and non-personally identifiable information, like IP address.
- **Engagement data** detail how prospects and customers are interacting with the company's website social media pages, apps, emails, ads, and customer service interfaces.
- **Behavioral data** include purchase and usage info, along with a user's digital footprint.
- **Attitudinal data** are metrics on customer satisfaction, product preferences, and purchase criteria.

These data are used to improve customer experience, refine marketing strategies, and even secure other, more sensitive data to prevent fraud. For example, a bank may use voice recognition data to ensure an actual customer is authorizing a financial transaction via phone. By matching the customer's voice previously captured on a customer service call, the bank's tracking technologies can take human error out of preventing criminal access to an account.

Companies also use data to generate cash flow by selling customer information to third-party brokers (Freedman, 2020). Advertisers and companies with a similar target audience use these data to leverage their own access to a potential customer base. As demand for consumer data grows, so, too, do *data privacy* regulations that mandate what information is collected, how people are informed, and what control individuals have over their own data (Ramirez, 2020). At the time of this writing, no single comprehensive federal law regulates data privacy in the United States. Twenty-five U.S. states have enacted their own privacy data laws, with the *California Consumer Privacy Act* (CCPA) being the most comprehensive to date. CCPA requires businesses that sell personal information to give consumers the right to opt out of having their information sold. Internationally, the *General Data Protection Regulation* (GDPR) is the most far-reaching, governing the collection, use, security, and transmission of data from residents in any of the 27 European Union countries. Fines up to 20 million euros for violating GDPR can be imposed on organizations failing to comply, regardless of their geographical location.

Cybersecurity Risk Management

Data breaches have become commonplace, either from malicious intent to steal data or from organizations leaving data unprotected and exposed (Swinhoe, 2020). In the first six months of 2020 alone, 540 reported data breaches affected more than 163 *million* individuals (Leonhardt, 2020). That staggering figure is actually a significant drop in an alarming trend, in large part because companies are becoming "hypervigilant" about cybersecurity risk management. However, cybercriminals are becoming more vigilant, too. There's a time lag between hackers obtaining data and finding new ways to use it. Although the drop in data breaches is encouraging, cybersecurity experts expect the rate to rise again.

Here's an overview of the operating environment companies are facing in a data-driven economy (Milkovich, 2020):

- **Government, retail, and technology** are the most popular targets for cyberattacks.
- **Every 39 seconds** a hacker attacks, affecting one in three Americans.
- **43% of attacks** target small business.
- **$3.9 million** is the global average cost of a data breach for small to medium-sized businesses (SMBs). For publicly traded companies, the average cost is **$116 million**.
- **Reported cybercrimes increased 300% since COVID-19** as office work moved to homes.
- **93% of healthcare organizations** have experienced a breach in the last three years.
- **User training and behavior** is the best defense against *phishing attacks* posing as a trusted source to steal information. **95% of cybersecurity breaches** are due to human error, not the IT department.
- **$6 trillion** has been spent globally on cybersecurity defense as of 2021.
- **75 billion** *IoT* (Internet of Things) devices will be connected by 2025. IoT devices include any device with a sensor that can transmit data without human intervention. The IoT market was 31 billion devices in 2020.
- **More than 4 million** cybersecurity jobs went unfilled in 2021. Demand far outpaces supply.

- **More than 77% of organizations** do not have a Cyber Security Incident Response Plan.
- **Six months** is the time many companies take before realizing their data have been breached, including majors ones like Equifax, Capital One, and Facebook.
- **7.27%** is the average share price drop after a breach is announced. Finance and payment companies take the largest hits to share price.
- **Cybercriminals have cost victims more than $1 trillion globally** – just as of 2018. Victims include both organizations and individuals.

What's a company to do? Aside from working with cybersecurity experts, having a data breach response plan, and training employees, consulting firm Deloitte ("Data Privacy," 2019) suggests companies minimize the data they keep, develop an enterprise data governance strategy, and conduct internal audits of privacy controls. Data breaches are blatant breaches of customer trust that impart significant reputational risk to a business. Internal and external communication are vital to strengthen corporate defense and resilience in an increasingly connected global economy (see Sidebar 7.1: Blockchain 101).

Sidebar 7.1 Blockchain 101

(Reiff, 2020)

The term *blockchain*, most frequently tied to banking, investing, or cryptocurrency, refers to digital information-storage "blocks" chained together. Here are some fundamentals on how this evolving data protection and transmission technology works:

> When you make a purchase on Amazon, it is verified by a network of computers. Your transaction is stored with thousands of others in a block.

> Once the entire block if verified, it is added to a blockchain that anyone can view. Check out Bitcoin's blockchain at https://www.blockchain.com/btc/blocks

> Blockchains are referred to as distributed ledgers. Thousands, even millions, of blockchain copies appear on each computer in the network. A hacker would need to manipulate every copy to edit transactions, which is highly unlikely.

> Blockchain security comes from its ability to receive and distribute info, but not edit it. Blockchains are theoretically hacker-proof.

> Currently, blockchains are used most in banks, cryptocurrency, healthcare, property records, contracts, supply chains, and voting.

Competitive Advantages of Data

Despite data's darker side, data-driven business strategies provide a competitive advantage when the benefits of data outnumber the cost of deep dives and complex technologies.[1] How's a firm to know when enough is enough? *Harvard Business Review* offers some guidelines (Hagiu & Wright, 2020):

- **How important is data-enabled customer learning?** Not every application requires the same level of customer data gathering. An advanced driver assistance system used to avoid collisions and improve road safety is much more reliant on gathering customer data than an online photo organizer for which customer outcomes aren't nearly as crucial.
- **At what point does the marginal value of more data begin to decline?** A customer's willingness to pay[2] must be accounted for when making the decision of whether to collect additional data points. If additional costs cannot be recouped in a higher price, is the extra data really worth it?
- **How quickly does the relevance of customer data fade?** For Google Search, years of customer data continue to inform developers and provide an increasingly high barrier to entry[3] to those attempting to compete with Google's dominance. Conversely, data regarding customer fashion preferences are going to shift frequently over time.
- **Are the data proprietary?** Or, can they purchased, copied, or obtained elsewhere? Having customer data with few or no substitutes provides a competitive advantage, but they are more costly, too.
- **Do data lead to hard-to-copy product or customer service improvements?** If so, data provide a competitive advantage. If not, competitors can replicate the same improvements without investing in data themselves.
- **Who benefits from data-driven product improvements?** Pandora's platform serves the preferences of an individual customer, whereas Spotify and Apple Music enable users to search and listen to other people's stations. This broader leveraging of data creates a valuable *network effect* across loyal users. For context, Pandora was acquired by Sirius XM in 2019 for $3.5 billion. Spotify went public later in 2019, valued at $26 billion.[4]
- **How quickly can customer data insights be incorporated into products?** The quicker the company's learning cycle, the greater the competitive advantage, and the more difficult for competitors to keep up. This faster application of customer data also generates a network effect when more users means a better experience for all. Google Maps is a great example.

Data-Driven Communication Strategy

There were two communicators in my MBA class of 80 working professionals: Kenny Diggs and me. Kenny is a political strategy savant based in Washington, D.C. and one of the most (truly) helpful people I've ever met. He's spoken to my students numerous times, and I always learn something new from Kenny. Relevant to our discussion on data is Kenny's take on three essential sources of knowledge (see Figure 7.2: Three Essential Sources of Knowledge):

- **Institutional knowledge** is what you know about your organization and how things get done internally and externally. A SWOT analysis (Strengths, Weaknesses,

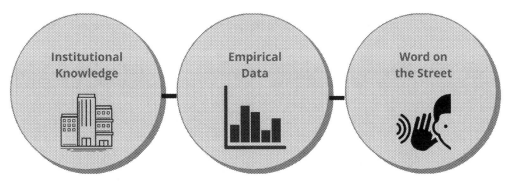

Figure 7.2 Three Essential Sources of Knowledge

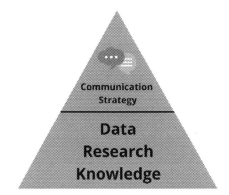

Figure 7.3 Data-Driven Communication Strategy

Opportunities, Threats) captures your institutional knowledge alongside your insights on workplace culture, team dynamics, and management's openness to change.
- **Empirical data** is the primary stakeholder data you're collecting plus the voluminous other data points your data scientists are gathering daily.
- **Word on the street** is just that, realizing "the street" includes social media and other venues you use for listening to your stakeholders. What are they saying, thinking, feeling about your company and its products?

Effective communication strategy relies on all three of these sources. Use only one or two of these, and you run the risk of overlooking some important information. Before you devise a strategy, you need to know what's doable (and not) in your organization. You need to know the trends and insights hidden in your customer (or other stakeholder) data. And you need to be aware of rumors, misinformation, naysayers, and fans floating around online and elsewhere. Use data to your communicating advantage. Work with data scientists to get the data you need. Help your data team realize the communication opportunities their data findings reveal. Flawed communication strategy erodes stakeholder trust in the organization as a reliable source of information. When data, research, and knowledge drive communication strategy, you're much more likely to be on point (see Figure 7.3: Data-Driven Communication Strategy).

Notes

1 See Chapter 2 Capitalism: Its Benefits and Discontents for discussion of cost-benefit analysis.
2 See Chapter 6 Marketing Envy and Other Observations for discussion of willingness to pay (WTP).
3 See Chapter 3 A Micro and Macro View of the Economy for discussion of barriers to entry.
4 See Chapter 5 How and Why Finance Rules the Business World for discussions of going public and company valuation.

References

Bulao, J. (2020, July 28). *How much data is created every day in 2020?* Retrieved from https://techjury.net/blog/how-much-data-is-created-every-day/#gref.
Data privacy as a strategic priority. (2019) Retrieved from https://www2.deloitte.com/content/dam/Deloitte/us/Documents/risk/us-data-privacy-as-a-strategic-priority.pdf.
Desjardins, J.(2019, April 17). *How much data is generated each day?* Retrieved from www.weforum.org/agenda/2019/04/how-much-data-is-generated-each-day-cf4bddf29f/.
Freedman, M. (2020, June 17). *How businesses are collecting data (and what they're doing with it).* Retrieved from www.businessnewsdaily.com/10625-businesses-collecting-data.html.
Grossfeld, B. (2020, May 15). *Deep learning vs. machine learning: A simple way to understand the difference.* Retrieved from www.zendesk.com/blog/machine-learning-and-deep-learning/.
Hagiu, A., & Wright, J. (2020, January–February). When data creates competitive advantage…and when it doesn't. *Harvard Business Review*, 98(1), 94–101.
Leonhardt, M. (2020, July 14). *The number of data breaches is actually down 33% so far this year – here's why.* Retrieved from www.cnbc.com/2020/07/14/number-of-data-breaches-down-33-percent-in-first-half-of-2020.html.
Lo, F. (2020). *What is data science?* Retrieved from https://datajobs.com/what-is-data-science.
Milkovich, D. (2020, June 20). *15 alarming cyber security facts and stats.* Retrieved from www.cybintsolutions.com/cyber-security-facts-stats/.
Parthasarathy, S. (2020). *Top 5 predictive analytics models and algorithms.* Retrieved from www.logianalytics.com/predictive-analytics/predictive-algorithms-and-models/.
Ramirez, N. (2020, June 25). *Data privacy laws: What you need to know in 2020.* Retrieved from www.osano.com/articles/data-privacy-laws.
Reiff, N. (2020, February 1). *Blockchain explained.* Retrieved from www.investopedia.com/terms/b/blockchain.asp.
60 incredible and interesting Twitter stats and statistics. (2020, January 2). Retrieved from www.brandwatch.com/blog/twitter-stats-and-statistics/.
Swinhoe, D. (2020, April 17). *The 15 biggest data breaches of the 21st century.* Retrieved from www.csoonline.com/article/2130877/the-biggest-data-breaches-of-the-21st-century.html.
Thakur, N. (2020, April 16). *The differences between data science, artificial intelligence, machine learning, and deep learning.* Retrieved from https://medium.com/ai-in-plain-english/data-science-vs-artificial-intelligence-vs-machine-learning-vs-deep-learning-50d3718d51e5.
Use big data – and small data to understand your customers. (2019, May 3). Retrieved from www.inc.com/focusvision/use-big-data-and-small-data-to-understand-your-customers.html.

Chapter 8
Why You Cannot Ignore Operations Management

Operations management is the central nervous system of a company. In the simplest of terms, it enables the company to conduct whatever business it is in. Without operations, you have no company. There are no products to offer without a comprehensive management system to coordinate the sourcing, production, and delivery of those products. Ops management, as it's usually called, doesn't get the same attention as finance and accounting in business school, and I've never heard it mentioned in a communication course I've taken. But spend a short time in industry, and you soon realize that every other function depends on and supports in some way the operations side of the business. And you know what? Ops management offers some of the most interesting insights into how your company ticks. Get to know operations management, and you'll be amazed at how understanding this side of the business can enrich your communication strategies.

A Focus on Efficiency

Profits flow from reliable revenue streams and efficient operations. Revenue is the top line, and efficiency ensures expenses are well managed so the bottom line can be maximized (Kenton, 2019).[1] Ops management is in charge of business practices ranging from securing supply sources, to overseeing production, to preparing goods for delivery to customers in the most efficient means possible. What struck me most when I first starting learning about ops management is the function's overwhelming reliance on *relationships* for success. As corporate communicators, we are in the business of relationships, and so is ops management.

Ops management covers a lot of terrain, including manufacturing capacity, raw materials acquisition, materials handling, project management, quality control, inventory levels, maintenance policies, and even information technology networks that support each of these systems. (Kenton, 2019; 2020). Whether a company manufactures pencils or automobiles, a key function of ops management is balancing revenues with costs. The calculation of *economic order quantity* (EOQ) is central to efficient operations. EOQ is an algorithm that determines the optimal number of units (of whatever the company makes) to order so that purchasing, delivering, and storing costs are minimized. Think about it: Having too much inventory on hand, whether raw or finished goods, ties up cash and increases storage costs. Having too little inventory frustrates customers and sends them to competitors looking for alternatives. There's a lot of math and logic behind order

DOI: 10.4324/9781003000600-9

and inventory management, and that's the purview of ops management. Additionally, ops management leaders understand:

- Local and global trends
- Customer demand for the company's products (or services)
- Availability of resources needed for production
- Material acquisition
- Timely, cost-effective use and productivity of labor and facilities
- Vendor/supplier quality and cost-effectiveness
- Delivery of goods to customers on schedule
- Development of new production structures
- Continuous feedback loops that provide improvement in the operations process
- Process versatility and innovation required for adapting to market changes

The Supply Chain

At the heart of operations management is the supply chain ("What is a Supply Chain," 2020). The supply chain is the network of business partners required to acquire raw materials, transform them into products, and then deliver those products into customers' hands. For a supply chain to be efficient and value-adding, each participant must adhere to standards of quality, timing, and delivery for this interconnected system to run smoothly.

A conventional supply chain is shown in Figure 8.1 ("What is a Supply Chain," 2020). The process begins with sourcing or extracting *raw materials*, which are taken by a logistics provider (e.g., transportation, warehousing) to a supplier. If we follow the supply chain of a t-shirt, the raw materials are bushels of cotton taken to a supplier that acts as a *wholesaler*. The supplier makes cotton fabric and sells it to manufacturers that convert the fabric into *finished products*, or t-shirts. Distributers deliver those t-shirts to retailers that market them to customers. Customers drive demand for more t-shirts, or perhaps t-shirts of different styles, colors, and fabrics. And the process repeats itself, many times over. Note, too, that raw materials must be purchased at a low enough price for each participant in the supply chain to profit from the process. Figure 8.2 shows a slightly revised supply chain for an e-commerce company. The process begins when orders are placed on a company's website, paid electronically, and then sent to a warehouse for shipping to the customer. The conventional process in Figure 8.1 is still working behind the scenes in Figure 8.2 to supply the online retailer. Until you begin to understand the supply chain, it's easy to underestimate the process, time, and logistics required to get any product from your company to your customer.

Companies consistently regarded as excellent in supply chain management include Amazon, Apple, Proctor & Gamble, McDonald's, and Unilever ("Gartner Announces," 2020). Companies best able to respond to *supply chain disruptions* are those that best manage their supply chain relationships. Challenges facing supply chain managers include (Howells, 2020; "What are the Main," 2020):

- **Increasing costs** of transport fuel, raw materials, labor, and international logistics.
- **Customers buying products across multiple channels** requires more flexibility and adaptability in supply chain management.

Why You Cannot Ignore Operations Management 161

Figure 8.1 Conventional Supply Chain
Reprinted with permission from Corporate Finance Institute

Figure 8.2 E-Commerce Supply Chain
Reprinted with permission from Corporate Finance Institute

- **Customers expecting** delivery within a few days of quality products that are ethically sourced, environmentally friendly, and reasonably priced.
- **Pressure on any part of the supply chain network** affects the entire network. New regulations, geopolitical unrest, additional steps in the supply chain, and lack of communication across the supply chain adds complexity to the process.

Add to these challenges a number of risks to supply chain security, including pandemics, trade wars, raw material shortages, safety recalls, severe weather impacts, and cargo thefts and/or fires that impart significant disruptions to an entire system of production and delivery (Jaegar, 2019). Supply chains are particularly vulnerable to cybersecurity attacks because companies are not always able to control security measures taken by supply chain partners (Duca, 2020). *Blockchain*, covered in Chapter 7, holds promise to address supply chain security concerns. Specifically, blockchain systems add transparency to transactions within these complex networks, allowing suppliers, retailers, and banks to observe the status of information, inventory, and money moving through the supply chain (Gaur & Gaiha, 2020; see also "Using Blockchain," 2020).

Let's turn now to a few key principles in operations management: lean manufacturing, demand forecasting, and vertical/horizontal integration.

Lean Manufacturing

Toyota developed *lean manufacturing* techniques in post-WWII Japan to compete with Western automakers reliant on traditional mass-production techniques developed by Henry Ford (Chavez, 2018). Much of the world's production operations follow lean manufacturing principles, which focus on reducing waste, improving process flow, and increasing productivity across a production line. Based on the Japanese model of efficiency, lean manufacturing operates on smaller production batches, reduction of cycle time required to convert raw materials into finished products, and, ultimately, increased customer satisfaction resulting from these efforts. Lean manufacturing principles take a broad view of waste. The acronym DOWNTIME describes eight types of waste that, when avoided, increase productivity and reduce costs, thereby increasing profitability:

- Defects caused by low quality inputs or human error
- Overproduction of goods with disregard for actual demand
- Waiting while *bottlenecks* (delays/constraints in the system caused by a backup in the production process) are identified and addressed
- Not utilizing talent fails to realize human potential
- Transportation to and from docks and warehouses that can be circumvented with better layout design and process flow
- Inventory excess is avoided by closely managing productivity
- Motion waste is avoided by eliminated repetitive employee motions on the assembly line
- Excess processing refers to completing only parts of the production process that add value for customers and eliminating the rest.

Kaizen is a Japanese word meaning continuous improvement of the lean production process via ongoing feedback and adjustments offered by anyone on the assembly line. Lean manufacturing reflects a collective mindset toward excellence and near-perfect production methods. Other than Toyota, companies recognized for their lean manufacturing excellence include Nike, Kimberley-Clark, Intel, and Ford ("Top 10," 2018). Similar approaches to production developed in the U.S. decades after lean production include *Six Sigma* and *Total Quality Management (TQM)*. Each focuses on enhancing quality and reducing errors ("Six Sigma," 2019).

Demand Forecasting

Responding to customer demand is a central focus of lean manufacturing (Chavez, 2018). As such, lean manufacturing is described as a *pull*, or *demand-based flow*, *manufacturing* process in which customer demand defines what is valuable. Alternatively, a *push manufacturing* process is based on a product the company can provide, not necessarily the product the customer wants. In lean manufacturing, *Kanban Order Quantity* (KOQ) is used instead of the conventional Economic Order Quantity (EOQ) previously mentioned to manage inventories (Lyles, 2019). Whereas EOQ calculates product replenishment quantities based on projected annual demand along with expected purchase and storage costs, KOQ uses daily demand to replenish only what's been used (or sold). KOQ is a *just-in-time inventory* tool designed to place the smallest order possible that still meets customer demand.

Fashion retailer Zara is a model for optimizing just-in-time production methods. Zara produces approximately 450 million items a year for twice weekly, small batch deliveries to stores around the globe ("Zara's Supply Chain," 2018). Their superior speed in responding to just-in-time customer demands for on-trend fashion is fueled by their supply chain and lean approach to manufacturing. Zara keeps much of its production in-house and reserves up to 85% of its manufacturing capacity for in-season adjustments in style, frequency, and variety. Zara relies on store manager communications to understand customer demand. The retailer is well known for providing the latest "must-have" fashion, from their own factories, at supersonic speed. Zara pays employees higher than average wages and keeps 85% of the full price of its clothing, compared to an industry average of 60–70%. Unsold items account for less than 10% of their merchandise, compared to an industry average of 17–20%. Zara is an exemplar for managing the lean principles, communication, and relationships required for a profitable supply chain.

Motorcycle manufacturer Polaris produces off-road vehicles and snowmobiles that sell mostly in winter months (Popkin, 2014). Lean manufacturing helps businesses like Polairs manage *seasonality*, or demand that varies depending on time of year. Efficiency and production cost savings result from reacting to, rather than attempting to predict, market demand and producing only what customers want. Businesses focused on holidays, special occasions, and activities tied to certain times of year also manage seasonality concerns.

Horizontal vs. Vertical Integration

Both horizontal and vertical integration strategies are used to drive a company's growth. The type of growth a firm seeks determines the strategy it will employ. A company looking to increase market share, diversify products, gain access to new markets, or reduce competition will pursue *horizontal integration* by purchasing a similar company in its industry (Tarver, 2019). Instead of competing with a similar firm, a company can enhance its own *value chain* by acquiring another firm. Horizontal integration allows companies to consolidate their supply chains, which can enhance profitability but restrict consumer choices in that market. As discussed in Chapter 5, mergers are regulated by U.S. antitrust laws to prevent high concentrations of economic power that restrict competition. Examples of horizontal integration include Marriott's 2016 acquisition of Starwood Hotels, Facebook's 2012 acquisition of Instagram, and Disney's 2006 acquisition of Pixar.

Vertical integration is when a company acquires a company that is either before (i.e., *upstream*) or after it (i.e., *downstream*) in the supply chain (Tarver, 2019; see also Figures 8.1 and 8.2 for supply chain illustrations). Vertical integration can reduce production costs, increase efficiencies, capture new profits, avoid supply chain disruptions, and access new distribution channels for the buyer, but this approach is capital-intensive and expensive (see also Amadeo, 2020). *Backward integration* is when a company purchases an input or raw material provider for its products, or, like streaming service Netflix starting to create its own content, takes on activities that an upstream supply chain partner would normally provide. *Forward integration* is when a company purchases a distributer or retailer on the downstream side of its supply chain to increase its profits. Examples of vertical integration include Ikea's 2015 acquisition of Romanian forests to supply its own raw materials for furniture making (i.e., backward vertical integration) and Target, which manufactures, distributes, and sells its store brand products to reduce its reliance on outside suppliers and distributors (i.e., backward and forward vertical integration).

Understand Operations, Improve Communications

Supply chain communications is not a well-developed area of public affairs practice, but it should be. Operations is integral to a company's survival and more dependent on well-managed relationships across a system of upstream and downstream partners than any other function in the company. Consider some of the top challenges related to the sourcing, production, and transportation of a company's products (Crawshaw, 2017):

- *Risk management.* Companies rely on the authenticity, financial stability, legal practices, and safety practices of supply chain partners. A failure in any of these areas causes a troubling rippling effect throughout the entire system. Financial fraud, misrepresentation of goods and services, bribery, and violations related to international sanctions and human rights can bring supply chains to a halt ("Supply Chain Fraud," 2018). Lawsuits were plentiful in the wake of the COVID-19 pandemic, claiming businesses neglected to adequately protect workers' health – at a time when supply chain delivery of essential goods to customers became increasingly urgent (Devine, Burger, & Weck, 2020). Supply chains with fewer available partner alternatives are at greatest risk when major disruptions occur.
- *Reputation and brand image.* Allegations of child and slave labor abound in international sourcing markets. Customers, watchdog groups, regulators, and investors have become increasingly vocal about where and how companies source their operations. Even Apple, one of the strongest, most successful global brands, has grappled with unethical labor practices in its supply chain (Allgeier, 2019). Companies must be aware of not only their suppliers' practices, but that of their suppliers' suppliers, too.

Negative news regarding supply chain practices will invariably focus on the most prominent brands involved.
- *Corporate Social Responsibility (CSR).* Sustainability of natural resources, including water, forests, and wildlife, receives ongoing attention from activists and customers alike. Companies are expected to work with supply chain partners that adhere to social, environmental, and ethical standards (Villena & Gioia, 2020). Dell and HP have been criticized for sourcing electronics from overseas suppliers with hazardous working conditions. Nike and Adidas were found using suppliers dumping toxins into Chinese rivers. Difficulties arise in ensuring global partners are following agreed-upon standards, particularly those upstream of primary partners. Lower-tier suppliers – those supplying the primary suppliers – are the least equipped to adhere to demanding standards. Multinational corporations (MNCs) must work directly or collectively with supply chain partners to set, manage, and audit CSR practices.
- *Stakeholder engagement.* The need for effective communication and relationship building among supply chain partners is evident. Supplier onboarding and scheduled check-ins, along with a focus on helping partners reach their own profitability goals, are ways MNCs can better ensure supply chains add to, rather than detract from, a reputation for favorable business operations.

Operations management *is* a company's business. Effective communication is central to its success. Make sure you have operations in your internal network. Keep asking questions about supply chain partners so you can be proactive in managing reputation risk. Share stakeholder concerns, questions, or rumors with your operations contacts. Understand how your products are sourced, produced, and delivered to customers, and you'll have a comprehensive knowledge of operations that can inform every communication decision you make.

Note

1 See Chapter 4 The Art and Science of Financial Statements for discussion of top line and bottom line as they relate to the income statement.

References

Allgeier, H. (2019, September 4). *How the biggest brand in the world grapples with ethical sourcing.* Retrieved from www.interos.ai/how-the-biggest-brand-in-the-world-grapples-with-ethical-sourcing/.

Amadeo, K. (2020, May 28). *Vertical integration: Pros, cons, and examples.* Retrieved from www.thebalance.com/what-is-vertical-integration-3305807.

Chavez, I. (2018, August 14). *The power of lean manufacturing: A complete guide.* Retrieved from https://princemanufacturing.com/lean-manufacturing/.

Crawshaw, G. (2017, October 2) *The top six challenges facing procurement.* Retrieved from www.cips.org/supply-management/opinion/2017/september/the-top-six-challenges-facing-procurement-/.

Devine, R.G., Burger, J., & Weck, D. (2020, April 14). *It has started: Supply-chain, warehouse, and retail workers of essential businesses are filing suit.* Retrieved from www.whiteandwilliams.com/resources-alerts-Supply-Chain-Warehouse-and-Retail-Workers-of-Essential-Businesses-Are-Filing-Suit.html.

Duca, S. (2020, January 17). *Supply chain remains the weakest link in cybersecurity*. Retrieved from www.supplychaindigital.com/technology/supply-chain-remains-weakest-link-cybersecurity.

Gartner announces rankings of the 2020 supply chain top 25 [press release]. (2020, May 20). Retrieved from www.gartner.com/en/newsroom/press-releases/2020-05-20-gartner-announces-rankings-of-the-2020-supply-chain-top-25.

Gaur, V., & Gaiha, A. (2020, May–June). Building a transparent supply chain: Blockchain can enhance trust, efficiency, and speed. *Harvard Business Review, 98*(3), 94–103.

Howells, R. (2020, January 15). *5 trends set to disrupt global supply chains in 2020*. Retrieved from www.forbes.com/sites/sap/2020/01/15/5-trends-set-to-disrupt-global-supply-chains-in-2020/#2a39da031464.

Jaegar, J. (2019, May 6). *Top 10 supply chain risks for 2019*. Retrieved from www.complianceweek.com/risk-management/top-10-supply-chain-risks-for-2019/27024.article.

Kenton, W. (2019, June 26). *Operations management*. Retrieved from www.investopedia.com/terms/o/operations-management.asp.

Kenton, W. (2020, February 10). *Economic Order Quantity (EOQ) definition*. Retrieved from www.investopedia.com/terms/e/economicorderquantity.asp.

Lyles, A. (2019). *Kanban Order Quantity (KOQ) vs. Economic Order Quantity (EOQ): The best formula for setting standard replenishment quantities*. Retrieved from https://falconfastening.com/lean-learning/inventory-management/kanban-order-quantity-koq-vs-economic-order-quantity-eoq/.

Popkin, B. (2014, March 13). *This motorcycle maker is surging through seasonality*. Retrieved from www.fool.com/investing/general/2014/03/13/this-motorcycle-maker-is-surging-through-seasonali.aspx.

Six Sigma vs. Total Quality Management. (2019, February 16). Retrieved from https://project-management.com/six-sigma-vs-total-quality-management/.

Supply chain fraud: Risk management for retail companies. (2018, December). Retrieved from www.bdo.com/insights/industries/retail-consumer-products/supply-chain-fraud-risk-management-for-retail-comp.

Tarver, E. (2019, April 20). *Horizontal vs. vertical integration: What's the difference?* Retrieved from www.investopedia.com/ask/answers/051315/what-difference-between-horizontal-integration-and-vertical-integration.asp.

Top 10: Lean manufacturing companies in the world. (2018, February 1). Retrieved from https://ufuture.com/top-10-lean-manufacturing-companies-world/.

Using blockchain to drive supply chain transparency. (2020). Retrieved from https://www2.deloitte.com/us/en/pages/operations/articles/blockchain-supply-chain-innovation.html#.

Villena, V.H., & Gioia, D.A. (2020, March–April). *A more sustainable supply chain*. Retrieved from https://hbr.org/2020/03/a-more-sustainable-supply-chain.

What are the main supply chain challenges? (2020). Retrieved from www.blumeglobal.com/learning/supply-chain-challenges/.

What is a supply chain? (2020). Retrieved from https://corporatefinanceinstitute.com/resources/knowledge/strategy/supply-chain/.

Zara's supply chain analysis: The secret behind Zara's retail success. (2018, June 25). Retrieved from www.tradegecko.com/blog/supply-chain-management/zara-supply-chain-its-secret-to-retail-success.

Chapter 9

The Care and Feeding of Human Capital

The central focus of *human resources (HR)* is caring for employees. Here, we refer to the care and feeding of those all-important employees because they require more than a paycheck, office space, and health benefits to thrive in an organization. As a company's single most important asset, employees require ongoing *engagement*, growth opportunities, and professional development. *Human capital* doesn't appear on a company's balance sheet, but its intangible asset value flows from an employee's experience and skills (Kenton, 2019). Although the economic value of human capital differs across the firm (think intern vs. CEO), the company must invest in employees at all levels. Human capital investments improve productivity and profitability. The human resources department manages recruiting, hiring, training, and development of employees. We'll explore key issues in human capital management in this chapter.

The Future of Work and the Employee Experience

The global COVID-19 pandemic accelerated a business shift toward digital workspaces that was already underway (Sixt, 2020). Many firms demonstrated that business continuity during the crisis was not only possible, but also profitable. Employees are expected to continue preferring working remotely for the foreseeable future. This digital shift isn't limited to workspaces, however. Google, Microsoft, Slack, and other developers offer tools for streamlining virtual communication among team members. As Millennials rise to executive positions, they carry an "always on" work mentality driven by mobile technology while still striving for balance in life.

Add to these trends the increasing demand for a *scalable workforce*, that is, hiring according to demand and business need with the ability to add or reduce personnel on short notice (Sixt, 2020). Some *talent acquisition* firms specialize in providing workers on an as-needed basis to accommodate both employers and the labor force. This future of the workplace is not the 9-to-5, same desk, same job, same company approach that dominated the labor market for generations. Human resources is at the forefront of managing the changing landscape of how work gets done today.

Six areas that will dominate the Chief Human Resources Officer's (CHRO) attention in coming years include (DiClaudio, 2020):

- **Purpose and culture.** Human resources is expected to take a more dominant role in shaping, leading, and driving *organizational culture*. Part of that challenge includes actively engaging employees in experiences that reinforce and enhance culture and identifying which behavioral levers drive or detract from culture (see also Shin, 2020). Purpose and culture are the backbones of a happy, productive workforce (see also Kohll, 2018). When employees are motivated, engaged, and well prepared to do their jobs within a positive culture, several benefits ensue, including the ability to recruit top talent, retain top performing employees, increase job satisfaction and collaboration, sustain morale, and diminish job-related stress (see Sidebar 9.1: Sweetgreen's Company Culture and Sidebar 9.2: Employee Engagement).

Sidebar 9.1 Sweetgreen's Company Culture

(Morgan, 2018; see also Kohll, 2018)
(Logo reprinted with permission from Sweetgreen)

sweetgreen®

Sweetgreen is an American fast and casual restaurant offering healthy, seasonal food made with locally sourced ingredients. The chain was started in 2007 by three co-founders just three months out of college. Sweetgreen today has more than 90 locations and 4,000 employees across the East Coast, Midwest, and California.

Sweetgreen's CEO describes the company's culture as happy, humble, hardworking, curious, and coachable, which drives their purpose of investing in local communities. Inherent to Sweetgreen's culture is fostering a meaningful experience for employees and customers. Corporate headquarters is referred to as The Treehouse, and the general manager of each restaurant is known as the Head Coach.

Sweetgreen's CEO's advice for company culture:

- Connect to mission
- Convert values to action
- Allow teams to co-build cultural elements together
- Realize your culture will – and should – evolve over time

- **Workforce insights and analytics.** Data are everywhere and increasingly important in HR decision-making and talent management. Data science methods discussed in Chapter 7, including artificial intelligence (AI), help firms understand how best to recruit and retain top talent – as well as predict which employees are most likely to leave the company.
- **Employee experience.** Much like the customer experience of interacting with a brand, so, too, is the employee's personal experience with the company gaining attention. Employees expect an experience uniquely tailored to their career goals, lifestyle, and work preferences. The employee experience moving forward is expected to be mobile, social, physical, technical, and digital (see also Campbell, 2020). The best companies work with employees to develop *individualized development plans* (IDPs), which can

include opportunities for coaching, mentoring, cross-training, "stretch" assignments, job shadowing, and rotation to enhance an employee's skill set and experience (see also "Developing Employees," 2020). Employees identified as *high potential* are fast-tracked for leadership development. Whether employees are told they've been designated as "high po" depends on the company's approach to employee development. Other employees may be developed as *individual contributors*, or those without management responsibilities, to best offer their skills to the firm (see also "What Is," 2020).

- **Workforce shaping.** Agile workforce planning and shaping is the future of HR, akin to the scalable workforce demands previously mentioned. Data analytics is at the center of deploying full-time employees, short-term (also known as gig) workers, and machines to get work done on time and on budget. The "resources" leveraged by HR have expanded beyond human resources.
- **Enabling technology.** Human resources management requires tech-savvy approaches to maintaining a connected, productive workforce, ranging from cloud services and knowledge management to social, mobile, and AI innovations. Didn't think HR required technology know-how? Think again (see also Doel, 2020).
- **Organizing HR.** With expanding expectations for HR to utilize technology, manage an agile workforce, facilitate a winning culture, and customize the employee experience, CHROs will need to consider, too, how best to organize the HR function that now includes capabilities, partnerships, and budgets not previously seen as relevant to HR. The broadening of expected HR deliverables – and the consequent talents required of HR professionals in recent years – is remarkable.

Now that we've taken a look at the future of work, let's consider what is involved in bringing and keeping top talent in the company.

Attracting, Retaining, and Incentivizing Employees

People are the focal point of managing human capital (Carreau, 2020). The battle for acquiring and retaining top talent is real, with demand far exceeding supply. We've covered the expanding role of data science in all things HR. Beyond technology, however, HR additionally must develop and manage an *employment brand* that not only attracts, but also retains, talent. Successful talent acquisition and retention strategies center on the following:

- **Putting culture first** – specifically, a culture that drives employee satisfaction with a clear mission/purpose, high-quality leadership, and plentiful career opportunities.
- **A strong employer brand** – the need for cross-disciplinary brand management is obvious when studies reveal 75% of job seekers consider a potential employer's brand before applying.
- **Ongoing training and development** – companies must both forecast future skills needed and develop employee talent to fulfill those needs in a just-in-time manner.
- **Treating even those not hired as brand ambassadors** – job candidates will either receive an offer or walk away for other opportunities. In either case, the job candidate experience needs to be one worth remembering – and sharing with other potential seekers.

- **Using technology to enhance the human touch** – today's top recruiters are a combination of headhunter, data scientist, customer service expert, and digital strategist. The relational aspect of attracting talent may begin with data, but the human touch is essential in getting a candidate to choose one company over another. Having a prospect's future co-workers involved in securing an employment offer is one effective strategy.
- **Not giving up on the office** – although working remotely may be a desirable option, employees need in-person interaction to build trust, a sense of community, and collaborative work environments.

Sidebar 9.2 Employee Engagement

("Developing Employees," 2020)

Definitions of employee engagement vary, but the overarching idea is that engaged employees are personally invested in and actively contributing to the company's success. The following attributes differentiate the engaged from the disengaged employee.

Engaged Employee Behaviors	Disengaged Employee Behaviors
Optimistic	Pessimistic
Team-oriented	Self-centered
Goes above and beyond	High absenteeism
Solution-oriented	Negative attitude
Selfless	Egocentric
Shows a passion for learning	Focuses on monetary worth
Passes along credit but accepts blame	Accepts credit but passes along blame

---

Employee engagement starts with identifying, recruiting, and securing talent, but the process must continue if companies hope to retain that talent for a longer term (see Sidebar 9.2: Employee Engagement). Effective retention strategies reinforce an employee's decision to join the company and motivate employees to keep contributing (and growing) their talents to help the company succeed. *Turnover* is expensive (Halvorson, 2018). Firms can spend nearly double an employee's salary replacing an employee who's left, not to mention the time and effort involved in finding the right match for the vacated position. As one of my grad school professors used to say, "It's much easier to keep a friend than to find a new friend." My college sorority phrased the same idea as "keep rushing our pledges." Similar logic applies to retaining employees. Don't assume that once they're in the door, they're yours to keep forever. Much of a manager's work is keeping good performers convinced they're valued and making a difference.

So, how, you ask, do you intentionally work on retaining employees? Here are some suggestions (Halvorson, 2018):

- **Competitive salary and benefits** – HR has access to loads of related data to ensure a company's compensation is on par with its competitors. Money and benefits aren't everything when a candidate is looking for the right place to work, but the importance of these offerings being fair cannot be underestimated. Like HR, potential and current employees have access to data, too, including Glassdoor and other providers of salary-based info.

- **Hiring the right person from the start** – companies can feel the pressure of filling a position and fill it with the wrong person. It's much better to have a failed search, regroup, and start over than to hire the wrong person who can potentially harm productivity and morale.
- **Reduce employee pain** – finding and addressing employee pain points, and then addressing them to the extent possible, requires managers to remain personally connected with their people. Life will present occasional stumbling blocks to even the best employee's usual performance. The sooner a pain point can be recognized and addressed, the more likely the employee will stay with the company through a rough patch.
- **Provide leaders, not bosses** – *leaders* are much better at retaining employees and much more likely to be followed than a task-master boss. The best leaders know where the company is headed and how their team contributes to that vision, how to handle the inevitable challenges that will impact their teams, and the importance of high quality in their employees' work. Leaders also know that believing in and inspiring people drive success. Leadership can flourish at any level of the organization when employees are given the skills, trust, and ability to lead. Managers lacking leadership skills must have their development needs addressed, not ignored.
- **Value and encourage learning** – research tells us that employee learning and employee engagement go hand-in-hand. Employees learn from mistakes, too, and need opportunities to share lessons learned when things go wrong. Training and development should align with employee goal-setting and reward systems that encourage continuous learning.
- **Make advancement possible** – employees who know where they're going – and how to get there – are naturally more motivated and engaged. Even employees who are content to stay in their current role or work as individual contributors long for ways they can grow their skills, job satisfaction, and knowledge base. Advancement doesn't just mean climbing the ladder. Some of the most valuable employees are those who develop deep expertise right where they are.

Incentives are an important component of making the employee experience rewarding and productive (Rowe, 2018). Common types of incentives include:

- **Profit-sharing** can be offered via cash or stock bonuses or through *deferred compensation* when specified company goals are met. For example, a company can distribute a share of profits to employees on an annual basis or increase tax-free contributions to employee 401(K) retirement plans for later use.
- **Bonuses** can take the form of cash or commissions paid for outstanding employee performance, such as reaching sales goals, developing a new product, or securing new business referrals. Retention bonuses are used to incentivize essential employees or executives to stay with the company for a period of time after a major event, such as a merger.
- **Company stock shares** are awarded to employees in several ways. *Restricted stock* must be held for a specified period of time before shares can be sold, thereby incentivizing

employees to stay and share the company's interest in increasing the stock price for financial gain. *Stock options* allow an employee to purchase a specific number of shares at a specific (usually lower-than-market) price within a specific timeframe. Employees who leave the company before being eligible to *exercise* those options forfeit those stock options. *Performance shares* are grants of shares typically provided to executives or officers for reaching performance goals over a multi-year period.

- **Career development and training** works best as an incentive when employees have a say in the work-related area they wish to develop, such as a new language, an international assignment, or an opportunity to learn another part of the business.
- **Recognition and other non-cash incentives** can be offered at the individual or team level, including awards, featured accomplishments, gift cards, or paid time off for reaching stated performance objectives.

Attracting, retaining, and incentivizing employees to do their best work with the company requires managers with a keen ability to match employee needs with organizational needs. More often than not, however, optimizing skills and resources requires employees to work in teams.

The Psychology of High-Performing Teams

Much of human capital management focuses on developing individual employees, but teamwork is required to get organizational goals accomplished (see Sidebar 9.3: Three Types of Workplace Intelligence). As a manager, you may supervise a number of thoroughbred performers with the drive and expertise to get things done. Put them together on a team, however, and disaster can strike if individuals are primarily concerned about their personal interests, visibility, or recognition for a job well done. To avoid this dilemma, we now turn to the psychology of high performing teams. How does a team of superstars, average performers, or some combination thereof evolve into a well-oiled machine focused on a common purpose? Here's what research and experience tell us (Lino, 2020):

- **Bonded teams need each other to keep succeeding.** Interestingly, a superstar taken out of their usual team environment doesn't perform nearly as well without their team. Organizations fall prey to thinking that an outstanding team performer can be placed in a different setting on their own, with equal success. But experience proves otherwise, at least in the short term. A superstar without their usual team dynamic, resources, and processes needs time to recreate those dynamics in a different place. The effective functioning of a bonded team and their unique way of interacting – in many ways that are unspoken – takes effort to replicate. Connectedness matters in effective teams.
- **Trust among team members is essential.** Without positive expectations of the intentions of other team members, particularly in states of ambiguity or uncertainty, teams quickly degrade into hidden agendas, contradictory information, and higher levels of command and control. A trusting team will work faster and more effectively than a team mired in bureaucratic controls (see also Covey, 2008).
- **Teams require a sense of identity.** A sense of belonging brings enjoyment in working together, clarity to the team's mission, and loyalty among members that can help

teams maneuver the inevitable challenges they will face. A positive mood, expectations of success, and a sense of humor (and even fun) help create a collective "can-do" attitude.
- **Competition may or may not motivate team members.** Some teams thrive on competition. Others disintegrate in a competitive environment. Team composition must balance personalities to sustain a motivated team with stretch goals, increasing levels of responsibility, and reinforcement of successful outcomes.
- **Feedback mechanisms are a must for teams.** Effective communication and participation in group feedback focused on what is and what is not working are just as important for teams overcoming setbacks as they are for learning from achievements. Trust and connectedness among members ease the feedback process and significantly aid conflict resolution.
- **Teams must manage team-level stress.** Individual members have their own stress triggers, but one member's stress can impact the team's dynamic as much as a new constraint or change pressure placed on the entire team. The most effective teams ably diagnose and address pain points when they surface. They also realize that, in stressful times, division of workload may require some members to carry extra weight.

Teams function best when members are able to bring their authentic selves to the workplace. Diversity and inclusion initiatives are essential for optimizing human capital potential.

Sidebar 9.3 Three Types of Workplace Intelligence

(Kumar, Rose, & Subramaniam, 2008; Dixon Hall 2018)

Intelligence commonly measured as IQ is not a guarantee of professional success. Beyond job skills, academic credentials, and proven performance are three types of workplace intelligence required of leaders, managers, and others responsible for developing human capital. Likewise, employees aspiring to lead others should develop each of the following qualities. Each form of intelligence involves ways of behaving and adapting to changing work environments.

Social Intelligence	The ability to understand one's own thoughts and others' feelings, thoughts, or behaviors; interpret non-verbal cues; accomplish interpersonal tasks; and act appropriately in a situation that requires one to "get along" with others.
Emotional Intelligence	The ability to be self-aware in a given situation, control impulses, express empathy, and respond to emotional cues that are symbolically constructed and culturally transmitted. As such, someone with high emotional intelligence in a familiar culture may have very low emotional intelligence in another culture.
Cultural Intelligence	The ability to adapt to various cultural settings through a conscious effort to understand one's own and others' "hidden scripts" derived from cultural cues that drive behavior. Cultural intelligence goes beyond diversity and multicultural efforts to develop a deeper understanding of cultural identities and nuances related to race, ethnicity, political ideology, gender, sexuality, and religion.

Diversity and Inclusion

The U.S. Civil Rights era ushered in laws designed to protect individuals from discrimination, including the Equal Pay Act of 1963, Title VII of the Civil Rights Act of 1964, and the Age Discrimination in Employment Act of 1967 ("Diversity & Inclusion," n.d.). Subsequent laws in the 1970s and 1990s expanded civil rights protections, including those for the disabled. Organizational commitment to diversity and inclusion efforts can be tracked along four stages of evolution, ranging from basic compliance to an integrated business philosophy.

- **Stage 1: EEO and legal compliance.** Early corporate efforts focused on complying with laws regarding equal employment opportunities and reporting to the *Equal Employment Opportunity Commission* (EEOC). Organizations still at this stage are reactive in fulfilling legal mandates.
- **Stage 2: Affirmative action and hiring of diversity officers.** Affirmative action began in the 1970s as an effort to give preferential hiring treatment to underrepresented groups. Diversity officer positions were created to implement programming, scholarships, and other opportunities for minority employees and communities. Although this stage goes beyond mere legal compliance in equal employment initiatives, it falls short of an organization-wide commitment to diversity and inclusion.
- **Stage 3: Targeted diversity and inclusion recruitment and retention.** At this stage, diversity and inclusion are leveraged for recruiting and retention as a workforce imperative. The search for top talent is purposively designed to seek potential hires from diverse backgrounds and tailor the employee experience to retain these employees in ways they find meaningful.
- **Stage 4: Integrating diversity and inclusion into the corporate business model.** Organizations demonstrate a comprehensive commitment to diversity and inclusion when related efforts touch every major aspect of the business, including customers, markets, communities, and suppliers. Diversity and inclusion is managed as a competitive advantage, broadly articulated to internal and external stakeholders, and pervasive across business activities (see Figure 9.1: Target Corporation Diversity and Inclusion Goals and Results).

Workplace *diversity* is defined by differences in not only race, ethnicities, genders, ages, religions, disabilities, and sexual orientation, but also differences in education, personalities, skill sets, ideologies, experiences, and knowledge (Mondal, 2020). *Inclusion*, however, implies a collaborative and respectful work environment where employees feel supported. Although much focus has been placed on the diversity of human characteristics that are physically visible, such as skin color and able-bodiedness, the strategic value of diversity derives from a much broader set of attributes. Diversity goals met for the sake of diversity alone don't necessarily deliver inclusion. Without concerted attention paid to creating an environment where different traits are welcomed and valued, the full advantage of diversity is not realized.

Boston Consulting Group (BCG) defines inclusion as employees feeling free to be their authentic selves and believing their perspectives matter in the workplace (Krentz, Dean,

champion an inclusive society

At Target, diversity & inclusion are key to our business strategy. To be able to remain relevant with the products, services, experiences and messages our guests expect, we must have their perspectives represented in our team and work.

For us, diversity is about recognizing that our dimensions of difference are actually our greatest strength, and then building an inclusive environment in which everyone feels welcome, valued, respected, and free to bring their full selves... whether that's to work, to a shopping experience... or to their communities. We strive for parity and to give everyone equitable access to opportunities.

To advance diversity & inclusion, we champion a more inclusive society through creating an inclusive guest experience, having an inclusive work environment, ensuring we have a diverse workforce and leveraging our influence to drive positive impact on society.

Three years ago, we established commitments as a mechanism to help drive focus and measure progress within our broader diversity and inclusion strategy. While we are proud of the progress we have made, we recognize the opportunity ahead.

supplier diversity
↑64.4%
tier 1 spend

hispanic media marketing
#2 spend in retail

localized product
↑77% in sales
beauty, toys, food

corporate responsibility
51% of spending to diverse communities

diverse hiring
↑8%
exempt team members

diverse turnover
↓8%
in progress

diverse representation
20+%
across all position levels

D&I inclusive experiences
80+%

Figure 9.1 Target Corporation Diversity and Inclusion Goals and Results
Reprinted with permission from Target Corporation

& Novacek, 2019). Moving toward an inclusive environment may require a significant cultural shift in an organization, including a visible commitment to inclusion spanning from top leadership to frontline leaders, sharing and celebration of best practices, and accountability for maintaining behavioral standards at all organizational levels (see Figure 9.2: Diversity and Inclusion Best Practices). Diversity and inclusion must be effectively paired to optimize their value for organizational learning and competitive advantage.

A survey of HR executives reveals best practices in diversity and inclusion go beyond observable human characteristics to attributes associated with how an organization gets things done, including:

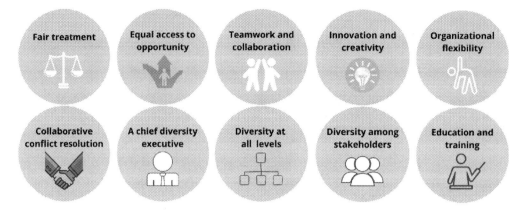

Figure 9.2 Diversity and Inclusion Best Practices
Mondal, 2020

HR Risk Management

The recruiting, retention, and care of human capital sustains the company's most important asset, but not without substantial risk. Four areas are particularly vulnerable to human resource risk, as follows (Friede, 2018):

- **Compliance.** Laws relevant to employment and benefits are plentiful, overlapping, and subject to changes over time. Issues including fair labor standards, medical leaves, pregnancy discrimination, mental health, and insurance coverage demand continuous monitoring and policy adaption to ensure the company stays in compliance and out of the courtroom.
- **Financial.** Employee investments are significant. Financial risk in an HR context refers to maximizing return on those investments through appropriate compensation, development, and incentive programs. The financial risk of losing top talent can be just as great as the risk of retaining employees who should be dismissed.
- **Operational.** Talent shortages, employee job satisfaction, performance, productivity, vendor management, absenteeism, safety, and retention of organizational knowledge each expose the company to the risk of interrupting operations. These areas of human capital risk must be managed across the organization.
- **Strategic.** Risk associated with the company's strategic direction resides in the selection and cultivation of leadership, including *succession planning* that requires the organization to consider not only what's next, but who's next, in the leadership ranks. When actively managed, culture, diversity and inclusion, and employee development programs expand the pool of potential leaders for the company.

Human resource risks are plentiful and, as such, need to be prioritized (Friede, 2018). Risks that are relevant, likely, impactful, enduring, and addressable demand the most time and resource allocation. As with any organizational crisis, several response strategies to

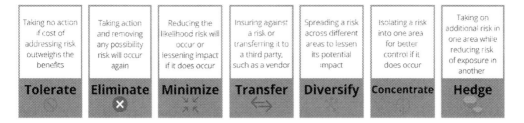

Figure 9.3 Human Capital Risk Treatment Options
Depending on the nature of human capital risk, managers across the organization have a number of treatment options available to address, lessen, or eliminate a risk.
Friede, 2018

human capital risks are available to HR and operations executives (see Figure 9.3: Human Capital Risk Treatment Options).

The Dual-Brand Challenge

Employees may be the company's most important asset, but they also pose the greatest risks to the enterprise. Their daily actions can bring both substantial rewards and liability exposure to a firm. The focus of human resources is attracting, developing, retaining, and leveraging the extraordinary potential of human capital. And herein lies a dual-brand challenge relevant to corporate communicators.

Branding is overwhelmingly related to the product and service side of the business, including how the company interacts with its customers, delivers on its promises, and performs among its competitors. Not as prominent but equally important is a company's employment brand. Job candidates base application decisions on their perception of how the organization treats its customers. Fewer companies are standouts in promoting how the organization treats its employees. The battle for talent will continue to intensify.

Granted, communication strategies vary when attempting to reach a potential employee versus a potential customer, but the fundamentals of branding apply to each audience. If a company wants to distinguish itself as an employer, it needs an employer brand. Obvious, too, is the need for alignment between a firm's product/service branding and its employer branding. Although messages will differ, the company's underlying attributes should be consistently conveyed. A highly innovative consumer products company, for example, should have an equally innovative employee development program. Applicants familiar with the company's products will expect as much.

On the public affairs side, it's important for elected officials and policy makers to know the employer side of a company, particularly in regard to local hiring practices and economic contributions to communities where it operates. As well, employees represent the company in their daily interactions outside of the office. The more informed they are, the more accurate the information they can convey to interested friends, family members, and other acquaintances who inquire about their work and employer. In essence, every employee is a walking, communicating representative of the company. Being a brand employees can be proud of on and off the job enhances both the work of public affairs and the realization of human capital potential.

References

Campbell, M. (2020). *Employee experience*. Retrieved from https://advisory.kpmg.us/insights/future-hr/future-hr-employee-experience.html.

Carreau, D. (2020, January 2). *How to win the war for talent in 2020*. Retrieved from www.entrepreneur.com/article/344360.

Covey, S. M. R. (2008). *The speed of trust: The one thing that changes everything*. New York, NY: Free Press.

Developing employees. (2020). Retrieved from www.shrm.org/resourcesandtools/tools-and-samples/toolkits/pages/developingemployees.aspx.

DiClaudio, M. (2020). *The future of HR*. Retrieved from https://advisory.kpmg.us/insights/future-hr.html.

Diversity & inclusion: An overview. (n.d.). Retrieved from www.diversitybestpractices.com/sites/diversitybestpractices.com/files/import/embedded/anchors/files/diversity_primer_chapter_01.pdf.

Dixon Hall, M.A. (2018). *The cultural intelligence initiative @ SMU*. Retrieved from www.ciqatsmu.com/home.

Doel, J. (2020). *The future of HR technology*. Retrieved from https://advisory.kpmg.us/insights/future-hr/future-hr-enabling-technology.html.

Friede, K.A. (2018, February 23). *Human capital risk management*. Retrieved from https://cacubo.org/wp-content/uploads/2018/03/Human-Capital-Risk-Management-CACUBO-02-23-2018.pdf.

Halvorson, C. (2018, May 30). *7 great employee retention strategies*. Retrieved from https://wheniwork.com/blog/7-great-employee-retention-strategies.

Kenton, W. (2019, May 28). *Human capital*. Retrieved from www.investopedia.com/terms/h/humancapital.asp.

Kohll, A. (2018, August 14). *How to build a positive company culture*. Retrieved from www.forbes.com/sites/alankohll/2018/08/14/how-to-build-a-positive-company-culture/#5ddd04fc49b5.

Krentz, M., Dean, J., & Novacek, G. (2019, April 24). *Diversity is just the first step. Inclusion comes next*. Retrieved from www.bcg.com/publications/2019/diversity-first-step-inclusion-comes-next.

Kumar, N., Rose, R.C., & Subramaniam (no first initial). (2008, November/December). The bond between intelligences: Cultural, emotional, and social. *Performance Improvement*, 47(10), 42–48. Retrieved from https://onlinelibrary.wiley.com/doi/pdf/10.1002/pfi.20039.

Lino, C. (2020, June 9). *The psychology of teamwork: The 7 habits of highly effective teams*. Retrieved from https://positivepsychology.com/psychology-teamwork/.

Mondal, S. (2020, June 13). *Diversity and inclusion: A complete guide for HR professionals*. Retrieved from https://ideal.com/diversity-and-inclusion/.

Morgan, J. (2018, October 8). *Sweetgreen's CEO on creating a meaningful company culture and positively impacting the surrounding community*. Retrieved from https://thefutureorganization.com/sweetgreens-ceo-meaningful-culture-impacting-community/.

Rowe, R. H. (2018, November 21). *Six types of incentive plans*. Retrieved from https://bizfluent.com/list-6557258-six-types-incentive-plans.html.

Shin, L. (2020). *Purpose and culture*. Retrieved from https://advisory.kpmg.us/insights/future-hr/future-hr-purpose-culture.html.

Sixt, A. (2020, July 28). *4 trends that are shaping the future of work*. Retrieved from www.entrepreneur.com/article/353861.

What is an individual contributor? (2020, April 17). Retrieved from www.indeed.com/career-advice/finding-a-job/what-is-an-individual-contributor.

Chapter 10

What is Strategy?

Strategy. It's a word frequently used in business circles. *Strategic thinking. Strategic planning. Strategic alignment.* But just what is strategy, and how does it apply to our work as communicators? We know we need strategy, and we want it to be good strategy, but what, exactly, does strategy entail? Strategy applies as much to a public affairs project as it does to a new business unit or an $80 billion merger, but knowing where to begin and what exactly to *do* with strategy can leave the best communicators perplexed. In this chapter, we'll explore strategy and its many related components, starting with the basics.

The Business Model

To understand strategy, you must first understand a company's *business model*. Essentially, a business model is a company's plan for monetizing its products and/or services. Have a business idea? Great. The first question a potential investor will ask is, "How are you going to make money with that?" Enter the business model, which identifies the following for new and established companies (Kopp, 2020):

- Products and/or services the business offers
- Target market(s)
- Projected revenues
- Costs
- Pricing
- Suppliers/partners
- Competitors
- Financing sources
- *Value proposition*, or why products and/or services are valuable to customers
- Marketing strategy

The channels through which businesses earn a profit can take a variety of forms. Direct sales, franchising, brick-and-mortar retail, and other options can be combined with internet retail to earn revenues.

DOI: 10.4324/9781003000600-11

MIT researchers describe four types of business models (Weill, Malone, D'Urso, Herman, & Woerner, 2005):

- **Creators** buy raw materials and then transform them into a product sold to buyers.
- **Distributors** buy products and resell essentially the same product to someone else.
- **Landlords** sell the right to use, but not own, an asset for a set period of time.
- **Brokers** facilitate sales by matching potential buyers and sellers.

They further classify these business types as dealing with four types of assets:

- **Physical assets** include durable (e.g., tools) and nondurable (e.g., food) items.
- **Financial assets** include stocks, bonds, and insurance policies.
- **Intangible assets** include intellectual property, knowledge, and brand image.
- **Human assets** include people's time, effort, and knowledge.

Examined together, it becomes apparent how these elements can be combined to solidify a working business model. For example, General Motors is a creator of physical assets, Target is a distributor of physical assets, Bank of America is a landlord of financial assets, Crunchbase is a broker of intangible assets, and Robert Half is a broker of human assets.

What Business Are We In?

Although the answer to "What business are we in?" may seem patently obvious, it's a question worth exploring, particularly when a company is facing opportunities for new products, brand extensions, and the like. Ask your colleagues this question about your own company, and you may be surprised by how many different answers you get. If your colleagues have varying responses, assume your stakeholders will, too.

Here's an example: If a company is in the airline business, it's going to focus on air travel. But if an airline instead sees itself in the transportation business, it's going to be open to acquiring rental car or bus services. If it envisions itself a travel business, it may invest in destination packages that get customers from point A to point B through a variety of means and strategic partnerships. Knowing what business your firm is in directs strategic thinking throughout the organization on how best to leverage assets and growth. Part of answering "What business are we in?" is noticing not what you're selling, but rather what, exactly, your customers are buying (Heaton, 2016). Related, and equally important, questions include:

- Who is our customer?
- What does our customer value?
- What customer needs are not currently being adequately met?
- What is the potential of this market?
- How is this market changing?
- Who is our competition?
- What emerging technologies will impact this market?

These are just a few of the questions to ask on the way to a guiding strategy. Let's next look at the building blocks of strategy.

The What, Who, Why, and How of Strategy

Harvard Business Review defines strategy as follows:

> *A business strategy is a set of guiding principles that, when communicated and adopted in the organization, generates a desired pattern of decision making. A strategy is therefore how people throughout the organization should make decisions and allocate resources in order [to] accomplish key objectives. A good strategy provides a clear roadmap, consisting of a set of guiding principles or rules, that defines the action people in the business should take (and not take) and the things they should prioritize (and not prioritize) to achieve desired goals.*
>
> (Watkins, 2007, para 2)

If strategy is the map of actions to take with guiding principles on how to achieve stated goals, we can, with equal confidence, then state what strategy is not (see also Kaplan & Norton, 2004). Strategy is *not* the mission or big picture of what leaders want to accomplish. Strategy is *not* the company's purpose, or the driving reason for its existence. Strategy is *not* the company's vision of where it wants to be down the road or the values it holds dear to get there. But strategy *is* the *outcome* and next important step following the development of these components. In other words:

- Mission is **what** will be achieved
- Stakeholders are for **whom** value is created, captured, and delivered
- Vision is **why** the organization is motivated to excel
- Strategy is **how** resources are deployed to align a company's what, who, and why from a financial, stakeholder, operations, and human capital perspective

Strategy isn't created in a vacuum. Mission, vision, and stakeholder identification, guided by a company's values, are interrelated precursors that provide a direction of where the company wants to go, and why. And strategy isn't executed in a vacuum. Rather, strategy is dependent on a number of competing forces we'll next address.

Porter's Forces: Strategy and Competition

No discussion of business strategy is complete without Harvard Business School Professor Michael E. Porter's (1979) seminal research on how competitive forces affect the strategic process. Corporate strategy may focus on increasing share price, market share, global presence, employee satisfaction, or other objectives. Regardless of its aim, Porter tells us several overlapping forces governing *competition* in an industry must be considered in strategy development. That is, the company must either overcome or positively influence the following forces to be successful, as each determines an industry's profitability (see Figure 10.1: Porter's Competitive Forces):

Threat of entry. New market entrants increase competitive pressures, but the seriousness of this threat depends on *barriers to entry* in the industry.[1] If barriers are high, the threat of new market entrants is reduced. Significant barriers make market entry more daunting and discourage new entrants. Barriers include economies of scale,[2] product differentiation, capital requirements,[3] cost advantages, access to distribution channels,[4] and government policies. An industry that enjoys economies of scale in production, offers differentiated products, requires major capital investments, and has low-cost production and experience advantages, access to broad distribution channels, and favorable regulation policies is going to be a difficult one for new firms to enter. Industries with high barriers to entry include telecommunication, parcel delivery, pharmaceutical manufacturing, and passenger air transportation (Pearson, 2019). Newcomers will have a difficult time overcoming substantial entry barriers that protect the profitability of firms already in these industries.

Power of suppliers and buyers. Powerful suppliers can affect entire industries by raising prices on key inputs (e.g., steel, concrete, soft drink concentrate, coffee beans), thereby limiting the profitability of firms dependent on those suppliers and possibly driving those firms out of business. Buyers, too, have powers that sway markets. Buyers, including customers and firms, place competitive pressures on an industry by refusing to pay higher prices or demanding higher quality products and better customer service. Each of these actions related to supply and demand affects the profitability of firms in an industry.[5] Suppliers are more powerful when they are fewer in number and the cost of switching suppliers is high.[6] Buyers are more powerful when they purchase in large volumes, have alternative sources for purchasing, and are able to influence consumer purchasing decisions. Powerful suppliers and buyers can restrict autonomy and compel firms to adapt to change pressures. Consequently, supplier selection and customer segmentation are key strategic decisions for businesses.[7]

Threat of substitute products. The availability of substitute products or services places downward pressure on a firm's profitability.[8] Substitutes are a competitive threat if the firm's products are not sufficiently differentiated from similar products. Without differentiation, consumers are willing to accept a cheaper substitute, particularly if

Figure 10.1 Porter's Competitive Forces
Porter, 1979

switching costs are relatively low. Acceptable substitutes are also within the eye of the beholder. A consumer may be willing to switch mobile service providers but remain staunchly loyal to a local dry cleaning service. Marketing uses consumer research and brand differentiation to minimize the potential for substitutes.

Rivalry among existing competitors. Porter explains how firms jockeying for position among their competitors use pricing, new products, and advertising as tactics to get ahead.

Competition is more intense when competitors are numerous and/or of similar size and reach, industry growth is slow, products lack differentiation or switching costs, fixed costs are high, and exit barriers are high[9]. Each of these factors contributes to declining profits.

Corporate strategy, then, must comprise a plan of action that assesses and addresses each of these forces (Porter, 1979). How best can the company position itself among its competitors? What influence can the company exert on suppliers and buyers? What is the likelihood of new firms entering the market or mature firms exiting the market? Understanding the causes and trends of competitive forces enables the firm to know where best to confront competition and where best to avoid it. Porter cites the case of Dr. Pepper, a soft drink producer much smaller in size than Coca-Cola or Pepsi, yet still successful at capitalizing on a unique flavor by marketing to a narrower segment of customers.[10] The key to growth – and survival – is to position the company to be less vulnerable to competitive forces while remaining nimble enough to adapt as industry conditions change.

In essence, Porter (1985; 2008) tells us that competition doesn't come from competitors alone but rather an intermingling of forces placing change pressures on the firm. He refers to the collective strength of these forces – threat of entry, power of suppliers and buyers, threat of substitutes, and rivalry among competitors – as a function of *industry structure*, or the underlying economic and technical characteristics of an industry. The strategist, then, needs a multiple stakeholder perspective of competition reminiscent of the stakeholder model of public affairs discussed throughout this book. The more intense the forces, as seen in airlines and hotels, the more difficult earning returns on investments becomes. Porter's forces help explain the limits on a given industry's profitability and reveal the most salient threats and opportunities in a firm's competitive environment. Strategy guides the company to improve its positioning, reconfigure its supplier relationships, enhance its customer service, or otherwise focus on addressing conditions that impact the bottom line[11] and leverage competitive advantage.

Competitive Advantage and Strategic Choices

A firm's *competitive advantage* makes its products or services superior to that of its competitors (Amadeo, 2020). How does that work, you ask? Companies with a clear competitive advantage know and act upon three things: 1) the benefits and value their products or services provide; 2) their target market(s); and 3) their competitors, including not only firms, but also trends and changes in the industrial landscape that compete with a firm's offerings.[12] Strategic communication informed by a company's internal and external operating environment and aligned with each of these elements is key to promoting and sustaining competitive advantage.

Let's return to Porter's (1985; see also as cited in Amadeo, 2020) work on strategy to understand how firms achieve and maintain a competitive advantage (see Figure 10.2: Achieving Competitive Advantage). Porter argues that a firm's *positioning* is critical to its success:

> *Positioning determines whether a firm's profitability is above or below the industry average. A firm that can position itself well may earn high rates of return even though industry structure is unfavorable and the average profitability of the industry is therefore modest.*
>
> (Porter, 1985, p. 11)

Sustainable competitive advantage is "the fundamental basis of above-average performance in the long run" (p. 11) even when industry structure is unfavorable. The two basic types of competitive advantage Porter defines are *low cost* or *differentiation*, as shown on the horizontal axis in Figure 10.2. A firm's strengths and weaknesses ultimately derive from its ability to manage costs or differentiate its products and services. The vertical axis in Figure 10.2 represents a firm's scope of activities, whether it be broad-reaching in a number of industry segments or narrower in scope. The road to competitive advantage, then, reflects choices about the type of competitive advantage sought and the scope of the market in which competitive advantage is achieved. We'll examine each quadrant of Figure 10.2:

Lower Cost + Broad Target = Cost Leadership Strategy. This strategic choice is for firms determined to become the low-cost producer in an industry. The breadth of the firm's reach is wide, giving it the advantage of *economies of scale*,[13] preferential access to raw materials, and proprietary technology. Lower production costs allow for consumer pricing at or near the industry average. As such, cost leaders produce generally standardized products but must still differentiate their products relative to competitors if they are to maintain above-average performance. Examples of cost leaders include WalMart, McDonald's, and Southwest Airlines (see also Leonard, 2019).

Differentiation + Broad Target = Differentiation Strategy. This strategic choice is for firms aiming to be unique in attributes that are widely valued by consumers in an industry. Points of differentiation can focus on the product or service, its delivery system, or

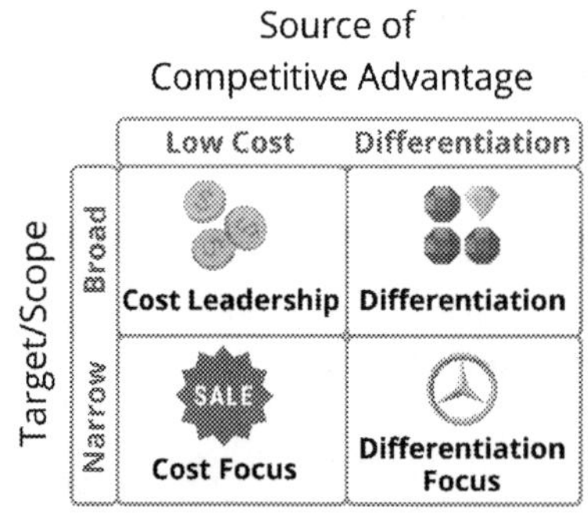

Figure 10.2 Achieving Competitive Advantage
Porter, 1985; see also Amadeo, 2020

even its marketing approach. Regardless, the reward for a successful differentiation strategy is the ability to charge a premium price. A differentiation strategy can sustain above-average performance as long as the premium price exceeds the cost of being unique. As such, differentiators must also be mindful of costs in all areas not related to its points of differentiation. Examples of broad differentiators include Nike, Toyota, and Apple (see also "Broad Differentiation," 2019; Meyer, 2019).

Lower Cost + Narrow Target = Cost Focus. This strategic choice is for firms seeking a cost advantage but in a target segment. Companies successful at finding a structurally attractive niche for cost leadership will sustain above-average performance in an industry. Examples of cost focus firms include Redbox, Claire's, and Papa Murphy's (see also Edwards, n.d.).

Differentiation + Narrow Target = Differentiation Focus. This strategic choice is for firms seeking a differentiation advantage but in a target segment. Companies successful at servicing the special needs of consumers in a particular segment will sustain above-average performance in an industry and, in many cases, with a premium price. Examples of differentiation focus firms include Mercedes Benz, Whole Foods, and REI (see also Edwards, n.d.).

Porter (1985) argues that firms must make a choice about which competitive advantage strategy to pursue, or else they get "stuck in the middle" with no competitive advantage and below-average industry performance. Most firms in a given industry are stuck in the middle, particularly those in mature industries[14] where ill-defined strategies become apparent over time and further separate competitors. Porter warns that attempting to combine strategies can be just as risky when firms fail to stick to their chosen strategy and attempt to be "all things to all people." In both airlines and hotels, premium brands are creating "no-frills" sub-brands to compete with low-cost entrants rather than diminish their differentiated strategies at higher price points (e.g., see Sargeant, 2016). The flipside of this strategy conundrum is when cost leaders like Walmart attempt to go upscale, which it attempted, and failed, in its clothing lines in the early 2000s (Pearson, 2018). Brand blurring related to competitive advantage strategy shifts can cause firms to lose focus on the areas of the business that made them industry leaders. In the case of Walmart, it's low prices, not high fashion, that makes the company a competitive behemoth. To sustain competitive advantage, strategy has to be implemented at multiple levels of the organization, and not just at headquarters.

Three Levels of Strategy

Strategy provides a competitive-based roadmap for the company, but it must be tailored for different levels of execution. Thus, strategy needs to be applicable at the corporate, business, and functional level for employees in each area to understand their specific role and contribution in fulfilling a strategic plan ("Three Levels," 2020; see Figure 10.3: Three Levels of Strategy).

- **Corporate-level strategy** is where the company answers, "What business are we in?" Corporate-level strategy sets the tone for business- and functional-level strategy. Major investment, acquisition, and divestment decisions are made at the corporate level to

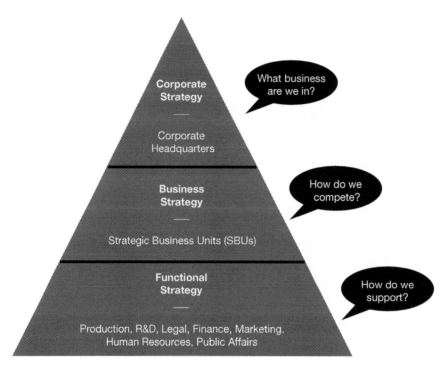

Figure 10.3 Three Levels of Strategy
"Three Levels," 2020

ready the firm for its strategic outlook. Corporate strategy is more predominant in multinational companies (MNCs) than in small-to-medium enterprises (SMEs).
- **Business-level strategy** focuses on "How do we compete?" and "How do we gain a sustainable competitive advantage in our industry?" Business-level strategy aligns with corporate-level strategy by concentrating on value created and delivered to customers as well as differentiating a firm's products and services in the marketplace. Different business areas are often referred to as *strategic business units* (SBUs).
- **Functional-level strategy** focuses on how supportive functions, including production, R&D,[15] legal, finance, marketing, human resources, and public affairs, are designing and implementing their operating strategies to align with and advance business- and corporate-level strategies.

Samsung is a good example of how multiple levels of strategy are constructed and applied ("Three Levels," 2020). The company is a conglomerate of multiple SBUs that manufacture and sell smartphones, kitchen appliances, cameras, chemicals, and televisions. Samsung corporate strategy determines if the company will add a product line to its already diverse portfolio or divest a product line that's no longer profitable. Business strategy for the SBUs must necessarily vary to accommodate the competitive environment in each product market. And functional strategy needs to address the specific needs, challenges, and opportunities in each SBU. For instance, the chemicals business may face more regulatory pressures requiring public policy management than, say, the cameras business that needs a more flexible work schedule for its employees. Although an overarching strategic direction is set at the corporate level, the nuts and bolts of strategy are executed at the business and functional levels where the work actually happens.

Innovation: The S Curve and Blue Ocean Strategy

Like strategy, the term *innovation* is commonplace. But what does innovation mean for business, and how does innovation relate to strategy? Continuous tracking of Porter's (1979) forces reveals an obvious need for firms to adapt to changes in their competitive environments. Innovation is a means of increasing value by introducing new processes, products, or services that have a positive impact across the firm (Cassidy, 2018). Ideally, innovation should result in higher profits and provide competitive advantage. Three primary areas describe where innovation can occur:

- **Revenue model innovation** can be as basic as changing pricing strategy or as radical as changing revenue models altogether. Netflix was a pioneer in using a subscription-based revenue model for on-demand movie access (see also "10 Examples," 2017). A number of newspapers, magazines, and journals – once solely accessed by subscribers – now provide certain content for free, with fuller access and benefits reserved for those paying a fee.
- **Business model innovation** can include new partnerships, products, or technologies to boost the company's profitability. Amazon began in 1995 as an online bookstore. Today, it is a leader in cloud computing, grocery delivery, and award-winning entertainment production (see also Landry, 2020).
- **Industry model innovation** is the most radical of approaches to innovation, which can include a major change to an industry or creation of an entirely new industry. Airbnb's brokering of lodging transactions using a peer-to-peer model is an example of *disruptive innovation* in the hospitality industry (see also "Airbnb," 2020). The *S Curve* (see Figure 10.4) and *Blue Ocean strategy* (see Figure 10.5) describe how these market-changing innovations occur.

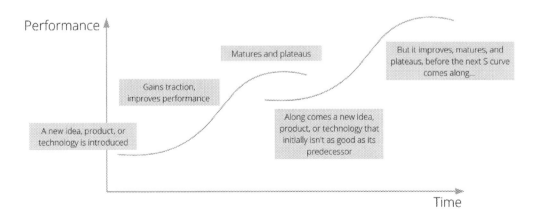

Figure 10.4 The S Curve
"S Curve," n.d.

188 What is Strategy?

The S Curve is typically used to describe technological shifts in an industry, but its overarching concept applies beyond just technology ("S Curve," n.d.). The "big idea" of the S Curve is how new ways of operating replace outdated ways of operating. As shown in Figure 10.4, the lower part of the curve of the letter "S" represents the initial introduction of a new idea or a new technology. At the onset, performance is lacking, but with experience and time, performance improves rapidly, which is represented by the steep upward slope of the middle of the "S" shape. As performance peaks, the new idea or technology reaches a plateau where further improvements are limited. Around the time of this leveling, a new S curve begins to develop as a new idea or technology is introduced and, like its predecessor, has a slower start followed by rapid growth. This new S curve will plateau, too, as the next innovative idea or technology sparks yet another S curve. And the process continues, fueled by innovative thinking each time.

The lesson of the S Curve is for businesses to know where they are on it ("S Curve," n.d.). Then, firms can either ride the curve as long as it's profitable and get out of the business, jump to a new S curve, or, take on the boldest of strategies and create a new S Curve.[16] Examples of S Curve innovations include digital watches, mobile apps, and electric cars. Tried and true methods of production or delivery give way to new approaches that begin slowly, accelerate rapidly, and eventually decline as the next innovation comes along.

Strategy professors at global graduate business school INSEAD W. Chan Kim and Renée Mauborgne wrote the iconic bestseller, *Blue Ocean Strategy*, to encourage businesses not to compete in an existing market space (what they refer to as red ocean strategy) but rather to create an uncontested market space (what they call a blue ocean) where no competition exists ("What Is," 2020; see also Figure 10.5: Red vs. Blue Ocean Strategy). A conventional following of Porter's forces aligns with their notion of red ocean strategy in that the firm makes a strategic choice of differentiation *or* low cost to beat the competition. A blue ocean approach, in contrast, is when the business creates an entirely new market. Without competition, the firm is able to garner value derived from *both* differentiation and low cost. Examples of blue ocean strategy include iTunes (2020) that unlocked a new market of digital music; Cirque du Soleil (2020) that redefined circus entertainment; and Curves (2020) that opened an untapped market of women seeking a fitness solution that was fun, interactive, and feasible within their busy schedules. Blue oceans provide entirely new venues for value creation, and the first to arrive reaps significant benefits before competition appears.

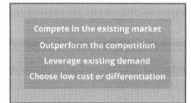

Figure 10.5 Red vs. Blue Ocean Strategy
"What Is," 2020

Strategic Communication

Put *strategic* and *communication* together, and we have yet another commonly used idiom worthy of closer examination. The functional execution of corporate and business strategy falls squarely into public affairs, along with other supporting functions in the company. Whereas production focuses on the product, R&D focuses on innovation, legal focuses on law, finance focuses on capital, marketing focuses on promotion, and human resources focuses on employees, public affairs is uniquely positioned to focus on negotiating relationships with a *variety* of stakeholders, both internal and external to the firm. And as we've discussed, it's necessary for public affairs managers to understand and draw upon the knowledge base of other supporting functions for communications to be accurate, sensible, and effective. As the primary interface for a broad swath of external audiences, public affairs has a direct role to play in implementing strategy as follows:

- **Knowing the business model** and understanding how each SBU contributes to that business model provides an overarching view of how the company makes money, manages costs, and prioritizes resources. This bird's eye view will provide you with an executive-level understanding of company operations, even if you're an entry-level employee in a narrowly defined role. You'll think, plan, and communicate better when you keep this broader business perspective in mind. You'll ask better questions, too, which will get you noticed (for good reasons). Demonstrate a deep understanding of the business model, and you'll greatly increase your value to the company.
- **Understanding industry structure and your target customer(s)** includes knowing what business you're in. Will you communicate as a clothing manufacturer when your company aims to be a lifestyle brand? Hopefully not. Are the barriers to entry in your industry high or low? How much power is wielded by your suppliers and buyers? Where is your company positioned among its competitors? How vulnerable is your product to substitutes? Answers to each of these questions help set the tone, content, audience, and venues for your communication strategy.
- **Knowing your competitive advantage** includes understanding whether your target market is broad or narrow and whether your strategic direction focuses on differentiation or low cost. What draws customers, suppliers, government officials, employees, and investors to your business? Know what matters to your key stakeholders, provide them with related information, and strengthen those relationships on behalf of your firm.
- **Listening and sharing stakeholder inputs** means serving as the company's active listener of concerns, praise, trends, and wants from the audiences most critical to strategy. Public affairs is well positioned to draw inputs from across the operating environment, but that vital feedback must be shared at the business and functional levels so the firm can adapt, when appropriate, to stakeholder expectations.
- **Aligning messages with strategic initiatives** may seem obvious, but the work of public affairs is central in *communicating* strategy. If your company focuses on differentiation, your communication strategies should focus on differentiation, whether you're interacting with customers, employees, suppliers, or elected officials. A differentiated product or service brings certain benefits to each audience. Your communication strategy should clearly identify and convey those benefits in ways that are meaningful to your stakeholders.

Communication is strategic when it aligns with corporate and business strategy. Understand well your company's business model and industry positioning and apply that knowledge to every decision you make as a communicator. Doing so enhances not only your value as a communicator, but also the company's likelihood in reaching its strategic goals.

Notes

1. See Chapter 3 A Micro and Macro View of the Economy for further discussion of barriers to entry.
2. See Chapter 3 A Micro and Macro View of the Economy for further discussion of economies of scale.
3. See Chapter 5 How and Why Finance Rules the Business World for further discussion of capital requirements, financing, and budgeting.
4. See Chapter 8 Why You Cannot Ignore Operations Management for further discussion of supply chain management.
5. See Chapter 3 A Micro and Macro View of the Economy for further discussion of forces affecting supply and demand.
6. See Chapter 6 Marketing Envy and Other Observations for further discussion of switching costs.
7. See Chapter 6 Marketing Envy and Other Observations and Chapter 8 Why You Cannot Ignore Operations Management for further discussion of market segmentation and supplier relations.
8. See Chapter 3 A Micro and Macro View of the Economy for further discussion of substitutes.
9. Meaning earning less is still less expensive than exiting an industry.
10. Dr. Pepper Snapple Group was acquired by Keurig Green Mountain in 2018 to become the third-largest beverage company in North America (Holtz, 2018). Keurig Dr. Pepper CEO Bob Gamgort noted how the company's product variety and its selling and distribution capabilities allowed it "to compete differently in the beverage industry" (para. 2).
11. See Chapter 4 The Art and Science of Financial Statements for further discussion of how profit, or the bottom line, is calculated.
12. Think, for example, of the impact of home schooling on demand for both public and private schools. A strategic disregard for home schooling as a "competitor" leaves conventional school systems at a competitive disadvantage.
13. See Chapter 3 A Micro and Macro View of the Economy for further discussion of economies of scale.
14. See Chapter 6 Marketing Envy and Other Observations for further discussion of the life cycle of products, businesses, and markets.
15. See Chapter 4 The Art and Science of Financial Statements for further discussion of R&D, or research and development.
16. See Chapter 6 Marketing Envy and Other Observations for further discussion of the life cycle of products, businesses, and markets, which is complementary to S Curve concepts presented here.

References

Airbnb. (2020). Retrieved from www.fastcompany.com/company/airbnb.
Amadeo, K. (2020, August 2). *What is competitive advantage?* Retrieved from www.thebalance.com/what-is-competitive-advantage-3-strategies-that-work-3305828.
Broad differentiation strategy. (2019, October 1). Retrieved from www.careercliff.com/broad-differentiation-strategy-examples/.
Cassidy F. (2018, August 28). *What is business innovation?* Retrieved from www.raconteur.net/business-strategy/business-innovation-guide/.
Cirque du Soleil. (2020). Retrieved from www.blueoceanstrategy.com/bos-moves/cirque-du-soleil/.
Curves. (2020). Retrieved from www.blueoceanstrategy.com/bos-moves/curves/.
Edwards, J. (n.d.) *Focused cost leadership and focused differentiation.* Retrieved from https://opentextbc.ca/strategicmanagement/chapter/focused-cost-leadership-and-focused-differentiation/.

Heaton, J. (2016, March 2). *What business are you in?* Retrieved from www.tronviggroup.com/what-business-are-you-in/.

Holtz, S. (2018, July 10). *Keurig completes acquisition of Dr. Pepper Snapple Group.* Retrieved from www.cspdailynews.com/beverages/keurig-completes-acquisition-dr-pepper-snapple-group.

iTunes (2020). Retrieved from www.blueoceanstrategy.com/itunes/.

Kaplan, R.S., & Norton, D. P. (2004). *Strategy maps: Converting intangible assets into tangible outcomes.* Boston, MA: Harvard Business School Publishing Corporation.

Kopp, C. M. (2020, July 3). *Business models.* Retrieved from www.investopedia.com/terms/b/businessmodel.asp.

Landry, L. (2020, May 2). *Business model innovation: What it is and why it's important.* Retrieved from www.northeastern.edu/graduate/blog/implementing-business-model-innovation/.

Leonard, K. (2019, March 11). *Examples of cost leadership and strategy marketing.* Retrieved from https://smallbusiness.chron.com/examples-cost-leadership-strategy-marketing-12259.html.

Meyer, P. (2019, June 5). *Apple Inc.'s generic strategy and intensive growth strategies.* Retrieved from http://panmore.com/apple-inc-generic-strategy-intensive-growth-strategies.

Pearson, B. (2018, March 22). *Walmart is going upscale, but it doesn't mean what you think.* Retrieved from www.forbes.com/sites/bryanpearson/2018/03/22/walmart-is-going-upscale-but-it-doesnt-mean-what-you-think/#78eda6ae1102.

Pearson, J. (2019, April 10). *Industries and commercial sectors with the highest barriers to entry.* Retrieved from www.theselfemployed.com/article/industries-and-commercial-sectors-with-the-highest-barriers-to-entry/.

Porter, M.E. (1979, March). *How competitive forces shape strategy.* Retrieved from https://hbr.org/1979/03/how-competitive-forces-shape-strategy.

Porter, M.E. (1985). *Competitive advantage: Creating and sustaining superior performance.* New York, NY: The Free Press.

Porter, M.E. (2008, January). *The five competitive forces that shape strategy.* Retrieved from https://hbr.org/2008/01/the-five-competitive-forces-that-shape-strategy.

S curve. (n.d.) Retrieved from http://strategictoolkits.com/strategic-concepts/s-curve/.

Sargeant, A. (2016, January 27). *Sub-brands for no-frills: Why service airlines are creating subsidiaries to compete with low-cost entrants.* Retrieved from https://pwc.blogs.com/industry_perspectives/2016/01/sub-brands-for-no-frills-why-full-service-airlines-are-creating-separate-subsidiaries-to-compete-wit.html.

10 examples of revenue models. (2017, November 20). Retrieved from https://medium.com/business-model-validation-101/10-examples-of-revenue-models-50af0078c58c.

Three levels of strategy: Corporate strategy, business strategy, and functional strategy. (2020, August 29). Retrieved from www.business-to-you.com/levels-of-strategy-corporate-business-functional/.

Watkins, M.D. (2007, September 10). *Demystifying strategy: The what, who, how, and why.* Retrieved from https://hbr.org/2007/09/demystifying-strategy-the-what.

Weill, P., Malone, T.W., D'Urso, V. T., Herman, G., and Woerner, S. (2005). *Do some business models perform better than others? A study of the 1,000 largest U.S. firms.* Retrieved from http://ccs.mit.edu/papers/pdf/wp226.pdf.

What is Blue Ocean strategy? (2020). Retrieved from www.blueoceanstrategy.com/what-is-blue-ocean-strategy/.

Chapter 11

And Here Comes Legal

The legal ramifications of conducting business are plentiful. The larger the business, the larger the presence of attorneys, regulatory mandates, and risk of legal action against the firm. On the surface, the relationship between communicators who err on the side of speaking and attorneys who err on the side of not speaking appears conflicting, though each side has the best interests of the business in mind. Including legal counsel in your internal network we discussed in Chapter 1 is essential. A system of law pervades the work of public affairs, and you don't want to venture into legal territory alone. When you proactively build relationships with your attorneys, you provide yourself a venue to understand the myriad of laws that impact your work. Likewise, those relationships provide you with an opportunity to present your case for communicating. Somewhere in between telling all and "no comment" lies a workable solution, but you need effective working relationships with Legal to get there. Don't wait for a crisis to hit to build those relationships. If your Legal relationship-building needs attention, focus on those relationships now. In this chapter, we'll review key aspects of corporate law that can get your discussions started.

A Global View of Enterprise Risk

We'll begin with an overarching view of business risks, in rank order, derived from an annual survey of C-suite level executives and directors from around the globe (DeLoach, 2020):

- **Regulatory changes** that impact the production and delivery of products and services. Heightened regulatory scrutiny in the areas of privacy, tariffs, environment, product development/approval, and social issues is potentially disrupting to business operations.
- **Economic changes** that restrict growth in certain markets, volatility in equity markets, uncertainty in major global financial markets, and trade policy disputes bring concerns of economic downturns that negatively impact firms.
- **Talent acquisition and retention challenges** threaten firms unable to quickly adapt to changing work environments, employee expectations, evolving skillsets, and growing demand for top talent.

Table 11.1 Major Laws Governed by U.S. Department of Labor (DOL)

Wages and Hours	**Fair Labor Standards Act (FLSA)** requires employers to pay eligible employees at least the federal minimum wage and overtime pay of one-and-one-half-times the regular pay rate.
Workplace Safety and Health	**Occupational Safety and Health Act (OSHA)** regulates safety and health conditions and recognizes employers as having a general duty to provide employees with a workplace free of serious hazards.
Workers' Compensation	Private company and state government employees must seek workers' compensation remedies at the state level where these wage and benefits insurance programs are administered. The DOL administers workers' compensation programs for certain maritime, energy, and federal employees.
Employee Benefit Security	**Employee Retirement Income Security Act (ERISA)** imposes a number of fiduciary, disclosure, and reporting requirements on employers providing pension or other welfare benefit plans to their employees.
Unions and their Members	**Labor-Management Reporting and Disclosure Act (LMRDA)** requires filing of financial and labor relations practices reports and establishes standards for the election of union officers.
Employee Protection	**OSHA** enforces whistleblower protections to employees who report law violations by their employers. **Uniformed Services Employment and Reemployment Rights Act** provides members serving in the armed forces the right to reemployment with the employer they had when they entered the service. **Employee Polygraph Protection Act** permits polygraph testing only in limited circumstances.
Garnishment of Wages	**Consumer Credit Protection Act (CCPA)** protects employees from discharge because of wages garnished for a debt and limits the amount that can be garnished in a week.
Family and Medical Leave	**Family and Medical Leave Act (FMLA)** requires employers of 50 or more employees to give up to 12 weeks of unpaid, job-protected leave to eligible employees for the birth or adoption of a child or the serious illness of an employee or an employee's spouse, child, or parent.
Veterans' Preference	**Veterans' Employment and Training Service** enforces special federal government employment rights of veterans to have preference in hiring and protections in reductions of force.
Government Contracts, Grants, or Financial Aid	Recipients of government contracts, grants, or financial aid are subjected to wage, hour, benefits, and safety and health standards regulated by the **Davis-Bacon Act, McNamara-O'Hara Service Contract Act,** and **Walsh-Healey Public Contracts Act.**
Migrant and Seasonal Agricultural Workers	**Migrant and Seasonal Agricultural Worker Protection Act (MSPA)** regulates hiring/employment practices for agricultural employers and wage protections and safety standards for employees. Related regulations are included in **Fair Labor Standards Act (FLSA)** and **Immigration and Nationality Act (INA)**.
Mine Safety and Health	**Federal Mine Safety and Health Act** regulates safety, health, and training standards for miners.
Construction	**OSHA** and related federal agencies issue safety and health, wage and benefit, equal employment opportunity, and anti-kickback standards for the construction industry.
Transportation	Most labor provisions regulating the transportation industry are administered outside of DOL. **OSHA** regulates longshoring and maritime industry safety and health standards.
Plant Closings and Layoffs	**Worker Adjustment and Retraining Notification Act (WARN)** provides eligible employees early warning of impending layoffs or plant closings.

("Summary," n.d.)

- **Digital and technological readiness** pressures concern firms that are slow to adjust the IT infrastructure and digital capabilities needed to compete in their industries and retain a growing base of digitally oriented customers.
- **Cybersecurity threats** continue to loom as the use of cloud computing, mobile devices, robotics, and machine learning increase across industries. Privacy and identity management are related concerns.
- **Corporate cultures** not attuned to risk identification and reporting are problematic if employees aren't involved in day-to-day risk management activities.

These concerns cut across the topics we've covered in previous chapters. Although talent acquisition may fall under the purview of HR, and digital readiness is guided by IT, each of these risks has a connection to Legal and the laws governing business conduct. *Enterprise Risk Management*, or ERM, is a broadly based business strategy that identifies, assesses, and prepares for risks most likely to interrupt a firm's operations (Kenton, 2020b). Legal, then, must be engaged in managing any risk type affected by the exercise of legal judgment ("In-House Counsel," 2019). We'll cover several categories of legal concerns in the following sections.

Key Aspects of U.S. Employment Law

The U.S. Department of Labor (DOL) enforces federal laws governing workplace activities for businesses, job applicants, workers, retirees, and contractors ("Summary," n.d.). A number of DOL regulations require workplace communication of their provisions to employees via posters, email, or other means. Table 11.1 outlines major aspects of U.S. labor laws.

The U.S. Equal Employment Opportunity Commission (EEOC) enforces federal laws prohibiting *discrimination*, *retaliation*, and *harassment* by employers with at least 15 employees, including labor unions and employment agencies. EEOC laws apply to all types of work situations, including hiring, firing, promotions, training, wages, and benefits. Key focus areas for EEOC are defined as follows ("Overview," n.d.):

- **Discrimination** is illegal on the basis of age, disability, compensation, genetic information, harassment, national origin, pregnancy, race/color, religion, retaliation, sex (including transgender status and sexual orientation), and sexual harassment (see also "Discrimination by Type," n.d.). Examples of discrimination include treating an employee unfavorably because of a disability, assigning an employee a non-customer contact position because of religious-based attire or grooming practices, and requiring fluent English for a position when fluency in English is not essential to job performance.
- **Retaliation** against employees asserting their rights in *protected activities* is illegal, including attempts to punish those who file or serve as a witness in an EEOC complaint, report harassment to a supervisor, participate in an employer investigation of an alleged harassment, resist sexual advances or intervene to protect others, request a disability accommodation, or refuse to follow orders that would result in discrimination (see also "Retaliation," n.d.). Examples of retaliation include making an employee's work schedule more difficult by purposefully having it conflict with family

responsibilities, transferring an employee to a less desirable position or location, and engaging in verbal or physical abuse.
- **Harassment** is a form of employment discrimination involving unwelcome conduct based on any number of factors, including race, religion, sex, and age (see also "Harassment," n.d.). Harassment is illegal when an employee must endure the offensive conduct as a condition of continued employment *or* the conduct is severe or pervasive enough to create an environment that a reasonable person[1] would consider hostile, intimidating, or abusive. Harassing conduct can include offensive jokes, threats, ridicule, objects or pictures, or other ongoing interference with work performance.

Disparate (or *adverse*) *impact* and *disparate* (or *adverse*) *treatment* refer to illegal discriminatory practices ("What are Disparate," 2020). An employment hiring practice that on the surface appears fitting for job screening, for example, may unintentionally eliminate a disproportionate number of minority applicants. Such a practice would be found to have an disparate impact on a protected group, even though not intended to do so. Disparate treatment, however, is intentional discrimination. Testing a particular skill only of minority applicants would be considered disparate treatment and prohibited under federal law.

Employees (or applicants) wanting to file a discrimination suit must first register their charge with the EEOC and receive a Notice of Right to Sue that permits a case to be filed in federal or state court ("Filing," n.d.). A lawsuit must be filed within 90 days of receiving the Notice of Right to Sue.[2] The EEOC can file suit on behalf of the employee if its investigation reveals there is reasonable cause to believe discrimination has occurred and attempts at *conciliation* (a voluntary resolution reached by parties involved) are unsuccessful.

Intellectual Property

Intellectual property, or *IP*, includes patents, copyrights, and trade secrets ("Is Intellectual Property," 2020). These intangible assets may be recorded on a company's balance sheet, but their true market value can be difficult to determine. Some IP rights are granted legal protection and warrant our attention here.

Companies hire and invest in employees to develop new ideas, technologies, processes, and markets (Syring & Boyd, n.d.). Intellectual property created by employees in the course of their employment is generally owned by the employer. As such, the employer is entitled to benefits derived from IP created by its employees. Essential to the employer's ownership is a written agreement known as an *assignment of inventions* or *ownership of discoveries* in which the employee assigns all rights related to IP created during employment to the company. To avoid disputes, such agreements are executed before the employment relationship commences and reflect that without the agreement the company would not hire the individual. If such an agreement is entered into after employment begins, the employer is expected to provide sufficient consideration to the employee in the form of a bonus, promotion, or stock options to support company IP ownership moving forward. Written IP agreements must comply with state laws and can be used with independent contractors as well as employees.

Employers may still successfully assert their IP ownership rights even when there is no employment agreement or related policies to assign rights to the employer (Syring & Boyd, n.d.). The work product in question, however, must have been created during the course of an employment relationship (see also Guerin, 2015). An employee may be able to demonstrate ownership of ideas developed outside of the employment relationship. The courts, however, look to the nature of the employment relationship. That is, if an employee was hired for the purpose of creating intellectual property, the employer is generally the owner of the intellectual property. Independent contractors without an employee-employer relationship generally own what they create unless there is a written *work for hire*[3] agreement or copyrights of the created work are otherwise assigned by the contractor. Copyrights are one of four intellectual property protections (Brewer, 2019):

- A *copyright* is the legal right for the creator of an original, tangible work to exclusively reproduce that work and grant authorization for others to do so (see also Kenton, 2020a). Copyrights protect authorship of literary works, computer software, architecture, music, art, and more. Copyright registration supports the legal defense of copyright protections.
- A *trademark* provides legal protection for phrases, words, or symbols that distinguish the source of a product or service. Whereas copyrights can expire, trademark rights derive from the use of the trademark and can be held indefinitely. Like a copyright, trademark registration is not required but offers legal advantages. Trademarks (and related slogans) are typically not the subject of ownership disputes because their legal protections flow from their use and not their creation (see also Syring & Boyd, n.d.).
- A *patent* provides legal protection, for a limited time, to inventions or discoveries that are new, non-obvious, and useful. Only the patent holder may make, sell, or use the product, such as a new machine, process, or formulation. Patent ownership presumptively belongs to the inventor (see also Syring & Boyd, n.d.). In the case of employment agreements, employee inventors are typically required to assign patentable ideas to the employer but can still retain nonexclusive, royalty-free rights to use an invention.
- A *trade secret* is specific, private information that gives a business a competitive advantage. Trade secrets include recipes, algorithms, processes, and client lists. Trade secrets need not be registered, but firms must actively behave in a manner that protects the information. Companies demonstrate active protection of trade secrets by marking them as confidential, limiting employee access, securing non-disclosure agreements with those who have access, training those with access on how to keep them secure, and having a notification and security process in place if a trade secret is stolen (see also Murray, 2019). Contracts and/or state law define ownership of trade secrets (see also Syring & Boyd, n.d.).

Employers use *non-compete* (or *no-poach*) clauses to protect intellectual property (Martinez, Lee, Donahue, Rigney, & Smith, 2020). Non-compete provisions prohibit employees who leave the company from working for a competitor and/or in a defined geographic region for a specific duration of time. *Non-solicitation* clauses likewise prevent former employees from soliciting a company's client base or employees on behalf of a competing firm. The enforceability of non-competes, as they're called, is governed by state law but is coming under increasing scrutiny, particularly for low-wage workers. At a minimum, non-competes must satisfy contract law requirements and be supported by adequate consideration for the restrictions imposed. That is, employees must be provided an additional benefit, such as a raise or bonus, highly specialized training, or promotion, in exchange for limitations on where and how they can work after leaving the company. States generally follow the principle that any restrictions placed on employees are no greater than necessary to protect the employer's legitimate business interests, also known as *protectable interests*. Any restriction placed on an employee's ability to work must be reasonable in duration and scope.[4]

Product Liability

The potential for *product liability* poses significant legal risk to a firm. Cases are decided not only on whether an actual injury incurred from the use of a product, but also whether the product was defective or unexpectedly dangerous ("Fundamentals," 2020). A *defective product* is one that causes damage or injury resulting from a flaw in the product itself, its labeling, or its intended use. States govern product liability laws. Both manufacturers and sellers can be held liable as *defendants* in defective product claims. There are three types of product defects *plaintiffs*, or injured parties, can claim:

- **Manufacturing defects** occur when the product was designed to be safely used but manufactured in a way that makes it unsafe, such as weak, poorly fitting, or cheaply manufactured parts that render the product dangerous to use.
- **Design defects** occur when the fundamental design of the product is faulty, thereby rendering the entire product dangerous to use. Design defects include how a product is packaged, such as failure to use child-proof medicine tops, or a lack of safety features, like automatic shut-off.
- **Insufficient instructions or warnings, also known as marketing defects,** occur when a product may meet safe design and manufacturing standards but doesn't include proper warnings or instructions for safe operation.

Consumer product misuses result from products being used for purposes they were never intended (Copenhaver & Angelino, 2018). Bizarre social media challenges to consume laundry detergent, swallow a spoonful of cinnamon, or combine ingredients for an explosive effect were never intended by product makers, but courts expect manufacturers to anticipate and take precautions against misuses that are "reasonably foreseeable." Under the reasonable foreseeability standard, a company may be held liable for injuries caused by a product even when the customer did not use the product as intended. Courts view a frequent, widely publicized misuse occurring around the time of the product's manufacture as a reasonably foreseeable risk and expect companies to warn consumers accordingly. Whereas some states may recognize teens attempting to shake a soft drink out of a vending machine without paying as not reasonably foreseeable, other states may. Manufacturers are expected to explore potential uses of their products and provide warnings against foreseeable misuses. Courts allow companies to update warnings, instructions, and designs over time as misuses are discovered.[5] No company is required to manufacture a fool-proof product but is expected to protect consumers from misuse that is both reasonable and foreseeable. Although it's reasonable and foreseeable that someone could stand on a chair to change a light bulb, it's not reasonable or foreseeable to expect someone to use an oven to dry clothes ("Defective Products," 2020).

Liable parties in a product liability suit include the manufacturer, sellers, and/or anyone who repaired or modified the product ("Fundamentals," 2020). Sellers potentially include all firms in the supply chain, regardless of their lack of knowledge or complicity in the defect. Product liability claims arise from ("Defective Products," 2020):

- **Negligence,** or failure to fulfill a duty to exercise reasonable care in the manufacturing or selling of a product;
- **Breach of warranty,** or violation of an implied warranty the law imposes on the sale of goods. In other words, even if not expressly stated, products are expected to be in proper condition, free of defects, and functional for the purpose intended; or
- **Strict liability,** which demonstrates manufacturer liability for the defect without needing to prove negligence. That is, if the product was used according to its intended use and not substantially changed from the time it left the seller's hands, the manufacturer is liable for the defect.

Available damages that can be recovered by plaintiffs in a product liability case include *compensatory damages* to cover medical bills, lost wages, and/or property damage caused by the defective product; *pain and suffering* compensation for related injuries; or *punitive damages* if the manufacturer's conduct was egregious and worthy of further punishment ("Fundamentals," 2020). In cases where a victim's own negligence played a role in the injury, known as *comparative negligence* or *comparative fault*, damages may be reduced or precluded. For example, a drunk driver injured by faulty car brakes would bear part of the responsibility for damages incurred.

Fiduciary Duty

The U.S. legal system defines a *fiduciary duty* as a relationship between two parties in which the *fiduciary* has a legal duty to act solely in the interest of the *principal* and takes strict care to ensure no conflict of interest arises between the two (Barone, 2019). Fiduciary obligations exist in relationships where trust, confidence, and reliance are paramount. Examples of fiduciary relationships include a trustee managing an estate on behalf of a beneficiary, an adult appointed legal guardian of a minor child, an attorney representing a client, and, most relevant to our discussion here, a *principal/agent relationship* that exists between investors and fund managers as well as between shareholders and the directors they elect to serve on corporate boards of directors. The fiduciary in these cases – the trustee, appointed adult, attorney, fund manager, and board member – have legal obligations to act in the best interest of the principals relying on their judgment and actions.

Corporate officers and board members, collectively known as directors, are charged with specific fiduciary duties ("Fiduciary Duty," n.d.; Johnson & Sides, 2004):

- **Duty of care** requires directors to inform themselves of all material information reasonably available to them before making business decisions. Directors are not expected to accept materials provided by the company at face value but rather have a critical eye to protect the interests of the corporation and its shareholders. Duty of care clearly focuses on a board's decision-making process in matters of electing,

evaluating, and compensating corporate officers; reviewing and approving corporate strategy, budgets, and capital expenditures; monitoring internal controls and financial reporting obligations; distributing profits to shareholders; and appointing and completing committee assignments. Directors must provide ample, informed oversight of the business affairs of the corporation.
- **Duty of loyalty** requires directors to act in the best interest of the corporation without personal financial conflicts and forbids directors from violating trust and confidence to advance their private interests. Directors may not improperly compete with the corporation or use corporate assets or confidential information for personal gain. Directors can be held liable for monetary damages for any harm caused by a disregard for duties to the corporation and its shareholders, intentional or not.
- **Duty of good faith** requires directors to fulfil their duties and advance the interests of the corporation without violating the law. Good faith relates to the director's state of mind, or whether the director was conscious of not devoting sufficient attention to assigned duties. Directors need not be grossly negligent to have their good faith brought into question. Deliberate indifference or conscious disregard of duties is sufficiently faulty to indicate lack of good faith. Approving or ignoring an irrational course of conduct, acting without sufficient knowledge, disregarding known risks, or knowingly violating the law are breaches of good faith.
- **Duty of confidentiality** requires directors to keep corporate information confidential and not disclose it to benefit their personal interests or give unfair advantage to competitors. Leaks of confidential information related to a company's products, strategy, or operations, whether intended or inadvertent, can violate federal securities laws (see also Stokdyk & Trotter, 2016).
- **Duty of disclosure** requires directors to act with "complete candor" in making decisions and disclosing to shareholders all relevant facts and circumstances used for decision-making. Delaware law[6] relies on a *material* standard to determine what information must be disclosed to shareholders. Information is considered material and must be disclosed if a reasonable shareholder would consider it important in deciding how to vote (see also Lafferty, Schmidt, & Wolfe, 2012).

Insider trading is a breach of fiduciary duty prohibited by the Securities and Exchange Commission (SEC) ("Insider Trading," n.d.). *Insiders* are persons with access to confidential and/or material information that is not available to the public yet has significant potential to affect share price if it were made public. Insiders include corporate officers, directors, and employees who, upon learning of a forthcoming transaction, such as a merger or a bankruptcy, have a legal duty not to advance their self-interest based on that confidential information. Specifically, insiders are prohibited from buying or selling securities for personal gain based on information they've been entrusted not to disclose. The SEC's reach is broad on insider trading, including prevention of insiders from "tipping" friends, business associates, family members, or others to trade securities based on non-public information. Government employees with access to confidential information are also prohibited from trading on that information for personal gain. Because insider trading undermines trust in the securities markets, detection and prosecution of insider trading is an SEC enforcement priority.

Foreign Corrupt Practices Act

Enacted in 1977, the *Foreign Corrupt Practices Act* (FCPA) prohibits both publicly traded and privately held U.S. firms, as well as individuals, from paying bribes[7] to foreign officials to advance business interests abroad (Kenton, 2020c; see also "Spotlight," 2017). FCPA likewise applies to related internal controls and accounting practices and is jointly enforced by the Securities and Exchange Commission (SEC) and the Department of Justice (DOJ). Violators can face sanctions, penalties, fines, and both criminal and civil actions, including imprisonment. In some cases, an independent auditor can be assigned to oversee a violator's business activities and ensure future compliance. The SEC posts violators and enforcement actions in press releases on its website.[8] Recent violations include:

- Alexion Pharmaceuticals, based in Boston, MA, agreed to pay $21 million for maintaining false accounting records and having insufficient internal controls to detect improper payments made to Turkish government officials for favorable regulatory treatment of Alexion's drug Soliris ("SEC Charges Alexion," 2020).
- Consumer loan company World Acceptance Corporation based in South Carolina agreed to pay $21.7 million for paying bribes to Mexican government officials in exchange for the ability to make loans to government employees. Bribes were paid via bank account deposits and through an intermediary distributing bags of cash to officials. The transactions were then recorded as legitimate business expenses on company books ("SEC Charges Consumer Loan," 2020).
- Herbalife Nutrition, a direct sales company based in Los Angeles, CA, agreed to pay more than $67 million related to a bribery scheme orchestrated by a China subsidiary executive to avoid government investigations into the company's business practices. Bribes made through gifts including cash, travel, meals, and entertainment were concealed through falsified expense reports ("SEC Charges Former Executive," 2019).

In 1998, the FCPA was amended to include application to foreign firms and persons who either act directly or through agents to make corrupt payments in the U.S. ("Foreign Corrupt," 2017). A 2020 case involved two Brazilian nationals and their affiliated companies that were fined nearly $27 million for engaging in a multi-year bribery scheme to facilitate acquisition of U.S.-based Pilgrim's Pride Corporation ("SEC Charges Brazilian," 2020). Bribery payments of $150 million made through intercompany transfers and dividend payments, along with undue influence to avoid an adequate system of internal accounting controls, led to the charges.

Legal Communication

The communication of risk, litigation response, liability exposure, and matters of employment law serves both a proactive and a reactive role in legal matters pervasive in the firm. An effective working relationship between attorneys and public affairs is essential for not only accuracy of communications, but also knowing when restraint and disclosure are appropriate courses of action. Enterprise risk is increased by a lack of, or ineffective, communication. To ensure your communications serve to minimize risk, solidify your legal relationships with each business client you advise. Ask and understand the greatest areas of legal exposure for the business. Think proactively about how you can help minimize risk through communication with employees, suppliers, investors, and other stakeholders *before* challenges arise. Pay attention to customer feedback, chatter, and complaints that provide early warnings of potential claims. Your understanding of the business and its legal implications informs the questions you need to ask and the actions you need to take.

Notes

1. The EEOC uses the "reasonable person" standard to evaluate the alleged harasser's conduct. If the challenged conduct would not substantially affect the working environment of a reasonable person, no violation should be found. The EEOC cautions, however, that the reasonable person standard should not be applied in a vacuum. That is, a workplace in which sexual slurs, displays of offensive images, or other harassing conduct is considered acceptable, the widespread presence of these behaviors can constitute a hostile work environment even if many people consider the behaviors harmless or insignificant ("Harassment: What is Meant," 2019).
2. Exceptions apply to age discrimination and equal pay lawsuits ("Filing," n.d.).
3. Independent contractors own the copyright to their created works unless they otherwise assign copyright to the company commissioning their work or if their work falls within a narrow legal definition of "works for hire" that provides copyright ownership to the company. The nine types of works for hire are: a contribution to a collective work, part of a motion picture or other audio-visual work, a translation, a supplementary work, a compilation, an instructional test, a test, answer material for a test, and an atlas (Syring & Boyd, n.d.; see also Guerin, 2015).
4. For example, fast food chain Jimmy John's was sued for imposing unlawful non-compete agreements on low-wage sandwich makers and delivery drivers, thereby preventing employees from seeking better paying, similar jobs elsewhere in the community ("Madigan Sues," 2016).
5. Courts generally regard enhanced or updated warnings favorably and do not consider them admissions that original warnings were inadequate or that the product was unsafe when initially sold (Copenhaver & Angelino, 2018).
6. Delaware law is often cited in corporate law because at least 65% of *Fortune 500* companies and more than half of all U.S. publicly traded companies are incorporated in Delaware ("Why Delaware," 2017).
7. The Act prohibits bribes from being paid by an individual, officer, stockholder, agent, consultant, director, distributor, firm, third party, joint venture partner, or other proxy representing a U.S. interest.
8. See www.sec.gov/spotlight/foreign-corrupt-practices-act.shtml.

References

Barone, A. (2019, September 11). *What are some examples of fiduciary duty?* Retrieved from https://www.investopedia.com/ask/answers/042915/what-are-some-examples-fiduciary-duty.asp.

Brewer, T. (2019, May 16). *What are the four basic types of intellectual property?* Retrieved from https://brewerlong.com/information/business-law/four-types-of-intellectual-property/.

Copenhaver, S.M., & Angelino, S.K. (2018, April 18). *When do manufacturers need to anticipate misuses – and abuses – of their products?* Retrieved from https://www.productliabilityandmasstorts.com/2018/04/when-do-manufacturers-need-to-anticipate-misuses-and-abuses-of-their-products/.

Defective products. (2020). Retrieved from https://www.bellbrigham.com/practice-areas/defective-products/.

DeLoach, J. (2020, February 11). *Top 10 risks for 2020.* Retrieved from https://www.corporatecomplianceinsights.com/top-10-risks-2020./

Discrimination by type. (n.d.). Retrieved from https://www.eeoc.gov/discrimination-type.

Fiduciary duty. (n.d.). Retrieved from https://www.law.cornell.edu/wex/fiduciary_duty.

Filing a lawsuit. (n.d.). Retrieved from https://www.eeoc.gov/filing-lawsuit.

Foreign Corrupt Practices Act. (2017, February 3). Retrieved from https://www.justice.gov/criminal-fraud/foreign-corrupt-practices-act.
Fundamentals of product liability law. (2020). Retrieved from https://www.lexisnexis.com/legalnewsroom/lexis-hub/b/commentary/posts/fundamentals-of-product-liability-law.
Guerin, L. (2015, April 9). *Who owns employee and independent contractor work product?* Retrieved from https://www.lawyers.com/legal-info/labor-employment-law/employment-contracts/ownership-of-work-product-depends-on-your-status.html.
Harassment. (n.d.). Retrieved from https://www.eeoc.gov/harassment.
Harassment: What is meant by the term "reasonable person"? (2019, September 11). Retrieved from https://www.shrm.org/resourcesandtools/tools-and-samples/hr-qa/pages/reasonableperson.aspx.
In-house counsel in the wake of Enterprise Risk Management: Implications for legal, compliance and risk. (2019, September 13). Retrieved from https://www.americanbar.org/groups/business_law/resources/materials/2019/annual_materials/in_house_counsel/.
Insider trading. (n.d.). Retrieved from https://www.investor.gov/introduction-investing/investing-basics/glossary/insider-trading.
Is intellectual property considered a capital asset? (2020, May 22). Retrieved from https://www.investopedia.com/ask/answers/061715/intellectual-property-considered-form-capital-asset-within-company.asp.
Johnson, L.P.Q., & Sides, M.A. (2004). *The Sarbanes-Oxley Act and fiduciary duties.* Retrieved from https://open.mitchellhamline.edu/cgi/viewcontent.cgi?article=1218&context=wmlr.
Kenton, W. (2020a, September 13). *Copyright.* Retrieved from https://www.investopedia.com/terms/c/copyright.asp.
Kenton, W. (2020b, September 17). *Enterprise Risk Management (ERM).* Retrieved from https://www.investopedia.com/terms/e/enterprise-risk-management.asp.
Kenton, W. (2020c, November 29). *Foreign Corrupt Practices Act (FCPA).* Retrieved from https://www.investopedia.com/terms/f/foreign-corrupt-practices-act.asp.
Lafferty, W.M., Schmidt, L.A., & Wolfe, D.J., Jr. (2012). *A brief introduction to the fiduciary duties of directors under Delaware law.* Retrieved from http://www.pennstatelawreview.org/116/3/116%20Penn%20St.%20L.%20Rev.%20837.pdf.
Madigan sues Jimmy John's for imposing unlawful non-compete agreements on sandwich makers and delivery drivers. (2016, June 8). Retrieved from https://illinoisattorneygeneral.gov/pressroom/2016_06/20160608.html.
Martinez, M.E., Lee, S., Donahue, L.N., Rigney, E.L., & Smith, B. J. (2020, November 7). *Competition in U.S. labor markets: Non-compete clauses increasingly under fire.* Retrieved from https://www.natlawreview.com/article/competition-us-labor-markets-non-compete-clauses-increasingly-under-fire.
Murray, J. (2019, March 27). *How to protect your business trade secrets from being stolen.* Retrieved from https://www.thebalancesmb.com/how-to-protect-your-trade-secrets-4590019.
Overview. (n.d.). Retrieved from https://www.eeoc.gov/overview.
Retaliation. (n.d.). Retrieved from https://www.eeoc.gov/retaliation.
SEC charges Alexion Pharmaceuticals with FCPA violations. (2020, July 2). Retrieved from https://www.sec.gov/news/press-release/2020-149.
SEC charges Brazilian meat producers with FCPA violations. (2020, October 14). Retrieved from https://www.sec.gov/news/press-release/2020-254.
SEC charges consumer loan company with FCPA violations. (2020, August 6). Retrieved from https://www.sec.gov/news/press-release/2020-177.
SEC charges former executive with FCPA violations. (2019, November 14). Retrieved from https://www.sec.gov/litigation/litreleases/2019/lr24666.htm.
Spotlight on Foreign Corrupt Practices Act. (2017, February 2). Retrieved from https://www.sec.gov/spotlight/foreign-corrupt-practices-act.shtml.
Stokdyk, S.B., & Trotter, J.H. (2016, February 15). *Maintaining director confidentiality.* Retrieved from https://corpgov.law.harvard.edu/2016/02/15/maintaining-director-confidentiality/.
Summary of the major laws of the Department of Labor. (n.d.) Retrieved from https://www.dol.gov/general/aboutdol/majorlaws.

Syring, T.A., & Boyd, F.J. (n.d.). *Employer and employee ownership of intellectual property: Not as easy as you think*. Retrieved from https://store.legal.thomsonreuters.com/law-products/news-views/corporate-counsel/employer-and-employee-ownership-of-intellectual-property-not-as-easy-as-you-think.

What are disparate impact and disparate treatment? (2020). Retrieved from https://www.shrm.org/resourcesandtools/tools-and-samples/hr-qa/pages/disparateimpactdisparatetreatment.aspx.

Why Delaware corporate law matters so much. (2017, July 24). Retrieved from https://www.delawareinc.com/blog/why-delaware-corporate-law-matters-so-much/.

Chapter 12
Last but Not Least: Business Ethics

Like legal issues, matters of ethics pervade the firm. Ethics also pervades the work of public affairs in supporting the firm. In this final chapter, we focus on the ethical conundrums of conducting a business designed to create value; generate profits; and navigate the many expectations of customers, investors, regulators, and other stakeholders who impact the firm's ability to reach its goals. Abysmal disregard for ethics and law at WorldCom,[1] Enron, and Tyco led to passage of expensive and extensive regulations in the 2002 Sarbanes-Oxley Act (SOX).[2]

The wide-reaching effects of these monumental ethics violations didn't stem from one incident or from one person but rather a series of lapses in corporate judgment and governance that required escalating means of deception, cooperation, and coverup. In this chapter, we'll explore how values, morals, and ethics can guide corporate behavior and how self-interest left unchecked can erode ethical behavior over time. We'll conclude with the important contributions communicators make to sustaining an ethical workplace.

Values, Morals, Law, and Ethics

Values are deeply held personal beliefs that provide a foundation for one's life and thus impact professional, political, religious, social, and personal choices (Heathfield, 2020). Values include ambition, honesty, efficiency, security, optimism, dedication, responsibility, quality, dignity, compassion, and so on. *Corporate values* should likewise guide business decisions but too often represent more prose than action (Lencioni, 2002). A company's *core values* are non-negotiable attributes adhered to despite market or management changes. As such, core values are fewer in number and effectively implemented only when they are woven into every organizational process, including hiring, firing, rewarding, and reminding employees that core values permeate every decision the company makes. Corporate *codes of conduct*[3] reinforce how employees enact corporate values in their everyday activities.

Morals provide a shared basis for cooperation, with variants across social and geographical conditions (Curry, 2018). Love of family, helping one's group, deferring to authority, respect for others, and fairness fall under ways of behaving that are generally accepted as good. Morals are developed neurologically and socially, drawing from experiences with family, communities, and culture ("Ethics," 2016). Morals inform understanding of the difference between right and wrong behavior.

DOI: 10.4324/9781003000600-13

Laws outline basic standards of behavior that are necessary for a society to function effectively ("Ethics," 2016). Where the law doesn't provide guidance, morals and ethics step in. For example, it may not be illegal to raise doubts about a competitor's credibility, but is it morally or ethically just to do so? Individuals and organizations can follow the law yet still behave in ways that are morally questionable. As well, some laws counter the moral code of individuals or organizations that, for religious or other reasons of conscience, would rather break the law than partake in what they believe to be immoral behavior.

Ethics is a branch of philosophy that investigates right and wrong actions as they pertain to moral propositions and applied situations (Annabelle, 2017). Professional codes of ethics prescribe behaviors to guide business operations (Hayes, 2020). Codes of ethics developed by individual firms or trade associations can focus on compliance-based behaviors that ensure lawful operations and/or core values that require more self-reflection and self-regulation than merely following the law.

The Psychology of White-Collar Criminals

Harvard business professor Eugene Soltes (2016) spent seven years interacting with prominent business executives convicted of white collar crimes including fraud, embezzlement, insider trading, and bribery. Soltes was curious: What drives otherwise successful, respected, and lauded professionals to commit such heinous violations of trust? Was it greed? Blind ambition? Fear of failure? Or, were these just bad people?

One financial executive whose actions robbed thousands of investors in his company told Soltes, "Morals go out the window when the pressure is on....When the responsibility is there and you have to meet budgetary numbers, you can forget about morals" (Soltes, 2016, para. 5). The former controller of WorldCom shared that he began thinking his role in one of the largest accounting frauds in history was somehow keeping the company afloat. Others were in stark denial they had done anything criminal or resentful that they were prosecuted for taking actions that were commonplace in their industry. Still others admitted their wrongdoing and were perplexed how they participated in illegal activity after decades of ethical conduct.

Soltes (2016) suspected white-collar criminals use cost-benefit analysis[4] in their ethical and legal lapses as much as they do in their everyday business decisions. He expected to find that they weighed the repercussions of getting caught against the potential benefits their illicit activities could bring. What he discovered through interviews, however, surprised him. Soltes learned that these normally thoughtful decision makers weren't thinking at all but rather relying on rush judgment, intuition, and gut instinct in the midst of an ethical dilemma. These wayward executives were not considering the broader, even devastating, consequences of their behavior. Their physical and psychological distance from potential victims made their crime seem less visceral than robbing someone at gunpoint, yet the outcome of stealing someone's money was the same. These executives either minimized the likely impact of their actions or were unable to relate to those potentially harmed whom they would never meet. To make matters worse, many were hailed for their brilliance in the business press while in the process of committing their crimes, thereby bolstering their behaviors.

Soltes' investigation led to a sobering conclusion:

> Most people like to think that they have the right values to make it through difficult times without falling prey to the same failures as the convicted executives I got to know. *But those who believe they would face the same situations with their current values and viewpoints tend to underestimate the influence of the pressures, cultures, and norms that surround executive decision making.* Perhaps a little humility is in order, given that people seem to have some difficulty predicting how they'd act in that environment. "What we all think is, 'When the big moral challenge comes, I will rise to the occasion,' [but] there's not actually that many of us that will actually rise to the occasion," as one former CFO put it. "I didn't realize I would be a felon."
>
> (Soltes, 2016, para. 15, emphasis added)

Moral hazard occurs when individuals violate a trust or duty while knowing the risks and consequences of their illicit behaviors will fall on another party ("Moral Hazard," 2020). As Soltes (2016) discovered, the more "distant" the victim, the less disturbing the infraction becomes. The classic example of moral hazard is someone driving recklessly while thinking any consequences of risky driving will be covered by the insurance company. Obviously, the insured isn't thinking of possible harm to self or others or the impact of increased rates across all insured parties. Interestingly, moral hazard results from misinformation, or differing information, among parties involved. The reckless driver isn't going to reveal a penchant for dangerous driving when applying for insurance, else a higher premium would be charged that could make insurance inaccessible. The 2008 financial crisis[5] resulted in the U.S. government bailing out a number of major banks. The moral hazard is that large banks could repeat their risky management practices assuming they would be bailed out once again, despite their assurances to regulators that policies have been amended to avoid another crisis. This misinformation, even deception, between parties in a business transaction who present themselves in one way yet act in an opposing way leads to moral hazard that can have detrimental impacts on countless "distant" others not party to the original transaction.

Keeping Self-Interest in Check

In Chapter 2, we reviewed the self-interest origins of capitalism explained by Adam Smith. From self-interest flows the motivation, risk-taking, and market adjustments necessary to earn profits that benefit numerous others beyond the founder of the business. Drawing on his writings in *Capitalism and Freedom*, classical economist Milton Friedman (1970) noted the importance of ethical, lawful operations in a free market economy:

> In such a society, there is one and only one social responsibility of business – to use its resources and engage in activities designed to increase its profits *so long as it stays within the rules of the game, which is to say, engages in open and free competition, without deception or fraud.*
>
> (Friedman, 1970, p. 6, emphasis added)

Self-interest left unchecked has resulted in dire consequences for employees, shareholders, and numerous others affected by the misconduct of business leaders. The WorldCom case discussed in Chapter 4 offers several cues that alert when focus on self-interest becomes excessive and potentially dangerous:

- **Skirting of internal controls.** Independent auditors, directors, and governance policies mandated by Sarbanes-Oxley are intended to provide multiple checkpoints to protect the integrity of financial and accounting information. Attempts to avoid, compromise, or otherwise diminish these controls is cause for concern.
- **Suppressing bad news.** Management should be open and responsive to the good and bad news that accompanies the business environment. A tendency to hear only the good and ignore (or silence) the bad is a warning sign that decisions are not being made on the full slate of information available. *Plausible deniability* provides unethical cover by claiming decision-makers weren't aware of material information, when, in fact, the information was purposely kept from them. A *hired gun* defense is similar when an attorney, spokesperson, or other public-facing representative of the company serves as a mouthpiece adhering to the "company line" without first establishing the truth or completeness of a statement made.[6] Attempts to avoid, alter, or punish messengers of negative but otherwise credible information along with practices of reporting a more favorable situation than reality dictates should raise ethical concerns. For example, a company maintaining historic growth patterns despite widespread market conditions to the contrary should raise questions to better understand its anomalous performance.
- **Using incentives to drive decision-making.** Every company wants favorable finances, and most have executive compensation and bonus incentives tied to financial performance. An ethical problem can arise when incentives, rather than the best interests of the business, drive decision-making.
- **Maintaining a short-term view.** Mackey and Sisodia (2014) warn in *Conscious Capitalism* of the dangers of excessive reliance on a short-term view of business performance. Looking at how the firm performs over the long-term provides a more accurate view of cause and effect and helps to avoid knee-jerk responses that may serve the firm initially but can prove detrimental over time. Related to this short-term view is a desire to please the changing whims of analysts and investors rather than focus on sustaining a successful business for all stakeholders over the long haul.
- **Coercing employees.** Berating, threatening, and coercing employees to conduct business practices against their will or better judgment is a clear indicator that something is wrong. Identifying and addressing aggression against employees enables HR to uncover what could lead to broader ethical violations if allowed to continue.

Whistleblower Protections

A *whistleblower* is a person who reports insider knowledge of illegal activities to authorities (Kenton, 2020). Whistleblowers include employees, clients, suppliers, or anyone with direct knowledge of illicit business practices. Whistleblower protections are provided by several U.S. agencies and include protections for federal employees (see Table 12.1: Whistleblower Protections). Companies named in complaints are prohibited from retaliating against whistleblowers with demotion, termination, threats, or other punitive actions. In certain cases, whistleblowers are eligible to receive a reward amounting to a percentage of

Table 12.1 Whistleblower Protections

Defend Trade Secrets Act	Provides whistleblower protections specifically regarding theft of trade secrets.
False Claims Act	Protects whistleblowers with evidence of fraud relating to government contracts. Also applies to reverse false claims in which the wrongdoer's actions prevents the government from collecting what it is owed.
Foreign Corrupt Practices Act	Extended protections provided under the Wall Street Reform and Consumer Protection Act (see below) allow eligible whistleblowers, including non-U.S. citizens, to receive financial rewards between 10-30% of monies collected.
IRS Whistleblower Program	Requires IRS to giver eligible whistleblowers 15-30% of amount recovered for reporting tax fraud.
Occupational Safety and Health Act	Enforced by the Occupational Health and Safety Administration (OSHA) to protect whistleblowers reporting workplace safety issues.
Sarbanes-Oxley Act	Initially protected employees of publicly traded companies from retaliation for claims made. A 2014 Supreme Court ruling extended protection to cover a public company's private contractors and subcontractors *and* employees of privately owned companies who provide services to publicly traded companies.
Wall Street Reform and Consumer Protection Act	More commonly referred to as Dodd-Frank, this Act requires the SEC to reward whistleblowers for reporting corporate fraud.
Whistleblower Protection Act	Initially protected U.S. federal employees from retaliation after reporting violations of law, abuses of authority, or dangers to public health. Was strengthened in 2012 to broaden the scope of protected disclosures.

("U.S. Whistleblower Laws," 2020; "Whistleblower Risk," 2019; Yahnke, 2019)

Private, public, and federal employees are protected in reporting illegal business activities. The U.S. has implemented dozens of laws at the local, state, and federal level to safeguard, encourage, and incentivize whistleblowers to report wrongdoing. A sampling of those laws is presented here.

the dollar amount recovered as a result of their reporting. Both Enron and WorldCom scandals were exposed by whistleblowers.

Communication and Ethics

It's disheartening to learn that white-collar criminals forego morals when business pressures intensify and that they can more easily justify their unethical behaviors when their potential victims are distant or unidentifiable. Often, illegal activities take place among a contained group of decision-makers, although whistleblower protections increasingly guard those willing to come forward and expose criminal activity. A corporate communicator may only witness the external effects of unethical behavior, which can include faulty praises from analysts and the business press who are likewise duped, at least initially, by the appearance of successful company performance. The enforcement framework against corporate fraud has proven effective, but what can a communicator do to reinforce ethics in the workplace? Several things, actually.

Before we delve into the particulars, let's recall the contributions of Ivy Ledbetter Lee, former journalist turned corporate spokesperson in the early 20th century (Bowen, 2007). His declaration of principles reminds communicators that neither the press nor the public can be fooled in the work of a press agent. Lee further called upon those working in public relations (most commonly referred to as public affairs in modern corporate settings) to serve as the ethical conscience of their organizations given their internal and external interface on behalf of the firm. The service of "ethical consciousness" should ideally fall across all aspects of the business. Communicators are able to support an ethical operating environment in several areas:

- **Reinforcing corporate culture.** Ethics should be engrained in a corporate culture that is modeled by executives and supported by training, rewards, and punitive actions against offenders. Codes of conduct, executive speeches, and internal communication channels provide opportunities to reinforce and highlight ethical ideals.
- **Making priority stakeholders known.** Communicators can do much to identify, humanize, and, just as importantly, quantify the numerous employees, retirees, suppliers, customers, and shareholders affected by the company's operations. Personalized storytelling that connects business decisions to stakeholder outcomes and rippling economic impacts throughout society can help lessen the "distance" that makes ethical lapses more tolerable to wrongdoers.
- **Asking questions.** If something seems too good to be true, unfavorable news is being ignored or suppressed, employees are being pressured to act against their will, code of conduct violations are going unnoticed, or there's an observable trend of "business as usual" taking an ethical downturn, ask questions. Leverage your internal network to make inquiries. You may find your suspicions are unfounded, or you may discover something is amiss and warrants additional attention. In either case, you're serving an important role by remaining ethically conscience of what's happening around you.
- **Would we be comfortable making this public?** Whatever "this" is, ask yourself and ask your colleagues whether the company would be comfortable if a questionable plan, decision, or action became public. If there's doubt, you've likely identified an area that requires further examination to keep self-interest in check. Ethical actions speak much louder than company prose written to promote ethical behavior.

Ethical strains are difficult and upsetting to navigate, particularly when otherwise good people make poor choices. Communicators are on the front lines of response when bad behavior goes public. The more informed you are, the more beneficial your counsel can be before, during, and after an ethical lapse impacts your company.

Notes

1 See Chapter 4 The Art and Science of Financial Statements for discussion of the WorldCom case.
2 See Chapter 2 Capitalism: Its Benefits and Discontents, Chapter 4 The Art and Science of Financial Statements, Chapter 5 How and Why Finance Rules the Business World, and Chapter 11 And Here Comes Legal (re: fiduciary duties) for further discussion of SOX.
3 See *18 of the Best Code of Conduct Examples* (2017).
4 See Chapter 2 Capitalism: Its Benefits and Discontents and Chapter 3 A Micro and Macro View of the Economy for further discussion of cost-benefit analysis.
5 Read more about the 2008 financial crisis in Chapter 3 A Micro and Macro View of the Economy.
6 Highly recommended is Frankfurt's (2005) short but compelling book, *On Bullshit*, which discusses plausible deniability, hired guns, and the important differences between lying and bullshit.

References

Annabelle, L. (2017, March 5). *Ethics defined*. Retrieved from https://medium.com/the-ethical-world/ethics-defined-33a1a6cc3064.

Bowen, S. (2007, October 30). *Ethics and public relations*. Retrieved from https://instituteforpr.org/ethics-and-public-relations/.

Curry, O.S. (2018, May 17). *Seven moral rules found all around the world*. Retrieved from https://thisviewoflife.com/the-seven-moral-rules-found-all-around-the-world/.

18 of the best code of conduct examples. (2017, August 29). Retrieved from https://i-sight.com/resources/18-of-the-best-code-of-conduct-examples/.

Ethics, morality, law – what's the difference? (2016, September 27). Retrieved from https://ethics.org.au/ethics-morality-law-whats-the-difference/.

Frankfurt, H.G. (2005). *On bullshit*. Princeton, NJ: Princeton University Press.

Friedman, M. (1970). *The social responsibility of business is to increase its profits*. Retrieved from http://umich.edu/~thecore/doc/Friedman.pdf.

Hayes, A. (2020, July 1). *Code of ethics*. Retrieved from www.investopedia.com/terms/c/code-of-ethics.asp.

Heathfield, S.M. (2020, October 29). *Identify and live your personal values for success*. Retrieved from www.thebalancecareers.com/identify-and-live-your-personal-values-for-success-1919216.

Kenton, W. (2020, March 30). *What is a whistleblower?* Retrieved from www.investopedia.com/terms/w/whistleblower.asp.

Lencioni, P.M. (2002, July). *Make your values mean something*. Retrieved from https://hbr.org/2002/07/make-your-values-mean-something.

Mackey, J., & Sisodia, R. (2014). *Conscious capitalism: Liberating the heroic spirit of business*. Boston, MA: Harvard Business School Publishing Corporation.

Moral hazard. (2020). Retrieved from https://corporatefinanceinstitute.com/resources/knowledge/other/moral-hazard/.

Soltes, E. (2016, December 14). *The psychology of white collar criminals*. Retrieved from www.theatlantic.com/business/archive/2016/12/pyschology-white-collar-criminal/503408/.

U.S. whistleblower laws. (2020). Retrieved from www.whistleblowers.org/major-u-s-whistleblower-laws/.

Whistleblower risk for private companies. (2019, February 1). Retrieved from www.convercent.com/blog/whistle-blower-risk-private-companies.

Yahnke, K. (2019, January 28). *A practical guide to whistleblower protections in 2020*. Retrieved from https://i-sight.com/resources/a-practical-guide-to-whistleblower-protections/#US.

Concluding Thoughts

We've covered a lot of ground across these many pages. Each piece of information provided adds to your business literacy, which needs to continue growing as inevitable shifts in economic, political, and social conditions impact your company's operating environment. I conclude this portion of our time together with a few thoughts I hope you find helpful.

When it comes to expanding your business literacy:

- **Take the approach of *and*, not *or*, as you continue learning and applying business principles.** Say yes to expanding your thinking about what makes business tick. Embrace the entirety of the complex, fascinating system of organization and stakeholder interactions that determine business success or failure. Sure, you may find some aspects of business more interesting than others, but trust that the more you know, the better strategist you'll be – whether you stay with your current firm, move to another, or even start your own business adventure.
- **Realize you need courage, credibility, and connections to communicate effectively.** All three of these attributes are required for you to navigate the C-suite and communicate to your stakeholders truthfully, accurately, and ethically. The courage to speak, act, criticize, defend, and offer alternative solutions comes from your determination to make a positive difference. When and where you speak up are your calls to make. Your credibility with other functions, managers, and executives is greatly aided by your demonstrated knowledge and shared concern for what's best for the business. Your connections – your self-made internal, interdisciplinary network we've repeatedly addressed – provide a sounding board, support base, and devil's advocate to help you succeed. You never have to address business challenges alone (nor would you want to).
- **Find a firm you love.** Love isn't a term often used in business, but why would you want to devote the 24/7/365 time required of corporate communicators to a firm you're not wildly enthusiastic about? Working with a company that reflects your values, gets you excited to get out of bed in the morning, and pursues a mission that ignites your passions will not only bring out the best of what you have to offer, but also not feel like work (well, most days). There will be days of doubt, frustration, and even failure,

but when you believe in the work you're supporting, you'll have the inspiration and determination to get you through the tough times.
- **Let me hear from you.** Have a question? Facing a dilemma? Need advice or info? Reach out to me at thecommunicatorsmba.com. My calling is helping communicators thrive in the business world. Let me know how I can help you.

Index

above the line 71
accounting fraud 81–84
accounts receivable 74
accrual (vs. cash) accounting 67
accumulated depreciation *see* depreciation
acquisition (of a company) 121
activism: against capitalism 22; against corporations 22–23; shareholder 106–111
adjusted present value (APV) in company valuations 125–126
adverse (disparate) impact 195
adverse (disparate) treatment 195
aggregate demand 49
aggregate supply 49
AI (artificial intelligence) 152–153
the American dream 22
amortization 71
analysts 114
angel investors 117
annual reports 111–113
antitrust legislation 122; *see also* monopolies
ARR (accounting rate of return) 93
assets 74; carrying value of 74; current vs. noncurrent 74; fixed 74; impairment in value of 75; tangible vs. intangible 71, 74; valued at historical cost on financial statements 66; write-down of 75; *see also* balance sheet
audits 69

B2B (business-to-business) marketing 137, 139
B2C (business-to-consumer) marketing 137, 139–140
balance sheet 73–77
bankruptcy 98–99; corporate vs. individual 98–99
barriers to entry 47; 181–182
baseline criteria for capital investments 92
bear market 105
below the line 71
Bernanke, B. 56
blockchain 155, 162
blogging marketing metrics 146
blue vs. red ocean strategy 188

board of directors 25–26; election at annual meeting 106–107; fiduciary duties of members 198–199
bondholders vs. shareholders (how paid) 98–99
bonds: corporate 97–98; coupon payments 98; face (or par) value 97–98; government 54; maturity date 97; ratings of creditworthiness 98
book value 74–75; reduction in 75
bottom line *see* profit
brand: communication 136; differentiation 135; as an employer 169, 177; equity 135; experience 135; extension 136; gap 136; identity 135; image 135; as intangible asset 72; personality 135; positioning 135; promise 140
branding: corporate vs. product 136; emotional 136; list of terms related to 135–136
breach of warranty 198
bright-line standards 26
budget 91; *see also* capital budgeting; deficit; fiscal policy; government spending; surplus
bull market 105
burn rate 77
business-level strategy 185–186
business model 179–180; innovation in 187; as part of startup pitch deck 118
buyer's journey (sales funnel) 141

CapEx (capital expenditures) 78–79; vs. operating expenses (OpEx) 84
capital 91; access to 100; seed 117–118
capital budgeting 91–96
capital gains 102
capital investments 91–96
capital projects 91–96
capital structure 98–99
capitalism: critics of 22–23; outside of the U.S. 23–24; market-oriented in the U.S. 21–23; *see also* freedoms
carrying value of assets 74
cash: burn rate 77; importance of 77; sitting on too much or too little 96–97

cash cows (and other product categories) 142–143
cash flow statement 77–79; indirect method of preparing 77
cash flows: capital project forecasting of 92–96; in company valuation 123–126; from financing activities 79; from investing activities 78–79; from operating activities 77–78
cautionary language (for forward-looking statements) 114
central banks 53
Chapter 7 bankruptcy *see* bankruptcy
Chapter 11 bankruptcy *see* bankruptcy
Chapter 13 bankruptcy *see* bankruptcy
Class A, Class B shares 100–101
codes of conduct *see* corporate codes of conduct
codes of ethics 205
COGS (cost of goods sold) 70–71
commodity 144
common stocks *see* Class A, Class B shares
comparative advantage *see* international trade
comparative negligence (or fault) 198
compensation *see* executive compensation
compensatory damages 198
competition: among existing competitors 183; forces governing 181–183; part of invisible hand 16–17; perfect (or pure) 47; *see also* antitrust legislation; blue vs. red ocean strategy; monopolies
competitive advantage 183–185
complements 42–43
conciliation in EEOC cases, 195
confidence (consumer, business, investor) *see* expectations
conservatism in accounting 67–68
consolidated financial statements 69
consolidated industries 48
conversion rate (in marketing) 141
cook the books 81–82
copyright 196; as intangible asset 71, 74
core values 204
corporate codes of conduct 204
corporate finance (three functions of) 91–102
corporate governance 25–34; Darden guidelines for 26–34; *see also* ESG
corporate-level strategy 185–186
corporate raiders 90
corporate reputation: related to accounting fraud 81; related to capital investments and budgeting 96; related to data breaches 155; related to supply chain 164–165
corporate social responsibility (CSR) 24–25; Milton Friedman on 24, 206; related to supply chain 165
corporate values 204

corporation: as a legal entity 47; privately vs. publicly held 47; redefinition of purpose by Business Roundtable, 90; in U.S. historical context 19–21; *see also* public vs. private companies
cost-benefit analysis 19; related to criticism of corporate interests 22–23; *see also* marginal analysis
cost focus strategy 185
cost leadership strategy 184
counter-cyclical industries 48
coupon payments on bonds, 98
cross-price elasticity 42–43
crowdfunding 118–119
cultural intelligence 173
culture *see* organizational culture
currency exchange rates 57–58; *see* currency peg
currency peg 57–58; currency peg break 58
cybersecurity risk management 154–155; in enterprise risk 192, 194; in supply chain 162
cyclical industries 48, 97

damages (in product liability): compensatory 198; pain and suffering 198; punitive 198
data: big 153; breaches 154–155; competitive advantages of 156; driving communication strategy 156–157; four customer types of 153–154; mining 151; privacy regulations of 154; science 151; scientists 151; small 153; use in HR 168–169, 170; *see also* AI; blockchain; DL; ML; predictive models
debits and credits 68
debt: advantages and disadvantages of financing 98, 100; financing 97–98; national/federal 51–52; securities 97; *see also* capital structure; leverage ratios; Wendy's ROE
defective product claims 197; design defects 197; insufficient instructions or warnings 197; manufacturing defects 197; marketing defects 197; *see also* product liability; product misuses by consumer
deficit: related to budget 51–52; related to spending 51–52
deflation 55
demand: demand curve 40–42; driven by price 40–42; forecasting in ops management 163; increase in demand 40–42; law of demand 40; *see also* aggregate demand
depreciation 71; accumulated 74; straight-line 71
depression 55; the Great Depression 19, 51, 55
differentiation focus strategy 185
differentiation strategy 184–185
dilution 102; in IPO 118
diminishing marginal utility 43–44
diminishing returns *see* diminishing marginal utility
direct vs. indirect costs 70–71

discounted cash flow (DCF) models 93–96; in company valuations 125–126
discrimination 194–195
disparate (adverse) impact 195
disparate (adverse) treatment 195
disruptors 48
diversification (in marketing) 134
diversity and inclusion 174–176; Target initiatives in 175
dividends 75, 101–102
DL (deep learning) 152–153
dollar *see* U.S. dollar
the Dow *see* Dow Jones Industrial Average (DJIA)
Dow Jones Industrial Average (DJIA) 104–105
dual mandate 52–53; during inflation 54
due diligence 123
duty: of care 198–199; of confidentiality 199; of disclosure 199; of good faith 199; of loyalty 199; *see also* fiduciary duty

earnings *see* profit
earnings call 114
earnings reports *see* quarterly earnings reports
earnings season 114
EBIT (earnings before interest and taxes) 72; in company valuation 124; *see also* operating income
EBITDA (earnings before interest, taxes, depreciation, and amortization) in company valuation 124
economic agents 17, 40
economies of scale 46; as a barrier to entry 47, 181–182; as part of cost leadership strategy 184
EEOC (Equal Employment Opportunity Commission) 174, 194–195
efficiency ratios 115
8-K (Form 8-K) 112
elastic demand *see* price elasticity of demand; cross–price elasticity
email marketing metrics 147
emotional intelligence 173
employees: attracting, retaining, incentivizing 169–172; engagement 170; experience with company 168–169; high potential 10, 169; individual contributors 169; *see also* HR (human resources); talent
employment 56–57; full 56; key aspects of U.S. employment law 194–195; non-compete (no-poach) clauses 196–197; non-solicitation clauses 196–197; protectable interests 197; *see also* dual mandate; unemployment
enterprise data warehouses 151
enterprise risk management (ERM) 192, 194
enterprise value 124–126
EPS (earnings per share) 72; in company valuation 124; diluted EPS 72; ratios including 116

equilibrium price 40–42
equity: advantages and disadvantages of financing 98, 100; financing 98; securities 97; *see also* capital structure
ESG (environmental, social, and governance) 24–25
ethical communication 208–209
ethics 205
exchange rates *see* currency exchange rates
executive compensation 90; disclosure in proxy statement 106, 112; discussion in Form 10-K 111
exit strategy 124
expectations: of analysts 114; role of in business confidence 51; role of in consumer confidence 50–51; role of in driving market 48; role of in inflation 55; role of in investor perceptions and confidence 105; role of in monetary supply 53; role of in stock market 103; role of in strength of U.S. dollar 58
expenses: depreciation 71; operating 71, 84; SG&A 71; operating (OpEx) vs. capital expenditures (CapEx) 84
external audit 69
extraordinary items 72

face (or par) value on bonds, 97–98
factors of production 39
FASB (Federal Accounting Standards Board) 66
the Fed *see* Federal Reserve
federal discount rate 54
federal funds rate 54
Federal Open Market Committee (FOMC) 54
Federal Reserve 52–56
fiduciary duty 198–199
financial crisis of 2008 56; the Great Recession 56
financial ratios 115–116
fiscal policy 51; contractionary 52; expansionary 52
fiscal year (FY) 70
fixed cost 46
fixed exchange rate *see* currency peg
float 118
footnotes (on financial statements) 79
forecasts 91; rolling forecasts 91
Foreign Corrupt Practices Act (FCPA) 200
foreign exchange market (forex) 57
forward-looking statements 114
fragmented industries 48
free rider problem 19
freedoms: associated with/necessary for capitalism 15, 17, 20–23; *see also* the American dream
Freeman, R.E. 14, 21
Friedman, M. 22, 24, 206
functional-level strategy 185–186
future of work *see* HR (human resources)

GAAP (Generally Accepted Accounting Principles) 66–69; ten basic standards of 66–68
GDP (gross domestic product) 50–51
general ledger account 68
global economy 58–59
globalization 22, 59
GNP (gross national product) 50
going concern 67
going public 103; *see also* IPO
goodwill 72; as an asset 74
governance *see* corporate governance
government *see* state
government spending 51–52; when federal tax revenues exceed 52; when greater than federal tax revenues 51–52; *see also* deficit; surplus
the Great Depression *see* depression
the Great Recession *see* financial crisis of 2008; recession
gross income 71–72
growth: market growth strategies 134; organic vs. inorganic 120–121; top-line vs. bottom-line 119–120; *see also* M&A (mergers and acquisitions)

harassment 194–195
horizontal integration 163–164; *see also* vertical integration
hostile takeover 110–111
HR (human resources): in the future of work 167–169; risk management 176–177; *see also* employees; talent
human capital 167; risks associated with 176–177
hurdle rate 92–93; effect on NPV calculations 96; in IRR calculation 95

income statement 69–73; multi-step 70; single–step 70
income taxes: on balance sheet as payable 75–76; on income statement 72–73
industrial organization 47–48
industry: classifications 48; model innovation 187; structure 183–184, 189
inelastic demand *see* price elasticity of demand; cross-price elasticity
inferior goods 140
inflation 54–55; decrease in purchasing power related to 57; *see also* dual mandate; monetary policy; nominal vs. real terms
innovation 187–188; in business model 187; in industry model 187; in revenue model 187
insider trading 199
institutional investors 100; attempts to influence company policies 108
insufficient instructions or warnings 197
integration: backward vs. forward 164; horizontal vs. vertical 163–164; upstream vs. downstream 164

intellectual property (IP) 195–197; copyright 196; as intangible asset 74; patent 196; trade secret 196; trademark 196
interest rates 53–54; and inflation 54; *see also* open market operations
internal audit 69
Internal Revenue Service (IRS) 80
international trade 58–59; comparative advantage in 59; specialization in 59
inventory: on balance sheet 74, 76; on cash flow statement 78; just-in-time demand forecasting for 163; in ops management 159–160; ratios related to 115
investment banks 118–119
investor relations (IR) 21, 100
investors *see* shareholders
invisible hand 16–17
IPO (initial public offering) 103, 117–119; preliminary prospectus 118; primary and secondary market offerings 118; red herring 118; S-1 registration statement 118
IRR (internal rate of return) 95–96

joint venture (JV) 124

Keynes, J.M. 51
KPIs (key performance indicators) 145

laissez-faire 17; in U.S. capitalism 22
large-cap corporations 105–106
laws (vs. values, morals, and ethics) 205
lean manufacturing 162–163
leverage ratios 115
liabilities 75–77; accrued 75; current vs. long-term 75; deferred 75; payable 75; unearned revenue 75
life cycle (products, businesses, markets) 141–142
line items 65, 70, 79
liquidity 74; ratios related to 115
loan types: cash flow 97; installment 97; revolving 97
long vs. short run 49
luxury goods 140

M&A (mergers and acquisitions) 121–123
macroeconomics: principles of 48–59
manufacturing defects 197
marginal analysis 43–45; *see also* cost-benefit analysis
market: capitalization (market cap) unchanged in stock split 102; capitalization (market cap) guidelines 105–106; classical view of self-regulating 16–17; clearing of 40–42; development of (in marketing) 134; failures 17–19; growth strategies 134; neoclassical view of self-regulating 17–19; penetration of (in marketing) 134; share of (in marketing) 134; structure 47–48

marketing: defects 197; list of types of 138–139; metrics 145–147; seven Ps of 136–137; shift in definition of 133–134
marketing metrics: email 147; general 145; pay-per-click (PPC) 147; SEO 146; social media 146; website and blogging 146
MARR (minimal acceptable rate of return) 92; see also hurdle rate
matching of revenues and expenses 67
material (information or items) 67; on Form 8-K 112
MD&A (management's discussion and analysis of financial condition and results of operations) 111
mental models 7–8
merger (of equals) 121
microeconomics: principles of 39–48
mid-cap corporations 105–106
missing markets 18–19
ML (machine learning) 152–153
monetary policy 52–54; contractionary 53; expansionary 53
money see time value of money
monopolies 18, 47
moral hazard 206
morals 204
multiples (used in valuation) 124–126

NASDAQ 104
NASDAQ Composite Index 104–105
national debt see debt
natural monopolies 18
necessary goods see normal goods
negative externalities 18
negligence 198; comparative (or fault) 198
net income see profit
New York Stock Exchange (NYSE) 26, 104
nominal vs. real terms 50
non-compete (no-poach) clauses 196–197
non-solicitation clauses 196–197
normal goods 140
NPV (net present value) 93–96

oligopolies 47
open market operations 53–54
operating company (in M&A) 124
operating expenses (OpEx) 71, 84; vs. capital expenditures (CapEx) 84
operating income 72; in company valuation 124
opportunity cost 45
organizational culture: as a driver of employee satisfaction 169; ethics engrained in corporate culture 209; impacts of primary focus on stock price 90; post-merger integration issues 123; role of HR in 168; at Sweetgreen 168; see also WorldCom scandal
overheated economy 52, 54, 56, 57

P/E (price-earnings) ratio 116; in company valuation 124
P&L (profit and loss) statement see income statement
paid-in capital 75
pain and suffering compensation 198
partnership 47
patent 196; as intangible asset 71, 74
pay "at risk" 90
pay-per-click (PPC) marketing metrics 147
payables 75
payback method 92–93
pegged currency see currency peg
pitch deck 118
political economy: and capitalism 15–16; origins of 13–14; and public affairs 14–15
Porter's forces 181–183
power of suppliers and buyers 182–183
PPE (property, plant, and equipment) 91
predictive models 151–152
preferred stock 101
preliminary prospectus (for IPO) 118
prepaid items 74
price: competing on 144; equilibrium price where market clears 40–42; takers 47; wars 144; willingness to pay (WTP) 140
price elasticity of demand 42
prime rate 54
principal/agent relationship 198
private company valuation 125–126
private equity (PE) firms 118–119
pro forma 92
product design defects 197
product development (in marketing) 134
product liability 197–198
product misuses by consumer 197
profit: attracts attention to the firm 81; bottom line 70–72; calculation of 69–73; part of invisible hand 16–17; pursuit of in market failures 18–19; pursuit of in private sector 16–17; as a signal to business owners 15; related to CSR and ESG 24–25; role of in creating value for others beyond the firm 20
profitability: index 95; ratios related to 116; related to NPV values 94–95; related to positioning 184
projections (financial): 91–92
protectable interests 197
protectionist trade policy 58–59
proxy: card 106–107; fight 109–110; statement 106, 112
public company valuation 124–125
public goods 18–19
public vs. private companies 102–103; see also corporation
pull vs. push manufacturing 163
punitive damages 198

purpose: and culture 168; of the firm 19–21; of market-oriented capitalism 21; redefined for the corporation 90

quantitative easing 56
quantity: driven by price 40–42; quantity demanded 40–42
quarterly earnings reports 113–114
quid pro quo exchanges 133–134
quiet period: related to quarterly earnings reports 113; related to IPOs 118

ratio and margin analysis 114–117
real vs. nominal terms 50
receivables 67; turnover ratio related to 115; *see also* accounts receivable
recession 51, 55–57; the Great Recession 56; leading and lagging indicators of 55; negative shocks related to 56; related to inflation 54; related to overheated economy 52, 54, 56, 57; related to unemployment 57
recognition of income and expenses 67; *see also* revenue
recruiting *see* employees; HR (human resources); talent
red herring 118
regulatory and reporting requirements 111–114
rent-seeking 58
reputation *see* corporate reputation
research and development (R&D) 71
reserve requirements 53–54
retail (or non-institutional) investors 100
retained earnings 75, 77, 101
retaliation 194–195
revenue 70; recognizing 68–69; top line 70; model innovation 187
reverse split 102
risk management: cybersecurity 154–155; enterprise (ERM) 192, 194; HR (human resources) 176–177; supply chain 164
rivalry among existing competitors 183
roadshows 118; non-deal roadshows (NDRs) 118
ROI (return on investment) 144–145

S curve 187–188
S-1 registration statement 118
safe harbor liability protection 114
safe haven *see* U.S. dollar
sales *see* revenue
sales funnel (buyer's journey) 141
Sarbanes-Oxley (SOX) Act 25–26, 111, 208
seasonality 163
SEC (Securities and Exchange Commission): and FASB 66; and Foreign Corrupt Practices Act (FCPA) 200; and insider trading 199; regulation of shareholder resolution process 106, 108; regulatory and reporting requirements 111–114; role in IPO 118; safe harbor liability protection 114
securities 97; debt 97; equity 97; *see also* bonds; shares
seed capital 117–118
self-interest: in capitalism 15–20; keeping in check 206–207; misdirected 83
SEO marketing metrics 146
serial entrepreneurs 124
series funding for startups 118–119
SG&A (sales, general, and administrative) expenses *see* expenses
share buyback (stock repurchase) 101–102
shareholder: activism 106–111; annual meeting 106; primacy 21, 90; resolution 106, 108–109; returns 100–102; value 21, 90, 100–101
shareholders: Class A, Class B shares 100–101; in corporate governance 25; how paid in corporate bankruptcy 98–99; how paid vs. bondholders 98–99; institutional investors 100; interests vs. other stakeholders 19–21; preferred stock 101; related to CSR and ESG 24; retail (non-institutional) investors 100; role in Darden corporate governance 26–33; types and classes of 100–101
shareholders' equity 75
shares (types of) 100–101
small-cap corporations 105–106
Smith, A. 13–17, 19–20, 40, 58–59, 206
social intelligence 173
social media marketing metrics 146
sole proprietorship 47
SOX *see* Sarbanes-Oxley
specialization *see* international trade
stagflation 55
stakeholders 14–15, 19–21; business shift toward stakeholder approach 90; corporate governance 25; creating value for 89–90; engagement in supply chain 165; and ethics 209; related to CSR and ESG 24–25; related to strategy 181, 183; and strategic communication 189
Standard & Poor's 500 Index 104–105
startup 117–119
state: minimal role of in a free economy 15–17; role of in political economy 13
stock exchanges 104
stock indices 104–105
stock listing (how to read) 103–104
stock market 103–106
stock price: and capital gains 102; effects of split on 102; in employee shares 171–172; following announcement of strong performance 114; impacts on culture when primary focus is increasing 90; related pressures on executive compensation 90; *see also* WorldCom scandal
stock repurchase (share buyback) 101–102

stock split 102
stockholders *see* shareholders
stocks *see* shares
strategic communication 189–190
strategy 181; blue vs. red ocean 188; and competitive forces 181–183; cost focus 185; cost leadership 184; differentiation 184–185; differentiation focus 185; Samsung example of 186–187; stuck in the middle 185; three levels of 185–186
strict liability 198
substitutes 42–43; threat of 182–183
sunk cost 45–46
supply: driven by price 40–42; law of supply 40; supply curve 40–42; *see also* aggregate supply
supply and demand 40–42; part of invisible hand 16–17
supply chain 160–162; blockchain use in 162; risk management 164
supply-side economics 52
surplus: related to budget 52; related to spending 52
switching costs 136
synergies 123

T accounts 68
talent: acquisition of 167; role of data in recruiting and retaining 168; role of purpose and culture in recruiting 168; targeted diversity and inclusion recruitment 174; *see also* employees; HR (human resources)
target company (in M&A) 124
tariffs 58
T-bills 54
T-bonds 54
T-notes 54
teams (psychology of high-performing) 172–173
technology: use in HR 169–170; using S Curve to describe shifts in 187–188
10-K (Form 10-K) 111–112
10-Q (Form 10-Q) 112
tender offer 110–111

threat of entry 181–183
threat of substitute products 182–183
time value of money 93
top line *see* revenue
trade *see* international trade; protectionist trade policy
trade secret 196
trademark 196; as intangible asset 71
Treasury securities 54; *see also* bonds
trickle-down economics 52

underwriter *see* investment banks
unemployment 56–57; cyclical 57; frictional 57; natural 56; structural 57; *see also* employment
U.S. dollar value 58; safe haven 58
utility 40; *see also* diminishing marginal utility

valuation (company) 123–126
value: chain 164; creation of 20–21, 65, 89–90; perceptions of in marketing 140; ratios related to market value 116; synergies 123; *see also* shareholder; stakeholders
value proposition 140
values 204; *see also* core values; corporate values
variable cost 46
venture capital (VC) firms 118–119
vertical integration 163–164; *see also* horizontal integration
volatility (in stock prices) 106
Volkswagen scandal 96

WACC (weighted average cost of capital) 99–100; in APV company valuation 125
wage-price spiral 55
website marketing metrics 146
Wendy's ROE 114, 116–117
whistleblower 207; protections for 207–208
white-collar criminals 205–206
willingness to pay (WTP) 140
workforce: insights and analytics 168; scalable 167; shaping 169
WorldCom scandal 81–84
write-off 71

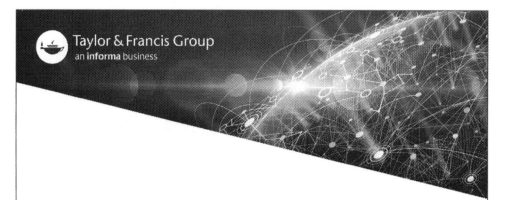

Printed in the United States
by Baker & Taylor Publisher Services